The Thought That Changed My Life Forever

What if one thought could change everything?

Like all great endeavours, this book started as a thought. One seed planted in two minds, giving life to a special vision—a vision that connected two people through one powerful phrase:

The Thought That Changed My Life Forever...

Meeting and working together in beautiful Vancouver, BC, Christian Guenette and Gillian Laura Roberts joined forces and invited 50 like-minded experts along to present this book to the World, with the desire to serve positive change in not just one life, but many lives...

Why Write This Book?

We know the power of the mind can manifest anything we desire, including health, happiness and success. We want others to understand, explore and benefit from this Truth, too, so together we can co-create a conscious, vibrant World...

Why Read This Book?

To learn how and why changing your mind can initiate powerful personal transformation; to be inspired by the stories of others who discovered the power of their thoughts; and to enjoy the positive effects this awareness can have on bringing dreams to life. *Your* dreams...

Why Share This Book?

We truly believe this awareness is a gift, and as more people on our planet awaken to the power within their minds, it will serve us all—benefiting the health of the Earth, all the amazing generations to come, and the very evolution of Consciousness itself.

This is **"The Thought Movement"**: Are you ready to add your spark to the enlightenment of the Universe?

Advanced Praise for

The Thought That Changed My Life Forever

"Through the openheartedness of their contributors and their own lives, Gillian and Christian provide factual evidence that there is no greater power than the power of thought, which informs our intentions, actions and manifestations. Important emphasis is given to the essentialness of making a commitment to our evolution of consciousness so we avoid using the laws governing the Universe simply for superficial gain, and instead, direct our thought-energy towards becoming a beneficial presence on the planet. I highly recommend this intelligent and compassionate book."

Michael Bernard Beckwith — Founder of Agape International Spiritual Center (Los Angeles, CA); Author of *Life Visioning: A Transformative Process for Activating Your Unique Gifts and Highest Potential* www.agapelive.com

"It is the case that most of us live our lives as automatons, without awareness, until or unless some event or thought jars us into consciousness and reflection. *The Thought That Changed My Life Forever* was birthed with just such an event, as were the testimonies of the 52 contributors who identify the moment when they woke up or were awakened from their trance—and became intentional about their destiny. This book is a testimony to the mystery and power of the human mind to create and transcend our ordinary reality. I recommend it as an inspiration and challenge to everyone."

Harville Hendrix — Author of *Getting the Love You Want: A Guide for Couples* www.harvillehendrix.com

"Every now and then a book comes together and opens the heart of everyone who reads it. *The Thought That Changed My Life Forever* is exactly what it sounds like: a lyrical journey, providing a rhythm and heartbeat that captivated my attention and moved my whole being right until the final word. What Gillian and Christian have compiled here is magical, and I know you'll agree. Most of all, it invites you to ask yourself the question, 'What is the thought that could change *my* life forever?' It's inside you right now waiting to be revealed. Reading this book will definitely light a spark and bring it to the surface of your awareness."

James F. Twyman — New York Times Bestselling
Author of *The Barn Dance* and *The Moses Code*
www.jamestwyman.com

"As Edgar Cayce said, 'Mind is the builder.' And Ambrose Worrall said, 'Thinking sets in motion spiritual forces to bring about change in body, mind, emotions.' Here you will find 52 more elegant ways to think!"

C. Norman Shealy, MD, PhD — Author of *Energy Medicine:
Practical Applications and Scientific Proof*, President, Holos
Institutes of Health & Professor Emeritus, Energy Medicine
www.normshealy.com

"An inspiring book of breakthroughs and a joyful call to personal awakening, *The Thought That Changed My Life Forever* demonstrates the power our thoughts really have. The book not only raises our individual consciousness, it breathes new life into the possibility of transforming our planet by helping us 'be the change we want to see.' This unique book so clearly affirms the principles I teach in my 'Breakthrough Adventures' program, I recommend it to every participant. I invite you to bear witness as 52 people each discover the power to create a new way of thinking—and dramatically change their lives forever."

Jason Sugar — Founder of Breakthrough Adventures, Inc.
www.breakthroughadventures.com

"Your thoughts truly create the life you are living right now. The chair, the couch, the phone, the TV, and all the things you are using in your daily life started with a thought. What if you could fully engage in the thoughts of an aspiring new generation of authors, spiritually inspired entrepreneurs, and master teachers of 'new thought,' all here to guide you to discover, know and mine the next greatest 'thoughts' within YOU? Here they are! This book can activate what is next in your life. Read it now."

Jennifer McLean — Host of *"Healing With the Masters"*
and Creator of "Body Dialog System of Healing"
www.mcleanmasterworks.com

"This book overflows with inspiration and reminds you of the thoughts that just might change *your* life, too."

Jared Rosen — Author of *The Flip* and founder of DreamSculpt Media, Inc.

www.DreamSculpt.com

"*The Thought That Changed My Life Forever* is clearly a work of dedication and love, and a heartfelt desire by Gillian and Christian to share their vision of enlightening and encouraging others to discover the mystery and power of the mind. By sharing their own stories and bringing together 50 other authors who willingly wrote about a thought which was life-changing to them, they have given their readers a gift. They have opened a door and invited you to walk through so you might change your life forever, too. Insightful, personal, touching, thought-provoking: it is an amazing body of work and well worth reading from cover to cover."

Sharon Ann Roberts — Registered Nurse (Ret.), MOM

"We live in a mysterious Universe where our thoughts connect us to our destiny. Inside these covers, you'll find 52 examples of people who found their deeper purpose through the power of positive thinking combined with bold action. If you've ever wondered whether thoughts can change the World, read this book…and allow your life to be changed."

Stephan Martin — Astronomer and Author of *Cosmic Conversations: Dialogues on the Nature of the Universe and the Search for Reality*
www.cosmicconversations.org

"This book will be worthwhile time spent for all its readers. Although you may already know some of the key points or may have glimpsed them in some form or fashion in the past, it is always a good idea to be reminded; this publication does so for its reader in an engaging, facilitating way. Light bulbs will go on with self-reflection and review, bringing to the forefront ideas and concepts dear to many people out there seeking a deeper experience of their lives."

Dr. Cindy-Ann J.N. Lucky — MBBS (MD), MSHA, CCFP (EM), FCFP
Clinical Associate Professor, University of British Columbia
Department of Family/Emergency Medicine

"This treasure trove of wisdom begins with a deceptively simple premise that leads the reader down a path winding and wondrous… Thank goodness, Christian listened to his muse when it whispered that phrase in his ear! You will love bearing witness to the vivid descriptions of these wordsmiths who have discovered that a re-frame can alter reality and shape outcome. These 52 'opti-mystics' who see the World through the eyes of possibility will dazzle you with their brilliance and invite you to explore your own soul's meanderings. Even if you haven't lived the same experiences as the authors, I imagine you will recognize your own journey in the turning of each page."

Edie Weinstein (a.k.a. "Bliss Mistress") — Journalist, Motivational Speaker and Author of *The Bliss Mistress: Guide to Transforming the Ordinary Into the Extraordinary* www.liveinjoy.org

"What a beautiful and powerful compilation of stories reminding us how one thought can change our life forever. These 52 stories represent the 52 moments that actually changed 52 *real* lives! I can only imagine how many more will be changed for the better by this inspiring book!"

Mary Allen (a.k.a. America's Inner Peace Coach) — Author of *The Power of Inner Choice* www.lifecoachmary.com

"20 years of marketing natural healthcare and wellness for thousands of doctors around the World has taught me much about how a transformation of attitude to maximize life's opportunities makes it possible for us to bring dreams to life. I thought I knew it all until I read this highly inspiring book. I honestly could not put it down, and I'm sure you will do the same."

Brian J. Crombleholme — President, *"Health Education TV"*

"Sprung from a thought, an idea, a dream…followed through with love and collaboration together with the intervention of Divine Order…*The Thought That Changed My Life Forever* is bound to be an inspiration to all who 'find' it. We are reminded to pay attention to our thoughts, to develop awareness of our own possibilities, and to realize we all have the potential to make our dreams come true. We are given tools to follow our path and are encouraged to forge ahead to live our passion through exquisite examples celebrated in fifty-two amazing success stories. Not only is it an exceptional read, it may change your life!"

Sylvia Green-Guenette — Certified Dream Therapist, MOM

"The concept is both elegant and profound: a single thought can change a person's life. The execution of *The Thought That Changed My Life Forever* is smart, clever, and yes, thoughtful. Christian Guenette and Gillian Laura

Roberts' collection of essays from spiritual thinkers on how they were transformed by a single thought is both inspirational and powerful. If you seek affirmation that your intuition and dreams should be your guide OR if you need motivation to learn to open up to the vast potential of your deepest consciousness through meditation and prayer, this is the book for you."

Tzivia Gover — Certified Dream Therapist, Proprioceptive Writing Instructor, and author of *Mindful Moments for Stressful Days*, and *Learning in Mrs. Towne's House* (about the life and work of Elizabeth Towne, a leader in the New Thought movement, 1865-1960)

www.tziviagover.com

"The inspiring stories found in this book remind us that an unexpected thought can permanently change a life and transform a world. One solitary thought can awaken a new direction and reveal who we truly are. A single thought has the potential to fully open our hearts and change everything—to make a miraculous shift in perception from fear of loss to love of Life. The thought can come from a book: it *has* come from a book! Keep reading this one. You'll see."

Dennis Rodriguez — Heart Circle Facilitator and Author of *The Super Human Effect: My Quest for the Moment When Everything Changes*

www.thesuperhumaneffect.com

THE THOUGHT THAT CHANGED MY LIFE FOREVER

HOW ONE INSPIRATION CAN UNLEASH YOUR TRUE POTENTIAL AND TRANSFORM THE WORLD

Dr. Christian Guenette & Gillian Laura Roberts

Imbue Press

an imprint of MORGAN JAMES PUBLISHING
NEW YORK

The Thought That Changed My Life Forever
HOW ONE INSPIRATION CAN UNLEASH YOUR TRUE POTENTIAL AND TRANSFORM THE WORLD

ISBN 978-1-61448-294-9 paperback
ISBN 978-1-61448-295-6 eBook
Library of Congress Control Number: 2012945357

Imbue Press
an imprint of
Morgan James Publishing
The Entrepreneurial Publisher
5 Penn Plaza, 23rd Floor,
New York City, New York 10001
(212) 655-5470 office • (516) 908-4496 fax
www.MorganJamesPublishing.com

Cover Design by:
Olaf Strassner, OS Design
www.olafstrassner.com

Interior Design by:
Bonnie Bushman
bonnie@caboodlegraphics.com

In an effort to support local communities, raise awareness and funds, Morgan James Publishing donates a percentage of all book sales for the life of each book to Habitat for Humanity Peninsula and Greater Williamsburg.

Get involved today, visit
www.MorganJamesBuilds.com.

Habitat for Humanity®
Peninsula and
Greater Williamsburg
Building Partner

Heart Thoughts

CHRISTIAN
to Hady Quan:
Memories fade,
But our love for you
Never will.
Thank you, Hady –
For showing us how to *be*:
Generous,
Loving,
Kind,
Selflessly…
<u>You</u>.

GILLIAN
I dedicate this adventure to my grandfather
Dr. James Hector Moir—whose loving hands healed people all over the
World and, unexpectedly, a place in his own
granddaughter's heart.
&
To Sharon and Michael Roberts—your love is the treasured bedrock of my
life, from the beginning and *forever*.

Thank you

Table of Contents

SECTION I — *TO* ME

When nothing an eager family therapist is doing seems to be working, it's his young client who turns the tables and shakes him into seeing a new reality. Where do you start when all you want to do is save the World?

In his darkest moment, one man hears the voice of his grandfather echoing in his head—offering a lifeline from illusion to Truth. In a flash of insight, a new path of hope is illuminated, sparking the beginning of a miraculous journey from his head to his heart.

Apartment hunting in Paris becomes an important life-lesson: one small shift in how a foreign grad student thinks about fulfilling her desires completely transforms the outcome. Can what you want for *others* actually bring you closer to what *you* want?

is. How can we enjoy the fruits of our intentions without planting seeds—or getting our hands a little dirty?

Is just enough really good enough? Not if you want to experience *Greatness*! One lesson in his grandfather's gas station leads a young boy to understand how focus and attention to detail are important tools for finding success and living a life on purpose.

How can anything evolve if we accept the status quo? After inheriting an approach to life—involving a specific line of inquiry—from her courageous, revolutionary ancestors, this MD becomes the change she wishes to see in her profession.

A practical joke gone wrong leaves a committed healthcare worker physically broken. When years of pain and treatment yield no progress, an introduction to hypnotherapy and the wisdom of Dr. Wayne Dyer changes everything.

SECTION III — *THROUGH* ME

Haunted by unexplained feelings of fear and a picture of life beyond her known reality, one mother faces the unimaginable—the untimely death her young child. A search for meaning in a time of great despair leads her to profound revelations about a powerful gift within her.

Two relationship therapists with a desire to revolutionize family healing have both their professional and personal approaches to relationship transformed by a single statement from a 9-year old boy.

At the end of a long dinner party, the silence of the moonlit night and the company of dirty dishes allow one woman to see beyond appearances and into a new realm of beauty. How she sees herself, others around her, and even Love itself will never be the same again.

catches him off-guard, but offers him a new perspective for every choice that follows.

Being the life of the party doesn't always mean you're having a good time. When one man jumps on his bicycle and chooses to let his athletic abilities support rather than mask what's in his heart, a journey of thousands of kilometres takes him to a surprising place—perhaps where he desired to be all along.

Olympians are made, not born. Even at 6'5" and with talent to burn, it takes witnessing an unexpected moment of graceful, athletic perfection that leads this fledgling rower to claim not only a place on the World stage and Olympic podium, but a powerful belief in the potential within each of us.

Sometimes what we *believe* can cloud our opportunity for finding our true *faith*. Discovering a deeply-held place of sorrow allows an ordained minister to take on a new level of understanding about himself, his religion, and the nature of our role in expanding Consciousness on the planet.

SECTION IV — AS ME

What do you do when the label you've been given just doesn't fit anymore? This courageous Religious Science minister takes us with her on a soul-searching journey in which she not only calls forth a different name, but awakens a latent essence from within her*self*.

In a letter to her friend, this self-proclaimed over-planner shares her story about why letting go of controlling the details doesn't mean you have to lose the plot.

Even graduating at the top of his class cannot prevent this college student from feeling lost and unsure of his career path. With an ingenious plan to help him decide, his journey of discovery reveals much, much more than the answer he was originally seeking.

A professional hypnotherapist discovers how adept she is in helping guide others to answers for their life-long questions. But what will she do when she receives a message from a surprising source, prompting her to ask powerful questions of her own?

Plagued with her own intense back pain, a massage therapist discovers the source of her discomfort—finding not only a personal gift, but a critical choice that is key to her own well-being *and* the true healing of her patients.

A young man pursues a career in medicine to combat the many ills that afflict his family. After years of astutely observing his loved ones and his patients, he discovers it's not what's "out there" that makes us sick. Advocating for a new *perception* becomes his powerful new *prescription*.

With her most difficult moments behind her, this addiction therapist shares the three guideposts that not only provided a way out of her *own* despair, but may also serve as beacons of light to lead others along a path of least resistance.

When faced with a potentially life-or-death health crisis, this running coach decides to take ownership of her own future, creating a mental workout plan that will ultimately guarantee her success—and better the chances for all of us.

As a child, being aware of all the "energies" around her creates confusion and isolation. After a brief but powerful spiritual experience, she receives an answer to her most profound question—one that could transform the entire World.

This career coach and counselor bares it all to share his most powerful and personal life-lesson: being true to oneself means embracing not only our more admirable attributes, but also our vulnerabilities.

Sweet Thoughts
In Gratitude

How often do you get a chance to tell the World how much you really, *really* appreciate the special people in your life? When you win an Oscar®...on your wedding day... upon retirement, perhaps...or when you win the lottery? We feel like we've scored all these, infused with the magic of Christmas Eve and falling in love—all rolled into one...

It's our sincere joy to celebrate the power of collaboration: the amazing synergy that arises when brilliant hearts and minds come together to co-create something, especially when it's with the intention to move us all to the next level of happiness and evolution. We are thrilled to shine a light on these special people who helped us get here with their unique contributions:

Andrew Lyons: An instigator or visionary, depending on how you look at it! Your inspired match-making worked in the end—proving it really *is* all in the timing. And the golf swing, of course.

Kristen Moeller at Imbue Press: She makes us laugh and kicks literary butt—often from a sailboat in the Bahamas. We like that. We like sailboats in the Bahamas, too. (We're free to travel, now that the book is done...)

David Hancock plus the talented Team at *Morgan James Publishing*: Thank you for taking us on—we're so grateful! We're genuinely delighted to be part of your publishing family.

Our Contributing Authors: Where would we be without you? It's been sheer bliss to work with such an inspirational, diverse group of talented helpers and healers. We've been fuelled by your excitement for this project from start to finish and look forward to many more opportunities to share the World stage with each and every one of you. Thank you for contributing your voice to our song: our collective passion to serve others *is* changing the World, right now.

Dr. Joe Dispenza and Paula Meyer: We are so appreciative of your work and your willingness to be a part of our project. A big thank you for your wonderful contribution, and we know it forms such an important part of the manifestation puzzle: "How do I actually *do* this?" We are confident this will make a difference in so many readers' lives, and we've loved getting our neuroscience on!

Reverend Dr. Kathy Hearn: You have made such a significant contribution to the expansion of New Thought in the World, and we feel so blessed to have your words, energy and support flow through the beautiful Forward you wrote for us. Having your feminine strength and spiritual power within these pages is something we consider a major coup! What perfect balance and synchrony to collaborate with you.

Our Generous Testimonialists: We are humbled and so appreciative of your words of affirmation and support. Your own work—visionary, inspired and thoughtfully created—has spoken for itself, and we feel blessed to have you speak for ours. Many thanks to all who took the time to read and reflect: we're definitely standing on the shoulders of (enlightened) giants.

Olaf Strassner: Thank you for bringing on your unique brand of German brilliance just when we needed it most—we cannot thank you enough! Your wonderful, limitless creativity and depth of commitment to "finding the essence" made for some inspiring collaborative sessions in pursuit of the perfect cover. We love it!

Ronan Reinhart at *Bell Alliance*: Thank you for gently reminding us there is wisdom in not trying to edit our own legal contracts. Once editors, always editors— *mea culpas*!

The Local and the magic known simply as "chocolate porter." A big hug of appreciation for our newest, biggest fan **Dorothy**—for her great enthusiasm as we plucked away on our computers in the midst of the hopping joint (once or twice whilst enjoying said chocolate porter).

Our Treasured Friends & Colleagues: You not only cheered us on all the way but also pointed us in the direction of some of the great folks who became our collaborators on this project. Thank you for hanging in there as we burned the midnight oil (seemingly without end!) and fired up our minds to illuminate a world of dreams—and our dream for the World. You've truly helped smooth the way for us to express our belief in the power of every mind to create beauty, purpose and joy. We cherish each one of you.

CHRISTIAN

To **Cooper and Shelli**: A huge "THANK YOU." Thank you for putting up with the countless late nights and the occasional missed family events. Thank you for taking this journey *alongside* me—with infinite patience. You are 2 of the most important reasons why I do what I do. I love you dearly.

To **Sylvia**: You set the example of love and loyalty I strive to live up to. You have always been my rock, and I give you full credit for where I am today. I rejoice every day knowing you've found peace (and loving companionship) in your golden years. You so deserve it. A simple thank you just doesn't say enough, Mom.

GILLIAN

To my teachers, here and beyond: Thank you for modeling the conviction necessary for taking *leaps of faith* and what having the *faith to leap* truly is. **To my fellow/ sister Practitioners**: I'm in awe of your commitment to light up the planet, one mind at a time. Your support in my personal & professional evolution continues to be invaluable. (NB: When you want to know what really being *loved* feels like, find a Spiritual Practitioner!) **To my friends at Toastmasters Club 59**: You've been the joy in my Mondays, helped sculpt my professional expression, and championed my heart. I'm forever grateful you became my cherished family and a truly spiritual community when I needed it most.

To Connor, Calla and Alison: It's pure joy to watch your new minds grow and flourish! Someday I hope you will enjoy this "chapter book"—I love you so. **In honour of the Buddha:** Whose teachings provide a portal through which I've directly experienced the *Big Love*. I'm so grateful for every moment I remember your beautiful instructions for loving-kindness—and for affirming my belief that heart and mind are one.

Finally, To Our Readers: Our thoughts turned powerfully to each of you at every step of this process. You are our True North! Though you may be friends we haven't met yet, it is your experience we've considered faithfully, asking ourselves, "Will this make a difference in at least one person's life?" Or, as Ted Kuntz asks in his chapter (#36), "What would do the most good?"

We send this missive out to you with our love and respect—in anticipation of offering you many moments of good reading, an introduction to our fine colleagues, and with the wish that these stories both illuminate new thoughts and inspire bold action that will change your life for the better...*forever*.

With great appreciation,

Christian & Gillian

Never doubt that a small group of thoughtful,
committed citizens can change the World.
Indeed, it is the only thing that ever has.

Margaret Mead

Forethought

Reflections on Forward Thinking

by Reverend Dr. Kathy Hearn

I am so impressed by this book!

First, by the shared heart and commitment that propelled and guided Gillian and Christian to offer the World these wonderful stories about moments of true awakening and life change. As a New Thought minister and teacher who has for many years spoken about the creative power of thought and the personal transformation it supports, I was gratified to read these highly individual examples of how a new thought can generate such profound newness in *living*—even revealing an unexpected or expanded life purpose…

Each chapter is a treasure of *good* to be received, a window into our own experience, and a doorway that leads us to an understanding of how a higher, expanded realization of our own capacity can manifest as an even greater revelation of good in and around us. In truth, *be-cause of us*—and our relationship with the mystery and source energy of Life.

What becomes clear in each story is that rising to any challenge or out of limitation is directly related to what moves through our consciousness—since our thoughts truly fashion our experience. The great opportunity we have is to take active and creative responsibility for our thoughts by lifting and expanding them toward greater truth and possibility. And to be open to those "ah-ha!" moments when a new idea or understanding seems to just "appear" in our minds. This is when Life becomes magical.

Just today in the New York Times, I read a report by physicists who discovered a new particle that may be the bridge between invisibility and matter. These words really caught my attention:

> **The finding affirms a grand view of a universe described by simple and elegant and symmetrical laws—but one in which everything interesting, like ourselves, results from flaws or breaks in that symmetry.**[1]

In chapter after chapter of *The Thought That Changed My Life Forever*, each writer uniquely shares how Life became more interesting, deeper and ultimately *happier*, as greater ideas pierced their awareness and "breaks in the symmetry" of their usual thinking became *breakthroughs*—changing life forever.

I find myself also moved by the container of consciousness that Gillian and Christian have created through the bookends of their writing: With clarity and energy, they engage us from the start in the story of their personal and shared inspiration, meeting and collaboration; then, following the story chapters, they call us to true reverence for our own mind, deep purpose and creative possibilities. I feel enlisted in a powerful, global project—"The Thought Movement"—to think and love, create and influence Life on behalf of my own full self-expression and joy… and for the blessing of all beings everywhere.

I am grateful for their care and commitment to forward *thinking*.

You are now at the beginning of your personal journey within these inspirational pages, holding an invitation to join others in unleashing your true potential in service of your best life—and the World. I know you will enjoy and savor every moment, and my hope is you will feel engaged, entertained, moved and guided to beautiful change and profound newness in your own life.

With blessings and gratitude,
Kathy Hearn, D.D.
Centers for Spiritual Living Minister, Writer, Consultant
Former Spiritual Leader, United Centers for Spiritual Living
La Jolla, California
July 5, 2012
www.kathyhearn.com

---

1   NYTimes.com 7/5/12

*The future belongs to those who believe
in the beauty of their dreams.*

Eleanor Roosevelt

He Thought, She Thought—*We Think...*

Pay attention to your thoughts. Pay close attention. For even the tiniest, seemingly inconsequential seed of today, when nurtured properly, could develop into the expansive, magical banyan tree of tomorrow. This book is evidence it actually can and *does* happen.

It all started as a thought...

He Thought — *Christian's Story*

It was mid-to-late summer in 2010, and the morning sun had just passed my patio. With floor to ceiling windows all around, the room still felt quite warm from its penetrating rays. Staring at a blank page on my computer screen, I thought: *If I'm going to win this writing contest, I sure could use some inspiration...*

Wait.

Before I get ahead of myself, let me back up a bit. You may be wondering why a chiropractor is sitting in front of a computer screen looking for inspiration, instead of looking into an x-ray screen searching for a spinal lesion. Let me give you a little background info:

As a chiropractor of more than a dozen years now, I have celebrated many truly wonderful (and sometimes miraculous) healing events with my patients, witnessing the awesome power of chiropractic first-hand. In fact, I still look forward to each and every treatment session I share with my patients.

However, what I've noticed over the years is a strange and somewhat surprising pattern emerging: When a patient presents to my clinic in pain and I ask them what caused their hurt, most often they provide me with a puzzled look and admit they have no idea. "Must have slept funny," is their most common attempt at a logical answer.

After I remind them that sleep is, in fact, the least physically-demanding event we experience in any 24-hour cycle, they usually look at me again and try to rationalize with me: since it was the last physical activity they participated in before their pain began, it *must* have been what caused it, right? But once I get them to delve a little deeper, it's not long before they can identify a different kind of (non-physical) stress occurring the day before the onset of their symptoms—like an argument with their spouse, trouble at work, etc. As a result, they get to see what I see: in almost all of the patients that present to my office with "mystery symptoms," there is a mentally or emotionally traumatic event that immediately preceded the onset of pain.

I've studied the work of many experts in the field of the mind-body connection, including such notables as Dr. Bernie Siegel, Carolyn Myss, Candace Pert and Bruce Lipton (to name a few), and they all seem to agree: increased periods of stress are <u>always</u> related to the onset of human disease. I was so relieved to discover that my observations and theories concerning stress and disease were validated by others working in the same field. But what they taught me next really opened my eyes to not only the *cause* of human suffering, but also the potential for a *cure*. It's a person's *perception* of their external environment (or an event), not the environment itself, which determines the formation and progression of an illness! What a person *thinks*—about themselves or where they find themselves—can either make them sick or help to keep them vibrantly healthy!

Armed with this knowledge and my own personal experience, I eagerly wanted to help share these insights with the World. An idea began taking shape in my mind: I could write a book highlighting all these principles in an inspirational and entertaining fictional story…

But like many budding writers, I suffered from two common afflictions: recurring self-doubt combined with a severe case of *procrastinitis.* I had a great idea, but I was neither confident enough in my writing skills nor did I think I could ever find the time to actually write my ideas down! Fortunately, the Universe sent me just the right message at the right time to break those bad habits. One of my patients, upon hearing me talk about my idea for a novel, asked, "Have you heard of that new, online spiritual-writing competition hosted by Robert Evans and James Twyman?" I hadn't, but thankfully my competitive spirit was sufficiently aroused. I looked it up on the computer as soon as I got home that day, and with a sudden flash of courage, I submitted my name and story idea for the competition. There was no going back—I was committed to becoming a writer!

This brings us back to that blank computer screen. It had been 4 months since the day I signed up for the writing competition, and although I started out of the gates running, fully inspired (two full chapters of the fictional story *Two Princes, One Crown* were written in the first month), my productivity was seriously waning when it needed to wax.

So, I did what any "Spiritual-New-Age-Guy" would do in that moment: I sought a quiet place to meditate and *ask* for inspiration. Wandering over to the couch and assuming my best lotus pose (barely a half-lotus, really), I dedicated the next 15-20 minutes to allowing whatever was meant to appear on that blank page to be downloaded from Source. My mind became more focused as I followed my breath to a deep state of relaxation...

At the end of 20 minutes, although the meditation itself did not bear any fruit that could be harvested immediately, both mind and body were definitely very relaxed and calm. Since it didn't look like the writing was going to go anywhere, the next best thing was to take advantage of this peaceful state and grab a quick nap before returning to the empty screen.

The precise details of what happened next are a bit fuzzy (falling asleep will do that to a person's memory), but to my best recollection, it was only mere seconds before my creative imagination was meandering through the land of make-believe in a dream. It wasn't the dream itself that I remember, but what happened while I was *in* the dream. Out of nowhere a sentence simply appeared, booming in my mind, **"*The thought that changed my life forever...*"**

First of all, this was very strange because I'm much more a visual person than an auditory person. To have something show up in a dream that was heard and not seen was odd to say the least. But even stranger, while still in my dream, I vividly remember thinking, *Wow—that would make a <u>great</u> book title!*

The thin veil that separates the conscious and unconscious can sometimes allow one mind to look in on the other. This must have been true in that moment, for the next thought was: *You should really get up and write it down!* And then, from the other side of the veil: *But I'm so relaxed and comfortable on the couch! Couldn't this wait until later?*

Tempted to remain in my relaxed position, but still acutely aware of *the thought* urging me to take action, my consciousness overcame my lazy tendency. Stirring myself awake, I went over to my work-station and wrote the inspirational phrase in my journal. Then, sitting back and gazing at what I'd written with a fist under my chin (doing my best impression of Rodin's "The Thinker"), I silently commented: *Wasn't the inspiration supposed to help with my fictional story?* This was a completely different animal altogether.

When you ask the Universe for a sign, it will appear—but sometimes in a completely different format than you originally expected. Knowing full well the benefits of visualization and meditation for manifestation, I knew enough not to question the form of the message—just to be thankful it was received. But to accept it gracefully was the real challenge. It was a precious gift, a compelling title for a book even. But why now? Immediately, another inspiring thought popped into my head: *Perhaps this will lead to even <u>bigger</u> things than the book I'm currently working on…*

All of a sudden, I could feel excitement again and the inspiration to keep pursuing this line of thinking. (After all, wasn't that the purpose of the first inquiry— *inspiration?*)

Taking a moment to reflect upon the previous forty years of my life, I was confident a great self-help book was just waiting to be filled with all my personal "a-ha" moments. Although it had the potential for great success (don't all authors believe this when they start out?), a nagging question still lingered: *Wasn't the intention to help millions of people with my personal insights?* A bunch of personal stories was sure to entertain friends and family, but wasn't mass appeal unlikely if the book was produced all by me? Self-doubt reared its ugly head once more, and my excitement proceeded to wane yet again.

But as quickly as I could feel the flame about to flicker out, a spark appeared in the form of a new thought, serving to rekindle my fire: *Why don't I get others of like-mind with a desire to have their messages published each contribute one chapter?!* What a perfect plan! (Wish I'd thought of that.) If constructed in this way, the collaboration could maximize our exposure (using all our collective social and professional networks), with chapters containing many different perspectives, yet based on the same question: "What was the thought that changed your life forever?"

Immediately, I began gathering names and email addresses for the other aspiring authors entered in the online spiritual writing competition…

And so, the idea was born.

If you believe in Divine Timing, you'll agree that everything happens in life at exactly the right time to teach us whatever we need to know in that moment. Once I'd set the wheels in motion, inspired by a single thought, the Universe just seemed to effortlessly click into the same gear, moving me rapidly ever-closer to realizing my dream of helping teach others on a global scale. The perfect people began showing up exactly as they were needed—most notably the equally passionate co-creator of this book and our company, Gillian Laura Roberts. If the title of the book felt like a gift, it was soon to be overshadowed by the brilliance of "everything Gillian." A writer herself, she also brought her own powerful world of vision, as well as a wealth of experience in editing, film-making, graphic design…plus, she's a *Licensed Spiritual Practitioner of New Thought*! How perfect could it get?

As perfect as I needed, apparently.

As they say, the rest is history. From the very first moment we met and started chatting, it was obvious we would make the perfect team to bring our dreams into reality. Thankfully, she echoed these sentiments, and it's been one of my life's most rewarding experiences to date. The Universe sure knew what it was doing when it brought us together!

But now let's hear *her* side of the story…

She Thought — *Gillian's Story*

For more than a year and a half, my friend Andrew had been trying to connect me and a guy he knew. It was his chiropractor, actually—a fella named Christian. Andrew was convinced we needed to meet one another because our respective conversations with him about our work and future plans sounded so energetically similar. He felt we were up to many of the same things in the World—helping others (and ourselves!) achieve greater vitality and authentic well-being. Maybe there was a valuable connection we could make?

For some reason, however, those introductory emails just hadn't caught on. After a final poke in my ribs one day on the golf course—and one last email—Christian and I finally caught the spark of our mutual friend's insight! In no time, we arranged a rendez-vous to discuss our work—and a cool book idea he'd had *just weeks earlier…*

When he asked me what I looked like so he could pick me out in the café, I said, "I have a feeling we'll recognize one another." We did! How does the song go, "… *when a tornado meets a volcano?*" Our first meeting was wonderfully energizing as we fed off one another's excitement about our philosophies and far-reaching plans. At the same time, it was really grounding to meet in conversation the way we did that day: I recognized a kindred spirit who, like me, came alive with a passion for life and giving, for creativity and expanding possibility. What beautiful synchrony! Notebooks came out, diagrams were sketched, visions were shared, and perspectives were illuminated. It was like two rocks striking together and sparking something new—yet refreshingly familiar.

My spirit smiled that day knowing we'd both met a newfound, long-lost friend. With simpatico visions—unique in detail, yet aligned in fire and intent—sweet spots of overlap slowly but surely revealed themselves, naturally catalyzing the possibility for partnership. It was done before we met, I'm sure of it.

When he told me the story of how the idea for the book had recently come to him during a meditative dream, I thought his inspiration was *really* wonderful—and indeed, a phenomenal book title! As a Science of Mind Practitioner (a faith and philosophy that holds the power of thought as a central tenet), I knew it was right on the money! It wasn't long before we decided to join forces to live into that powerful phrase—breathing life into this very book as a team. And we've been gifted with many, many more inspirations along the way.

Our clear, powerful *yes* had turned a key.

Even though starting another business and co-creating a book project right then was a somewhat surprising turn of events, I realized these wonderful prospects were simply manifestations of a long-cherished intention. You see, I'd been a writer for some time, but it had also been my secret practice (since about grade 2!) to dream up book titles and imagine the stories that would live into them. Though my writing experience had been varied, I had not yet written a book: however, given my personal and professional focus on spirituality, bringing such themes and philosophical queries to either fiction or non-fiction projects had become an anticipated element of my evolving, creative dream.

Now, *how* and *when* our dreams go from the invisible to the visible is part of the grand mystery of Life, but it was clear: so much of what I loved was being called forth in this wonderful meeting of the minds with Christian and me. And we were a team who would work tirelessly to bring out the best in one another.

The world of mind, neuroscience and psychology married with the arts, athletics and spirituality had informed my inner experience since my first memories. As a young child, I would stare at the ceiling each night until I imagined I could see its particles vibrating. My first meditation practice! When I was 11 or 12, I recall the impact of a quote I found: "*You're never given a dream without also being given the power to make it come true…*" It instilled in me a belief that no matter what limitation I (or others) perceived in a situation—whether it was economic "station," gender or being the tallest girl in the class—I felt empowered to use my inner awareness and gifts to achieve what I put my mind to. It seamlessly evolved my childhood belief in magic to an unspoken faith in the unknown power around me—and *my direct connection with it.* I felt plugged in, loved and cared for. Long before I would ever use the word "God," I felt like a child of a powerful, loving Universe.

In 1999, a rather large vision downloaded through me from that loving Source: It began the day I viewed a commercial space with a prospective business partner (my former choreographer) which was intended to be a new dance studio. As I walked through, suddenly myriad images and ideas began pouring into my awareness: not of a dance studio, but something much more. I saw a vibrant space radiating with the energies of vitality, creative expression, spiritual awareness and powerful connection. It would be a place where people come to thrive—exploring health, personal expression and the infinite nature of creativity. For me, creativity and spirituality were ultimately synonymous, so it would also provide a special opportunity for others to feel plugged in, too.

By the time I was home that afternoon, it had a name—"Centre Space"—and no fewer than 11 different elements had emerged. Each one could have been a stand-alone business! As amazing as it was, I found myself both excited and perplexed. What was I to do with all this?

Over the next few years, I dabbled in exploring its creative nature and business potential whilst simultaneously working in film. I came to wonder what the common thread was in all its many moving parts. During that same time, I discovered a wonderful New Thought community and minister, and began training to become a Licensed Spiritual Practitioner. As I neared the time of my licensing and contemplated my next steps, I realized what had been there all along for me to find: the common thread to all the seemingly disparate parts of Centre Space was that every element was about *elevating Consciousness*! After receiving the gift years earlier, I now understood my initial confusion had served to inform my journey since: I came to realize it had been necessary for me to *become the right person* to bring the vision to life for it to truly manifest. Becoming a Practitioner and seeing my life's path as preparation for this responsibility led me to believe I was ready to begin truly bringing it forward to benefit others, too.

I started where I could, establishing my company—Centre Space Spiritual Coaching—as an umbrella for my work as a Licensed Spiritual Practitioner. I began a spiritual counseling practice, taught meditation and New Thought philosophy, and served my church community. In time, I was speaking at Sunday services and leading meditation and mindfulness training in unorthodox (corporate) settings.

The first years were fast and furious—I could genuinely feel people yearning for spiritual nourishment wherever I went (even if they didn't choose to call it that). I sought to meet that need in any way I could, yet the pace began to feel unsustainable. How could I do this on my own and simultaneously build a team and unveil (read: finance) the much *bigger* vision of Centre Space? The *ultimate* iteration was intended to touch and serve throughout the World—yet my own world was stretched so thin. It started to feel untenable. I recognized I needed a new approach, but I just couldn't see it yet.

Around that time, I got a phone call. My parents had been shopping at an outdoor market when an elderly driver plowed his car right through the middle. My mom was struck directly, my dad pinned between the large crates—both left shocked and injured, my mom very seriously. A few inches either way would've meant their end. Even as a grown woman, the impact of nearly losing my cherished parents struck me deeply. In the days that followed, an acute, internal reckoning put me squarely at a fork in the road:

Should I move to their town to care for and be with them—or keep moving forward to build my dream?

As I lived with this question of where to be of service, I ultimately surrendered myself to Spirit, asking, *What do I need to embrace in order to manifest my highest calling?*

The one-word answer was swift, *audible* and clear: "collaboration."

In this beautiful truth, I finally rested, realizing I no longer had to endeavour on my own. Helping me to see that my parents did not need me to move either, I also rested in the wisdom of my good friend who said, *"This is the time to expand, not contract."* (Thanks, Jana.)

With these newly received gifts of insight, I relaxed into excited anticipation— knowing collaboration was the key to opening the next door in the beautiful manifestation of my dream…*and beyond.* As life would have it, just as my thought was coming to me, only blocks away, Christian was receiving his magical thought, too. Since we had now both asked the golden questions, the Universe could get busy crafting the perfect answer for both of us…

Through inspired thoughts, we came together; through powerful intention, *The Thought Publications, Inc.* was born. I'm so grateful for the lightning bolts that brought us here to create this book together, all in divine right timing. Now we know why those introductory emails hadn't worked a year and a half earlier!

Along the way, we've shared the same integrity and commitment, believing *it's not what you do, but how you do it.* So ultimately, this is a story of faith, commitment and friendship—the power of collaboration in service to not only happiness, but to an even greater vision than we could even imagine for ourselves as individuals.

I'm so pleased to have the World come to know this shared dream that also fuels and provides us the invaluable opportunity to express and explore our own personal visions. I especially cherish the chance to share my passion for the power of the mind and creativity as well as my love of possibility, alongside the amazing people we have gathered here—in service of *you.*

We Think

Was the Universe telling *you* it was the right time to create change in *your* life when you heard about this book? Maybe the phrase, **"The THOUGHT That Changed My Life Forever"** grabbed your attention, too?

"…Changed My Life Forever." We know—it's quite a bold statement. Yet it's absolutely true for every one of us telling our story here, and it can be true for you, too. Change is a *magical* thing. It can lead to the realization of goals and dreams for your future; it can also bring you joy, success and personal evolution. But isn't there a popular notion that change can also bring about your *worst fears*? Isn't that what often stops you from committing to the idea of change, even when your current circumstances are filled with things you really wish were different?

The beautiful thing about reading this book is it offers you powerful insights that can help make change magical instead of fearful.

Have you ever looked longingly at those who seem the most successful in life, imagining they must have never doubted themselves or were never afraid to take risks? You'd be wrong! We *all* have fears and doubts. People who achieve the success they desire are the ones who have come to recognize fear for what it is—a projection of "worst-case" scenario thoughts. They then overcome this fear by mindfully creating consistent pictures of themselves in "best-case" scenarios. This takes some serious resolve; this takes faith and desire stronger than fear; this takes a willingness to apply conscious thought over and over again until the dream is finally realized. It takes perseverance—against what may feel like incredible odds.

But does it also take special talents or great intellect to make this happen? No! Everything you need exists inside you right now. It's only a matter of recognizing your unique potential, then putting it into action.

Almost everyone who has achieved a lofty goal will admit it wasn't easy. Invariably, Life presents us with obstacles along the way that can sometimes feel insurmountable. But they're not. Those who ultimately persevere in the realization of their dreams are the ones who recognize their obstacles as challenges, not barriers—thereby *strengthening* their commitment to move forward, no matter what.

This book is all about individuals who faced their circumstances, fears or limitations and followed their inner guidance to achieve something they wanted (or never even knew they wanted): success, happiness, health, love, freedom. These are dreams we as human beings all share. We are here to offer you hope—if they can do it, so can you!

Although many of the authors we recruited for this volume are healing professionals—doctors, coaches, counselors, therapists, entrepreneurs—they're really just like *everyone* because we're all made of the same stuff! At some point along the way, when life was getting hard, each one of them had a thought—a single, solitary, catalyzing thought. For some, it was a voice; for others, it was an image. But for all of them, this thought served as a beacon of light, shining brightly in the moment and projecting onto their future—a future in which they saw themselves in a new, inspiring light.

They then made up their minds to keep following their thought despite any uncertainty they may have had. We're so grateful they did, as it brought them to these pages. Here, they share their life lessons hoping to inspire you to go for your own dreams—to trust in and follow your very own special "thoughts." In reading their stories, may you find the motivation to change your life, too!

Your Upcoming Thought Journey

In the opening chapter, Dr. Joe Dispenza will describe the process of changing your mind step-by-step, including how we all have the hard-wiring in our brains and bodies to make change both possible and *probable*. It should give you enough information to confidently believe you have the "stuff" inside you to make it happen. This same information has been used to teach thousands of individuals in workshops and seminars—in his typically wonderful "Dr. Joe" way—leaving most of his students spellbound (including us). He will highlight the beautifully complex nature of the human mind and its capacity to move dreams into reality, providing you with the tools that can change your life!

Then, as you read through each of the following carefully-crafted personal stories, see if you can relate to the person who is writing it and where they were at the moment *change* was initiated for them. Does it sound or feel familiar to you? Observe how each one of these individuals was changed forever by a single thought and how these personal moments of transformation led to their on-going tales of passion and purpose.

What's the best way to enjoy this book?

You may choose to savour one chapter each week or devour the stories section by section. We have arranged them very mindfully, though not conventionally. Each chapter "chose" where it wanted to be—by section and in what order. Just as this book is about the power of the mind and how our thoughts contribute to our individual and collective consciousness, we allowed our own awareness, together with guidance from higher Consciousness[2], to direct us as we assembled this book for you.

As the stories found their home in four groupings, our exploration of the sections' essential themes found they had emerged in perfect, mystical alignment with the tenets of the *Four Kingdoms of Consciousness (a.k.a. "Queendoms" or "Kin-doms")*. As Michael Bernard Beckwith, founder of the Agape International Spiritual Center, writes in his book *Life Visioning* (Sounds True, 2011), there are four levels of consciousness from which we live our lives. We have adapted them here:

Kingdom 1: I believe life is done *to me*—I have no control, I'm a victim;

---

2   We used "muscle-testing" methods akin to those described in David Hawkins' *Power vs. Force* (Hay House, 2002).

Kingdom 2: With a little more experience or insight, I come to believe I can have some authority over it all—life is done *by me*;

Kingdom 3: As I accept there is a Source of power to which I am connected, I come to feel life happens *through me*;

and finally,

Kingdom 4: As I achieve a sense of liberation from all other levels of consciousness—transcending attachment to realize true freedom—I directly understand that Life is living itself *as me*. In its pure state, this is *enlightenment*.

Although each chapter chose its place based on its story's theme, in the end, all roads led to one place for everyone: personal awakening. That is what enlightenment is!

Begin the Thought Journey

This is how a single thought—*the thought that changed my life forever*—multiplied and changed *our* lives. But it's only the beginning, for us and for you. These chapters are individual reflections of the miracle we call Life. May they serve to remind you of what amazing wonders your thoughts—divinely inspired, powerful thoughts—can bring into your daily living.

Whatever you get from reading this book, we all hope it's a rich experience and one that leads you to pay closer attention. Perhaps you will even have a transformational thought you'd be willing to share with us in future volumes of *The Thought That Changed My Life Forever*!

Ultimately, we trust you will take something positive from these stories and inject it into your *own* life. Perhaps this will help you re-fuel your belief in yourself, affirm your personal convictions or give you confidence to go for your own dreams. Maybe it will even help reinforce your faith in the Universe—that the "divine design" also includes *you*.

INTRODUCTION

When Our Thoughts Become Us:

The SCIENCE of Changing Your Mind

by Dr. Joe Dispenza

When I was approached to write a chapter for this book, naturally my first response was, "What's it about?" After I was given a brief explanation of the concept and its intention, my next thought was:

When do I start?

You see, for many years my work has also been focused on how giving our thoughts conscious attention influences our potential for happiness, success and perfect health. I've even written two books on the topic—*Evolve Your Brain: The Science of Changing Your Mind* and *Breaking the Habit of Being Yourself: How to Lose Your Mind and Create a New One*. I could see this new book would illustrate in real-time so many of the principles I've been passionately pursuing—in a truly unique and inspiring format.

So for me it was a no-brainer: Christian and Gillian were going to demonstrate for their readers how the impossible becomes possible—simply by paying closer attention to our thoughts and making choices congruent to the new path opened up in front of us. I was both excited and honored to do my part! Not only was I confident I could give an expert summary of my broad-based knowledge related to

1

the power of the mind, but I knew I could also contribute a compelling personal story—because I *lived* it in the summer of 1986.

This was the year I had the privilege of getting hit by a truck while I was competing in a triathlon.

It might sound crazy to say it that way, but it's true. While in the hospital, I received the diagnosis: I'd broken six vertebrae, had bone fragments pressing against my spinal cord, and was told I'd probably never walk again. Faced with the grim prognosis of paralysis, I was presented with "radical spinal surgery" as my best chance for recovery—by four different experts. As a doctor of chiropractic, I had been taught, *"The power that made the body heals the body,"* and I'd been sharing this wisdom with my patients ever since. But would I be able to lay my *own* future in the hands of this principle—let this incredible thought direct the creation of my own new reality? It was the moment of truth for me, and it put my faith to the test. The rest of my life would depend on what I decided to do next.

Luckily for me, my faith won. I opted against the surgery and left the hospital with a heightened determination to create healing on my own terms. My mission was set: I would make contact with the Innate Intelligence that gives us life, and then use my own *personal* intelligence to create the specific healing template for getting well again. As a final display of my belief, I would surrender my healing to this infinite power.

The power that made the body heals the body…

I certainly had nowhere to go and really had no other upcoming plans. Nor did I (now) have any triathlons I could participate in for awhile! So, it was the perfect opportunity for me to put the theories to work on myself—using the power of my mind to heal my body. For two hours, twice a day, I went within and began creating a picture of my intended result: a healthy, flexible, vibrantly functioning spine. I also committed to the belief that it was possible, such that I was able to feel the joy of that vision being true before it actually was! If my mind wandered to any extraneous thoughts, I would start from the beginning and recreate the whole scheme of imagery over again. I reasoned that the final picture had to be clear, unpolluted and uninterrupted for this Intelligence to take my vision to the next level.

Over the course of the following ten weeks, I observed first-hand a miraculous and veritable healing! At eleven weeks, I was back in my office seeing patients once again *without surgery or even a body brace* (both of which were recommended by the physicians at the time of my injury). As a result of this triumph more than 25 years ago, I've dedicated my life to investigating and researching the mind-body connection, as well as the powerful—and in my experience, *indisputable*—concept of mind over matter.

One thought had truly changed my life—forever.

When we are confronted with a potentially life-altering trauma or crisis, we *must* change our minds if we want to transcend the situation. We need to think, feel and act in ways that restore balance and produce a new, more desired result. Unfortunately, it often takes major traumatic events for many of us to shift our focus to ourselves and what might be possible beyond the status quo—that is, to consider our predilections and even our *true potential*. The good news is, consciously choosing to create and experience positive change in our lives does not require waiting for an emergency. We need only imagine what we want to see in our lives tomorrow then recruit thoughts that support this new vision—today. Whether a new way of thinking is set into motion by a flash of insight and inspiration or is consciously generated to support the "next steps" in the pursuit of a personal goal, the possibility for transformation in our lives is awaiting our focused and powerful attention.

The key to creating real and lasting change in our lives is to commit to that newly desired ideal in every moment, regardless of what our environment tells us—including our bodies. We seek comfort, but change usually means *dis*comfort because we are stepping into the unknown. If we can conjure up enough internal motivation to go after our goals with tireless focus—keeping our "eyes on the prize"—change will be inevitable! And when we have mind and body working together, we have the power of the Universe behind us. *No one* is excluded from this phenomenon.

Since I appeared in the hit movie "*What the Bleep Do We Know!?*", I've been very busy traveling around the World talking to audiences about how our unconscious thoughts and feelings are records of our *past*, whereas our conscious thoughts can be the very blueprints of our *future*. I've also been fortunate enough to spend the last ten years investigating hundreds of medical cases in which ordinary people experienced "spontaneous remissions" from a host of different diseases. I discovered there is a common thread to all of their healings, and it brought me to the realization that the same techniques they (and I) had used to achieve wellness could also be applied to manifest most anything the heart desires.

As a result of my own experience and years of research, I'm now convinced the same science and biology that created these healing miracles also support the process of *all* personal transformation. Independent of race, gender, culture, social status, education, religious beliefs—or even past "mistakes"—there is a power within each of us that can transform our dreams into our new reality. We are all connected to it. This invisible Consciousness is both personal and, at the same time, universal—it is the giver of life. This refined, mindful energy is conscious enough to support, protect and heal us in every moment, and, at the same time, is creating supernovas in distant galaxies, keeping planets rotating around the sun and bringing lilies into bloom!

When we take the time to develop an active relationship with this Mind—creating 2-way communication, asking for evidence of Its presence, and choosing to express Its power, love, and intelligence through us—we become more like It. We (re)claim our inherent divinity. As we take time each day to emulate the Creator, as the Buddhists say, "horse and rider become one."

Our *thoughts* are the keys that open us into this magical realm of possibility.

But how do we go about doing it? In the next few sections, I will break down for you the "traditional" method of taking any thought, concept or desire through to the development of a new experience. It takes three, concrete, sequential stages I call *thinking, doing* and *being*. Then, I will show you how to make a *quantum shift* directly from thinking to being—creating change in life using your mind alone.

As I've been teaching this principle to hundreds, even thousands of people, I'm always amazed at how such a simple concept consistently leads to incredible moments of personal transformation in people's lives! The truth is, we are all equipped to do this; the brain, as it turns out, is *designed* to assist us in evolving our lives!

Let's start with the basics behind the neurology of how our thoughts influence our behaviors.

Neurons that fire together, wire together[3]

With this statement, neurologist D.O. Hebb summarized the fundamental principle that not only explains the neuro-physiological basis of human behavior, but also points us to the possibility for consciously changing the human brain.

---

3   Hebb, D.O. (Wiley, 1949) *The Organization of Behavior: A neuropsychological theory.*

Think of the human brain like the CPU of a computer. All information necessary for human survival and behavior is processed in this area. Like the computer, information is passed from one component to another via dedicated pathways. However, where the computer has wires, the brain has neurons. For every thought or behavior, there is a corresponding circuit of neurons, all firing together to ensure a response is facilitated in the brain and then relayed efficiently to the body.

Hebb's credo also highlights how the brain *learns*. The more often any neurological pathway is stimulated, the more firmly established it becomes—thus making it easier for the body to repeat the corresponding behavior when signaled. The neurons that get accustomed to firing together under certain circumstances will become "hard-wired" together—solidifying the connection between our brains, our environment and our experience. When these same pathways are used often enough, we can begin to perform the same actions (or reactions) automatically—without having to *consciously* think about them. Just like a newly blazed trail, each time it is subsequently travelled, the path deepens—making it more likely it will be travelled again because it is so familiar and easily accessible. Pretty soon, the horse will get you back to the barn, even if you are daydreaming along the way.

Think about your typical day: You get up around the same time, follow the same process of getting ready for work or play (shower, shave, brush, get dressed, etc), take the same travel route, repeat similar tasks at work, eat from a familiar selection of foods at each meal, interact with a similar group of people in familiar social or professional environments...and so on. What's happening in your brain? The same neuronal pathways are activated so often by these familiar environmental cues that your body eventually learns to repeat the behavior without needing to be prompted by your mind. Like the trail, these pathways are so well-worn you could find your way through it in your sleep!

This process is incredibly helpful for behaviors that ensure our survival—like automatically looking both ways before crossing the street. However, it can also become harmful for behaviors that present a threat to our well-being—like mindlessly lighting up a cigarette in times of boredom or stress. Since this simple principle defines the process by which all patterns of behavior are created in our lives, the great news is we can also learn to mindfully and consistently apply it to serve our best interests. This is really the intended focus of not only this educational chapter, but this incredible book of inspiration: To reveal how tapping into this process more consciously provides you the opportunity to create a new way of *being* by altering an old line of *thinking*. New thoughts equal new experiences—and new experiences can change your life.

The Science of Changing Your Mind: Thinking — Doing — Being

All change begins with thinking. New neurological connections are constantly being formed, reflecting our new thoughts. And nothing gets the brain more excited than when it's learning—assimilating knowledge and experiences. Every second, it processes billions of bits of data—it analyzes, examines, identifies, extrapolates, classifies, and files information which it can instantaneously retrieve for us on an "as needed" basis. Truly, the human brain is this planet's ultimate supercomputer.

When I spoke of "evolving your brain" in my first book, what I was really referring to was taking advantage of the brain's biology—in particular, the most recent and highly evolved addition to our human brain, the frontal lobe of the neocortex. This part of the brain allows us to consciously build new neuronal circuits ("sprouting") and abandon outdated, no-longer-needed ones ("pruning"). The frontal lobe literally is the key that allows us to create a *new mind*.

The gift of *neuroplasticity*—this ability of the brain to rewire itself and create new circuits—is what allows for a neurological "out with the old, in with the new." It's what I call *unlearning* and *learning*, and it creates the opportunity for each one of us to rise above our current limitations and to be greater than our conditioning or circumstances.

Even though change can sometimes seem scary, thankfully we've actually got a few things going for us behind the scenes. Besides being neuroplastic, we could also say we have more than one brain to work with. In effect, we have three of them! For our purposes, this chapter will limit its focus to those functions of the "three brains" that relate specifically to creating change in our lives.[4]

THINKING—The Neocortex: "Knowledge is for the mind"

Our "thinking brain" is the *neocortex*, the brain's walnut-like outer layer. This is humanity's newest, most advanced neurological hardware—the seat of the conscious mind, our identity and other higher brain functions. Essentially, the neocortex is the brain's architect or designer. It allows you to learn, remember, reason, analyze, plan, create, speculate on possibilities, invent and communicate.

---

4   My first book *Evolve Your Brain: The Science of Changing Your Mind* (Health Communications, Inc. 2007) covered this topic in more detail. There are additional resources for study, including Breaking the Habit of Being Yourself: How to Lose Your Mind and Create A New One (Hay House, 2012) plus my website: www.drjoedispenza.com.

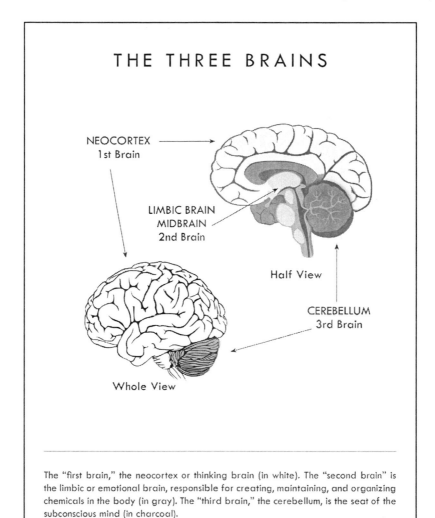

THE THREE BRAINS

NEOCORTEX
1st Brain

LIMBIC BRAIN
MIDBRAIN
2nd Brain

Half View

CEREBELLUM
3rd Brain

Whole View

The "first brain," the neocortex or thinking brain (in white). The "second brain" is the limbic or emotional brain, responsible for creating, maintaining, and organizing chemicals in the body (in gray). The "third brain," the cerebellum, is the seat of the subconscious mind (in charcoal).

© Dr. Joe Dispenza, used with permission. Originally appearing in *Breaking The Habit of Being Yourself: How to Lose Your Mind and Create a New One* (Hay House, 2012)

Since this area is where you log sensory data (such as what you see and hear), the neocortex plugs you into the external reality of your world. In general, the neocortex processes knowledge and experience. You gather knowledge in the form of facts or *semantic* information (philosophical or theoretical concepts and ideas you learn intellectually), and this prompts the neocortex to add new synaptic connections and circuits. That's what learning is.

If the neocortex had a motto, it might be, "Knowledge is for the mind." Simply put, knowledge is the precursor to experience. Your neocortex is responsible for processing thoughts or ideas you have not yet experienced physically, but that exist as a potential for you to embody at some future time.

Now it's not enough to just take in that information. As you entertain new thoughts, you begin to think about modifying your behavior to apply and demonstrate the knowledge you have acquired to change something about yourself or to create a new experience. New experiences enrich the brain. Everything we're seeing, smelling, tasting, feeling and hearing provides information from the environment and sends it rushing back to the neocortex. This causes jungles of neurons to organize themselves to reflect the event. This causes new *neural networks* to form, reinforcing the circuitry of what you learned intellectually and triggering the activation of the second brain (the limbic brain)—which facilitates the communication of thought with the body.

DOING—The Limbic Brain: "Experience is for the body"

The *limbic brain* is located under the neocortex. Think of the limbic brain as the "emotional brain" or "chemical brain." The moment those networks of neurons fire with a pattern unique to a new experience, the emotional brain is triggered to manufacture and release chemicals in the form of peptides. This chemical cocktail has a specific "signature" that reflects the emotions you are experiencing in the moment. Since emotions are the end products of experience, a new experience creates a new emotion—a unique "feeling." These emotions signal the body to record the event chemically, and we are now *embodying* what we've been learning intellectually.

Using this process, the limbic brain assists in forming long-term memories. Isn't it true you can remember any experience better when you recall how you felt while the event was occurring? We are all marked emotionally by highly charged experiences. Anybody who has been married can tell you where they were and what they were doing when they either gave or received the proposal. Perhaps they were eating a great meal on the patio of their favorite restaurant, enjoying the balmy breezes and the sunset as Mozart played softly in the background—when their beloved got down on one knee and held out a blue box. Of course the same could be said for any highly charged or norm-altering experience. Most people can readily recall where they were and what they were doing when, for instance, JFK was assassinated or Princess Diana passed away or when they became aware of the events unfolding in New York City on 9/11.

We can more easily remember these events because the combination of everything we were experiencing in that moment made us feel very different from our normal selves. The typical internal chemical balance that our "identity self" had memorized got knocked out of order by what we saw, heard and felt. In a sense, we woke up from the familiar, routine environmental stimuli that typically bombarded the brain, causing us to think and feel in predictable ways. Novel events have the tendency to surprise us to the point that we become more aware of the present moment. If the limbic brain had a motto, it might be, "Experience is for the body." And, if thought is the language of the brain, then emotion is the language of experience for the body.

It is important to remember: knowledge without experience is merely philosophy; experience without knowledge is ignorance. You have to take knowledge and *live* it. And, to create long-lasting and memorable change, you must engage new experiences emotionally.

If you're still with me as I've been discussing how to change your life, you've now learned about acquiring knowledge and then taking action to have a new experience—which produces a new feeling. Next, you will have to *memorize* that feeling so well that what you've learned can move from the conscious mind to the subconscious mind, making your chosen way of thinking and behaving a *positive* habit. You've already got the hardware to do that in the "third" brain.

BEING—The Cerebellum: The seat of your subconscious mind

We've all had the experience of not being able to consciously remember a phone number, ATM PIN or lock combination—but because we've practiced it so often, the body knows better than the brain, and our fingers automatically get the job done. Right? That may seem like a small thing, but when the body knows equal to or *better than* the conscious mind—when you can automatically or unconsciously repeat an experience at will without much conscious effort—you have subconsciously memorized the action, behavior, attitude or emotional reaction to the point it has become a skill or a habit.

When you reach this level of ability, you have moved into a state of *being*. In the process, you've activated the third brain area that plays a major role in changing your life—the *cerebellum* or the seat of the subconscious.

The most active part of the brain, the cerebellum is located at the back of the skull. Think of it as the brain's microprocessor and memory center. Every neuron in the cerebellum has the potential to connect with up to a million other cells to process balance, coordination, awareness of the spatial relation of body parts, and the execution of controlled movements. The cerebellum also stores certain types of simple actions and skills, however, most relevant to our discussion, it also houses our hardwired attitudes, emotional reactions, repeated actions, habits, conditioned behaviors, and the unconscious reflexes and skills we have mastered or memorized. Possessing amazing memory storage, it easily downloads various forms of learned information into programmed states of mind and body.

When the cerebellum makes that new state of being an implicit part of your subconscious, that means you have practiced and repeated a behavior so many times that you know how to do something, but don't consciously track how you know that you know. That is, you don't have to think about it because it's become *automatic*. When that happens, you will arrive at a point when whatever attitude, behavior, skill or trait you've been focusing on mentally or physically will become an intrinsic part of your new self.

From Desire to Reality—An Example

Let me give you a familiar, true-to-life example of how these three brains take us from *thinking*, to *doing*, and then to a new state of *being*:

When we reach our early teens, most of us have the dream of being able to drive a car. When we envision ourselves behind the wheel, don't we also *feel* the excitement associated with that imagined experience? It absolutely becomes an emotionally-significant event for us.

Finally coming of age, we begin this monumental task by acquiring all the necessary semantic knowledge required to drive a car: we become familiar with the licensing requirements and study the manuals describing the "rules of the road"; we observe our parents when they drive, noticing how they sit and where they put their hands and feet, what levers and buttons they press when they want the car to do different things, etc. We do our best to remember where everything is and what it's for. Then, we read those manuals over and over again, unknowingly reinforcing the neuronal circuitry in our thinking brain, allowing us to more easily recall the information whenever our parents quiz us. This ultimately leads us to passing the written licensing exam, at which point we could proudly proclaim, "I have *learned* what it takes to drive a car."

Once we've passed that first hurdle of knowing how to actually operate a vehicle, we set about putting our "theory" to the test—we put the information into action. We climb behind the wheel of the car, and step-by-step begin to apply the principles we learned so the car will do what it's supposed to (of course, all the while crossing our fingers, hoping we don't mess up!). We become incredibly attentive to every detail, and with each action step our brains are flooded with sensory information (sights, sounds, feelings) that reinforce what we intellectually learned, feeding the neuronal networks we established as we went through the learning process. As new sensory data is coming in, the combination of that information travelling to the brain through five different sensory pathways signals the limbic brain to make a chemical. This is the new feeling of *freedom* that comes with actually driving a car! We consciously take note of each time we do something right or wrong, emotionally reinforcing this new learning process by emphatically celebrating our successes and likely berating ourselves each time we forget some important detail. As we get a good "feel" for the application of all the required elements, we could say we are actually "*driving* a car."

With time, these patterns of thinking and doing "driving" become easier and easier to repeat because we have neuro-chemically conditioned the body to know how to drive a car as well as the mind. As mind and body become one, we begin to perform certain functions without even consciously thinking about them: we automatically press down on the turn signal to go left; we naturally shoulder-check to make sure the road is clear to change lanes; we always put the car in "park" before we turn off the engine, etc. Driving a car has now become a skill or a habit. We may even refer to "driving" as a part of our being. When we speak to others, we could confidently announce, "I *am* a good driver."

Haven't you ever found yourself at a stop-light, wondering how you got there—with your last memory being at an intersection five blocks back or even...when you first left the house? Your mind can sometimes be so consciously focused on something else while you are driving that you allow your unconscious mind-body to take over and operate the car for you! If this has ever happened to you, it's clear evidence you have progressed through all three stages of learning: from thinking and doing to being. Although not necessarily a *safe* way to drive, it demonstrates perfectly how what started as conscious thinking and doing—when repeated enough times— became a way of (unconsciously) *being*.

The preceding example of becoming an accomplished driver—gaining knowledge, applying it through actions that created new experiences (and thus, new feelings), and then repeating them enough to have them become automatic—led to shifting your dream to your reality. Driving became as automatic and familiar to you as the habit of dreaming about it was previously.

Now all three brains are working together, and you are biologically and neuro-chemically in a state of being a driver.

If we want to change *any* pattern of behavior and make a significant shift in our life's experience—in essence, to create our *desired* memories of tomorrow—then we can! But first, we must become aware of the existing patterns and our feelings about them. We need to become more conscious of our unconscious programs and choose what to retain, what to release, and what to create anew.

A good student will put all valuable lessons into practice, helping
to evolve the brain—breaking the habit of being the old neuro-
chemical self—leading to the actualization of a new personal reality.

A QUANTUM LEAP:
How to Use MENTAL REHEARSAL to Create A New You

Before I get to the magical process of quantum leaping, let me remind you of the initial stage of change for any human behavior—to become *aware* of what we want to change about our old self and what our new self would be like. This sets the stage for the grand performance.

I believe one of the greatest privileges of being human is having this ability *to observe our own thoughts:* that is, we have the capacity to be aware. If we choose to use this awareness, we can discern between what is favorable or unfavorable for us—not merely to survive, but to *thrive*. With recognition of where we are (now) versus where we'd like to be (soon), we must then choose how to focus our conscious attention. To change, grow, *evolve*—we need to think beyond our present environment, allowing our conscious thoughts to take authority over the emotional reactions of the body. Eventually we experience a new way of being because our mind and body are working together in alignment with our conscious desires. The trick in making the switch from actor to director lies solely in knowing what you want, then making decisions to *direct* your mind consciously: this is the first step in ensuring a life that more accurately reflects your dreams!

As I mentioned before, the next step is also (always) a good idea: acquire a healthy amount of knowledge, facts and figures regarding this newly desired activity or state of mind. Intellectual knowledge is fuel for the brain and can keep the mind motivated to continue moving forward when the vision hasn't quite yet manifested. The more knowledge you have, the better prepared you are for a new experience. Surely someone somewhere must have accomplished something similar to your desires and has written about what they learned and experienced! Gathering evidence of *possibility becoming reality* can help to prime the pump—your mind.

Both of those initial steps are part of the thinking stage, and comprise the very beginning of any worthwhile goal, aspiration or dream. It is the *next* step, however, that will allow you to skip over the arduous task known as "trial and error," (the *doing* stage) in the traditional process of *thinking*, *doing* and *being* described earlier. When you bypass that stage, you also get to avoid experiencing the deflating emotions often linked to realizing your own imperfections or potentially failing and having to get back up to start over again.

Not a great fan of missing the mark myself, I turn your attention instead to *mental rehearsal* as the key to unlocking your vision with greater ease and success. It is a tool that helps create that new state of being—your new personal reality—without the physical strain of doing anything other than using your mind.

When I use the term mental rehearsal, I am referring to the projection of an *actual* experience you want to have—before it happens—like a holographic movie in your mind. You generate a very specific wish, create it as real in your mind and then watch it come true—not only in your imagination, but in your life—just as you saw it. I know this may sound like the stuff of fantasy novels, but it's not hocus-pocus: it is a process that has been validated by a plethora of scientific studies. Let me show you an example of what I am describing using one such study from the mid-'90s which originally appeared in the *Journal of Neurophysiology*:[5]

In this experiment, four different groups of individuals were recruited for a 5-day study involving the playing of a simple piano arrangement:

- The first group was taught the exercises and then asked to practice the scales and chords for 2 hours per day, for 5 days.
- A second group was asked to play anything they wanted on the piano (other than the specific piece) for the same amount of time as the first group.
- A third group learned the same piece of music as the first, but then asked to only *mentally* rehearse it (without touching the piano), playing it in their minds as if they were performing it flawlessly. They were also asked to do this daily, for the same amount of time as the other two groups.

5   Pascual-Leone, D., et al (1995) Modulation of muscle responses evoked by transcranial magnetic stimulation during the acquisition of new fine motor skills. *Journal of Neurophysiology* 74(3): 1037-45.

- The last group was asked to do nothing related to the piano for the entire span of the study.

After 5 days, each group of participants underwent sophisticated brain-imaging tests to see if there were any changes that had occurred in the way their brains worked after their specific tasks were completed. The results showed that neither the group that did "nothing" nor the group that was asked to play "anything they wanted" on the piano had any significant changes detected by the brain scans. Apparently, *randomness* had similar effects on brain function as *doing nothing* at all.

When the researchers observed the brain scans of the other two groups, however, they discovered something quite amazing: the first group who did the physical rehearsal showed significant changes to neural patterns in their brains—created by practicing the same thing, over and over again in a specific sequence. Their brains were now "wired" to play the piano arrangement with greater ease. Although this was somewhat expected, what really surprised the researchers was that these same changes were also seen in the group that only *mentally* rehearsed the same sequences! Similar "wired" neuronal networks were detected in the brains of this group of subjects despite their never having touched the piano—showing unequivocally how powerful our thoughts can be to create actual physical changes in our brains *without doing anything physical.*

With respect to the possibilities mental rehearsal offers, this simple experiment represents the mere tip of the iceberg. The most valuable point it makes is that when you are truly focused, your brain does not know the difference between your experience in the outer world of reality and your experience in the inner world of mind. Sports psychologists have used this phenomenon for years with their elite athletes, having them visualize and rehearse in their minds hitting the perfect shot, crossing the finish line ahead of the field, and breaking through the previously unachievable heights, speeds or distances. They utilized this invaluable tool because they knew the same neurological pathways required to achieve peak performance could be activated by either physical *or* mental rehearsal! The bottom line is this: if you change your brain by having it believe you have already experienced a future event *before* it happens in your physical world, you increase the likelihood that it *will* because a new emotion has been generated in your body—and you are on your way to creating a new state of being.

Not to be overlooked, another promising thing to note here is the results in the music study were accomplished by average individuals like you and me, after only

5 days of mentally rehearsing the desired behavior. Knowing that mental rehearsal is a repeatable, verifiable skill, imagine what's possible when we incorporate these principles over a lifetime!

Think about it: in 5 days, what dream could you be living if you gave mental rehearsal a try? Does this make you excited to start your own personal experiment? I bet! However, before you endeavor to begin making this kind of change in your life, let me show you where our current reality ends and the real magic begins. Let me take you under the surface to witness the much larger part of the iceberg—the one that can shift you into a *quantum reality*.

From the Invisible to the Visible: Quantum Creation

Quantum physicists remind us that although things around us appear solid, the atoms that are considered the building blocks of all matter are comprised of 99.99999% empty space—filled with energy or frequency patterns of information. The other 0.00001% is the only portion dense enough to be measured as matter. So, as far as we can tell, all matter is more "no-thing" than "something."

And, when scientists began to study the tiny bits of matter inside the atom (particles called electrons), what they discovered truly amazed them. First, they found these microscopic particles seemed to have a split personality—sometimes they behaved like waves (energy) and at other times, like particles (matter). Second, it was difficult to locate them in time and space—they seemed to appear and reappear, shifting back and forth between wave and particle all the time. Finally, and most incredibly, from all the available evidence, quantum theorists and researchers concluded that it was the person measuring or observing these tiny structures that would affect the behavior of energy and matter, eventually resulting in a recordable reality.

It seems unbelievable, but according to this research, it's true: electrons exist simultaneously in an infinite array of possible "locations" in an invisible field of energy. Yet it's only when an observer focuses attention on any one location of any one electron that it actually appears! In other words, a particle does not manifest in reality (ordinary space-time as we know it) until someone observes it. Quantum physicists call this the "observer effect."

Why is this important for us here?

As a direct result of this discovery, mind and matter can no longer be considered separate; they are intrinsically related. And, our subjective minds produce *measurable* changes on the objective world! At the sub-atomic level, energy responds to our mindful attention and becomes matter. It's a scientific fact.

Think about it: everything in the Universe is made up of sub-atomic particles such as electrons. By their very nature, these particles exist in an energetic wave state with pure, infinite potential—they are "everything" and "nothing" until they are observed, at which point they become a measurable reality. Therefore, we as observers are potentially capable of collapsing into existence an infinite number of possible realities; if your mind can influence the appearance of an electron, then theoretically it can influence the appearance of *any* possibility! This means that the quantum field already contains a reality in which you are happy, healthy, and possess all the qualities and capabilities of the idealized self that you hold in your thoughts. That reality is just waiting for you *to serve as a witness to it* by focusing on it as your desired outcome!

How exactly does mental rehearsal facilitate quantum creation? If the brain looks like it has already experienced an event (e.g. learning a musical piece), then there is physical *evidence* that the event has already happened. As the piano experiment shows, the effect of mental rehearsal is that the brain now looks like it has experienced physical learning even when it has only happened in the mind. The quantum field now responds to the new way of being—knowing how to play the piece of music without thinking about it—because mind and body (thought and emotion) are working together as one. The one possibility has been collapsed into reality, and the desired outcome—playing the piece of music easily—has been achieved.

Learning *how* to harness the power of this observer effect and direct its properties to change your reality—this is where we are headed next. Mental rehearsal becomes your number one tool. If you follow me all the way to the end of this chapter, you will see that with willful attention, sincere application of new knowledge, and repeated daily efforts, you can use your mind as the observer to collapse quantum particles and organize a vast number of sub-atomic waves of probability into a desired physical event—a new, *inspiring experience* in your life.

For the purposes of this chapter, the entire process of quantum creation is much simplified and summarized. However, if it tweaks your interest, as we hope it does, please consider going to my website for a more thorough explanation and more information (www.drjoedispenza.com) or read my latest book: *Breaking the Habit of Being Yourself: How to Lose Your Mind and Create a New One* (Hay House, 2012). In both resources, you will find a much more detailed guide for performing the tasks I'm about to describe here.

Quantum Leaping: Step by step

The process of making the quantum jump from *thinking* to *being* has several requirements, and each one contributes significantly to the ultimate success of manifesting your desired intention. Those requirements are: 1) making a commitment to carving out specific time in a specific location to get quiet and focus (regularly); 2) making the subject of your mental rehearsal appear so real, it feels like you are already having the experience; and 3) applying the "wired" neurological circuits primed during your mental rehearsal to "sync-up" new experiences with your consciously-generated goal. In essence, giving thanks to the Universe for your new reality before it actually appears…and then looking around for signs of it showing up in your environment—just as you imagined it would.

1. Carving out specific time to get quiet and focus—regularly

At first, it's recommended you get away from the usual people, places, and events that make up your daily routine. To create an environment for change, you must *change your environment*. I marvel at the number of people who tell me how overtaxed and over-stimulated they are, longing for a few moments of peace and quiet. Yet that "peace and quiet" they settle for often ends up being some kind of mindless diversion (like television, drugs or alcohol). What I'm suggesting here is that a *mind-full conversion* is more what you need—and mental rehearsal in a quiet place of solitude is exactly that.

For the first few weeks at least, make the commitment to finding a special place and time to perform your mental rehearsal routine. A quiet room with soft light and sounds would be a great start. For the duration of your mental exercise, you also want to ensure you will not be disturbed. Turn off all electronic devices—or better yet, leave them out of your immediate environment. By doing all of these things, you will give your mind a better opportunity to focus on what you want.

Later on, after you've become proficient with the basic skills—feeling confident in using your new tool—instead of changing your environment, you can choose to simply "tune it out." When we want to be, aren't we all masters of selective hearing and selective action-taking? (Think of how easily we can tune out our spouse or partner when watching our favorite TV show!) In order to become the creators of our new destiny, we must put these skills of selectivity to better use and focus singularly on the task at hand. Creating significant life-change is not a multi-tasking exercise!

Once you prepare the environment for performing your mental rehearsal exercises, you must also prepare your mind and body. To make the kind of shift in the state of being we are alluding to here, mind and body must become one—you should be able to hold a clear, conscious intention in your thinking brain, all the while creating a receptive internal state in your subconscious mind (the body) to plant the seed of this new thought or experience.

To best accomplish this feat, you will need to conjure up an altered state—one in which you are relaxed, yet continually awake. Find a place where you can comfortably sit upright, then close your eyes. By removing a large amount of sensory information (visual) from coming into your brain, you immediately begin to shift your brain to a more appropriate brain-wave state, that is *alpha* instead of *beta* (a more in-depth discussion of brain-wave activity and its importance can be found in my first book or in the article *The Waves of the Future* on my website).

At the same time, also bring your focus to the body—to your breath, your position in space, etc. In order to facilitate a new state of being, you will want to stimulate the cerebellum. Since the cerebellum receives and monitors huge amounts of nerve information related to proprioception (body awareness), by bringing your awareness to the body, you immediately begin to engage the cerebellum. And, by taking your attention away from your external environment, you simultaneously de-activate the analytical brain, that part of your mind that keeps you thinking instead of feeling.

Together, these two effects prepare your brain for the processes of sprouting and pruning neurological pathways that will reinforce the projection of your new experience and rid you of your "old self."

2. Making the subject of your mental rehearsal so real, it feels like you are already having the experience

To take advantage of the full potential mental rehearsal has to offer, you must imagine yourself having a new experience with as much sensory detail as you can muster. It's time to take all the knowledge you've accumulated from the thinking brain and convert it into a newly envisioned experience—one that is so real in the moment, it evokes an emotional response.

Just like when we were previously "doing" something to have this emotional response, this "experience in the mind" produces the same chemical response to the body—that is, peptides are released into the bloodstream affecting heart-rate, blood pressure, etc. The experience is being embodied—without us actually moving.

We now have mind and body working in unison aligned to the intention (or vision) we've generated. Many experts agree the best way to make mental rehearsal more effective is to imagine the event as if it's *already happened*. Because of the size of the human frontal lobe, you have the privilege of *making thought more real than anything else*. And when you truly focus and pay attention, there comes a moment when your brain does not know the difference between what is real in the external world and what you've imagined in your mind. In fact, the thoughts you are embracing will become just like a real life experience in your mind and body. The moment this occurs, your brain upscales its hardware to reflect what you're intentionally thinking about. As we "memorize" the event mentally, emotionally, and physically as our *inner* reality, we move into a new state of being. And the quantum field tends to respond to who we *are*—not so much to what we want, but who we're *being*.

Our thoughts have become *us*—our lives. And because they now reflect our desired reality, they *become* us, too.

What's the simplest way to know we've actually achieved this new state with mental rehearsal? When you get up from your session, you *feel different*. You know that a change has occurred in your state of mind as well as your body At this point, you are ready to move to the third and final stage of mental rehearsal: *witnessing* the magic in real time.

> *Rehearsal lays down tracks so that the mind*
> *has a path for the body to follow.*

3. Applying the "hard-wired" neurological circuits primed during your mental rehearsal to align new *actions* with your consciously-generated goal

We now understand our routine thoughts and feelings will perpetuate a state of being which creates the same behaviors and the same reality to which we've become accustomed. The new ways of thinking and feeling developed during mental rehearsal have created a foundation for a new way of being. However, while mental rehearsal sets the stage, unless you show up for the performance, you are destined to lead a life of dress-rehearsal.

From a quantum standpoint, we have now created a different state of being as an observer and generated a new *electromagnetic signature* for an event by combining intentional thoughts and feelings. You see, thoughts create an electric charge and feelings create a magnetic field. When we project this vision into the Universe, we are asking to match it with a potential reality in the field that exists as an electromagnetic *potential*. According to the Law of Attraction, when we do, we will find ourselves pulled toward that potential reality—or it will find *us*.

I know it's frustrating when Life seems to produce an endless succession of minor variations on the same negative outcomes. But as long as you stay the same person, as long as your electromagnetic signature remains the same, you can't expect a new outcome. To change your life is to change your energy—to make an elemental change in your mind and emotions. If you want a new outcome, you will have to break the habit of being yourself!

Moreover, those outcomes that we attract to ourselves as a result of changing ourselves should be a *surprise*—maybe even astonishing us—in the way they come about. We should never be able to *predict* how our new creations will manifest; they must catch us off guard. If you can predict an event, it is nothing new; it's routine or automatic, meaning you have experienced it many times before. The same "you" has produced that familiar outcome. In fact, if you're trying to control how an outcome will occur, you just went "Newtonian."

Newtonian (classical) physics was about trying to anticipate and predict events. "Going Newtonian" is when the external environment is controlling your internal environment (thinking/feeling). That's *cause and effect*. Instead, you want to change your internal environment—the way you think and feel—and then see how the external environment is altered by your efforts. That's putting the quantum model of reality into action.

Strive to create an unknown, new future experience. These manifestations should leave us with no doubt that our consciousness made contact with the quantum field of Intelligence—so we are inspired to do this again! When we do, we just became "quantum creators." Can you hold a clear intention of what you want, but leave the "how" details to the unpredictable quantum field? It may seem counter-intuitive, but if you can, you are *more* likely to see the dream eventually appear in your reality.

Trust that the quantum field will orchestrate an event in your life in a way that is just right for you. It always does. If you're going to expect anything, expect the unexpected. Surrender, trust, and let go of how a desired event will unfold. This is the biggest hurdle for most to overcome because we human beings always want to control a future reality by trying to re-create how it occurred in a past reality.

At this juncture, I should mention another important point: While you are busy going about exercising your manifestation muscles, consider that life may not always reflect *exactly* what you envision. Nothing's perfect. However, like most things, the more you practice, and the more belief you have in yourself and the process, the more likely you are to succeed. Be patient and recognize that every step along the way you are achieving what you want to accomplish— it's just happening one step at a time. This is how anything worthwhile actually happens.

In my case, not every day of recovery was filled with measurable progress. With painstaking slowness at times—even an absence of any noticeable improvements—I had to forge ahead, maintaining my diligence, fueled by an unwavering faith in the power of Mind to re-create my health. I knew if I honored my commitment to mentally rehearse each and every exercise beforehand, my body would be primed and ready to rebuild. And it was.

The same can be said for any type of experience you would like to realize in your life. Mental rehearsal, meditation, visualization—whatever you prefer to call it—is the perfect tool to prepare yourself for the actualization of your dreams. Then, when you witness your actions reflecting in the physical world that which you have conjured up in the mental realm, your life will ultimately merge with the dream. Mind and body have become one. If there is not this integrity of vision with action, you will continue to live with the dream only in your head.

Let me ask you these very important questions: Can you feel the elevated emotions associated with a desired event before it occurs? Can you imagine that reality so completely that you begin to be in that future life now? In terms of quantum creating, can you give thanks for something that exists as a potential in the quantum field but has not yet happened in your reality? If so, you will move from cause and effect (waiting for something outside of you to make a change inside of you) to *causing an effect* (changing something inside of you to produce an effect outside of you). When you are in a state of gratitude, you transmit a signal into the field that an event has already occurred. Gratitude is more than an intellectual thought process—you have to feel as though whatever you want is in your reality at this very moment. Thus, your body (which only understands feelings) must be convinced that it has the "emotional quotient" of the future experience, happening to you now.

For example, in my situation I intellectually understood that the body heals itself: but when push came to shove and I faced the physical reality of my trauma, I had to choose to commit time and energy to aligning my mind-body with that understanding. I had to focus intently on every bit of understanding I had about the science and philosophy of healing and generate feelings of joy and gratitude in order to take it to a whole new level—to generate a true experience of healing.

By using the methods explained here, you can eliminate the act of living in stress by removing the worry about what might happen in a future moment. Through mental rehearsal, we can change our brain before the external experience happens—making the brain no longer a record of the past, but a blueprint for the future. To rise above the familiar and to become inspired is the true energy of creation! To think beyond how we feel is a great endeavor for any human being—being greater than our environment is what it's all about.

Let me close out this chapter by giving you an example of how this all comes together:

Let's say that your partner mentions (again) how abrupt you've been with your children lately—blaming them for everything negative that happens around the house, criticizing them for not getting good grades, telling them they are wearing the wrong clothes or the wrong hair-do, etc. You think to yourself: *Great. As if I don't have enough stress to deal with at work—now I have it at home, too!* In addition, he or she tells you the kids have brought this up secretly and are very afraid to tell you because they fear retribution. To add insult to injury, your partner confides in you that they aren't the *only* ones you've been in the habit of verbally attacking…

You bite your tongue as you feel like you're being cornered. "Me? Attacking? That's crazy-talk!" It takes all your will power at this point to not lose it altogether (like you usually do). You feel angry and hurt—upset by the mere suggestion that you've been less than a model parent and spouse. Your thoughts turn to how under-appreciated you are given how much work you do for the family. You get a familiar sickening, burning feeling in your stomach, and you just want to run away. You throw your hands up in the air and call your best friend to see if they don't mind meeting you for a drink.

At the pub, your friend listens quietly as you rant for 15 minutes straight about this most recent situation, and then turns to you and says, "What if what they're saying is true?" Shocked, you look back at your friend in disbelief, but something inside you tells you he's right. Every time you react in anger to your loved ones, you wish you could take it back. You've even wondered why you can't seem to stop yourself. But, what can you do?

Fortunately, your trusty friend reaches into his bag and pulls out a popular book on mindfulness, compassion, forgiveness and love. Included with the book is a how-to guide using mental rehearsal which shows you how to incorporate these characteristics into your daily life. You've heard about it, but kept telling yourself you didn't have the time to commit to yet another task. Knowing how much you love your family, in the moment you express how grateful you are for having such a caring friend. You silently promise yourself you'll *make* the time.

In short order, you become enthralled by the information in this book—you spend hours reading from its pages late at night as the other members of your family are fast asleep. Driving in your car, you review new ideas from the book by listening to the companion CD. As you continue to review this information in your head over the following days and weeks, all the new information you learn, contemplate and memorize in your head causes neurons to begin to develop a long-term relationship. "Nerve cells that fire together wire together," means you are wiring new information in your brain philosophically, and you've put some hardware in place to reflect this. As a matter of fact, every time you've thought about it, and every time you've repeated the thoughts over in your brain, you were reminding yourself and reinforcing those circuits.

So now, all this information is stored in your thinking brain. It is weeks later, and it's come time for you and your partner to sit down and plan the family vacation. Your partner shares with you how disappointing the last few vacations have been because they always seem to involve family squabbles, with the children often vowing they'll never go on another one. As you start thinking about going on the *next* vacation, you're all excited because for the last few weeks, you've shared with your friends all this great information from the book you've read. You haven't experienced it quite yet, but you've sure thought a lot about it. You could tell anyone what it is like to forgive and how to love and what personal transformation is. You could give advice at parties—you've become an excellent philosopher. But it's still theory.

As you're continuing the conversation with your partner, you start to think about your old self—what you've said, how you've reacted to things, and how you really don't want to repeat that pattern again. As you begin to think about your old familiar ways, all of a sudden you have these thoughts: What piece of knowledge did I learn from that book that I could actually apply? What could I demonstrate? How could I change my behavior and do exactly what the book says in order to have a new experience?

In other words, how can I get my behavior to match my intentions?

While you remind yourself of who you no longer want to be, how you no longer want to act, how you're not going to feel—as you begin to become conscious of those unconscious propensities—the mere fact you are reviewing them means you're restraining certain neuronal circuits from firing. And the principal in neuroscience says that nerve cells that no longer fire together, no longer wire together. In other words, if you don't use it, you'll lose it.

You tell your spouse to go ahead and plan the vacation—this one's going to be *different*. You can't say how, but you know it will. Leaving your partner with this proclamation, you decide to put mental rehearsal to the test. You set aside time each and every day to get quiet and contemplate everything you've learned. You announce to the family that during that time, you are not to be disturbed. Before each session, you review the information from the book so it is fresh in your mind. Then, you follow the steps as outlined in the guide, all the while focused clearly on your intention to feel and act differently than your old self would.

In each session, you see yourself relating to your kids with more patience, understanding and compassion. You hear yourself speaking to your spouse and your children with a lighter, a more loving tone. You feel their embrace in your mind as they express their gratitude for this change in attitude while on your next summer vacation near the beach. You internally express gratitude yourself for this new experience, and for everything it offers you and your family.

Each time you get up from these sessions, you feel an internal shift, like something heavy has been lifted from your shoulders. After three or four weeks (feels like a day), you begin to notice your stomach pains becoming less intense. When you look at your spouse, you feel something…different. It's like you've turned back the clock, and you're starting to feel like newlyweds again. When your kids approach you with demands for your time (and money), you find it easier to listen and respond with kindness, as you imagine you would have liked *your* parents to respond to you. You are surprised at how loving they are being *back* to you. It's like they read the same book—but you know they didn't. You're in a new experience, and the body is learning emotionally what the mind has understood philosophically.

As you became conscious of those old, automatic, knee-jerk reactions—and began to think about a new way of being—you cultivated new hardware neurologically and put the circuits in place before the experience actually happened. So now when you find yourself on the actual vacation, instead of responding in a predictable way, you decide now to do exactly what the book says. You forgive. You let go. You no longer get frustrated or impatient or angry with the ones you love most. You find it rather easy to no longer revisit the same emotions. As you flow through this process and approach this experience as your new self, you begin to feel this sense of love. You feel this sense of personal transformation and freedom as each moment happens.

You are incredibly shocked how Life showed up for you exactly as you envisioned it. As a result, you decide to practice it at every opportunity! Through repetition and with each experience, you begin to move into a new state of *being* as your mind and body are working together, in perfect alignment—eventually an internal order is established, so great that no condition in your life can move you from it. The quantum field responds to this state of being and collapses into your life more experiences that confirm your new reality.

As you can see, the beauty of mental rehearsal is this: it requires nothing except you, your thoughts, and your willpower to make it happen. Without any need for external resources, you have everything you need already within you to bring you that much closer to your dreams.

When you bring into reality that idealized vision you've created, what you receive in return will far exceed the sacrifices you have to make. The clarity of that vision and the depth of your commitment will ultimately pay off in ways that you have just begun to imagine. Aligning your intentions with your actions—matching your thoughts with your behaviors—leads to personal evolution. Mental rehearsal prepares the mind-body; physical rehearsal (demonstration) is the very last stage of this process. The union of mental and physical rehearsal working in harmony, however, showcases the mind-body connection in action, serving to create the opportunity for a new state of *being*.

And, when we project a new, improved version of ourselves into *our* world, the energy of the *entire* World can change as a result. The elegant beauty of this is it can all start with a single thought. Once you set the intention, consciously making the decision to follow that thought through to fruition, the miracle that is your envisioned dream becomes your personally-designed *destiny*.

Each of the incredible chapters that follow illuminates this beautiful Truth. Carve out some quiet time to enjoy, embrace, imagine and begin...

The <u>only</u> thing that's getting in the way of you being everything you want to be—and experiencing everything you want to experience—is taking the time to make it happen. If you truly believed in the power of the mind to create your reality, would you ever miss a day?

> *We are what we repeatedly do.*
> *Excellence then, is not an action, but a habit.*
> **— Aristotle**

The Think-Tank:

The Thoughts That Changed
Our Lives Forever

SECTION I

TO ME

We all have places in our life from
which we need to get unstuck.

— Michael Bernard Beckwith

CHAPTER 1

If It's Meant to Be,
It Starts With Me

by David Jan Jurasek

In my first year as a full-time family therapist, I was given a very sensitive case. I was introduced to a family that had been through several schools and assistance programs for their challenging son and found nothing had worked. I welcomed the challenge: With my creative nature and zealous dedication, I was confident I would be able to give them something new and useful.

Within the first five minutes of the family settling into my office, Jake—the 10-year old who was the "identified client"—insulted his dad and poked his mom three times while laughing at her. When his parents launched into reading his rap sheet to me, Jake cursed under his breath and leapt off his chair, ready to fight anyone who seemed to imply he had any flaws, including me.

It is important to note that Mom and Dad were very well-educated and highly accomplished professionals. She was a bank manager, and he was the head of a hospital. They dealt with high-stress situations daily in their work, yet both admitted to dreading coming home and facing their son. They didn't think they could survive another phone call from yet another school informing them how Jake had trashed the principal's office or poked another child's eye with a pen. This often led to expulsion and left them to face their worst horror: staying home to babysit their own "demon child."

As our times together continued, I devoted myself to doing whatever it would take to help them find relief. I pushed our sessions late, sometimes extending them to two and a half hours, eagerly hoping to see a break in the dark clouds of their daily battles. At the time, I was proud of my abilities as a therapist, and truly believed I could help *any*one with *any* problem—if only I tried hard enough.

So imagine my reaction one year later, when things were clearly no better (although not really worse either). Jake was still exploding daily, and his parents were pulling out their few remaining hairs. Both parents could see how their own attempts to correct Jake's behavior—through humiliation, blaming, shaming, and their own bursts of violence—only fueled his rage and taught him exactly how to behave. They came to me for my expert guidance, but every attempt I gave to show understanding, offer support or ask insightful questions seemed to get sucked into a vacuum. Any small step I suggested they might take (often their own idea) evoked in them a "Yeah, but…" response. Over the years, I have come to notice how this kind of stance is so common within families that are stuck.

What's truly remarkable is how this case evolved. One day, admittedly at my wits end, I leaned back in my chair and asked the boy quite matter-of-factly, "What do you think we should do, Jake?"

Jake looked up wistfully and proceeded—without hesitation—to give a detailed account of what he wanted his parents to change to make things better, including:

"They could stop yelling at me when I screw up."

"They could tell me when there's something I'm good at."

It sounded not only reasonable, but truly compelling. We all listened intently.

Next session, I was genuinely surprised when Jake's parents continued ranting about all his explosive behaviours, even after they acknowledged he had shown a 50% decrease in disruptive outbursts that week! Strangely enough, they appeared <u>adamant</u> nothing had changed—and they seemed to want to keep drilling that home. Meanwhile, Jake sat there quietly. Sometimes he would pump his fists in response to his parents' reporting, but he held back his temper. Near the end of the session, Jake finally leaned in to ask if he could see me alone.

In private, I realized what a delight he could be away from the firing squad— or anyone demanding anything of him. It became so clear that he was extremely lonely. He laid out his cards for me:

"My parents have been making me come here. I hate it. They make me crazy. They just want to see you fail and suck. You *do* suck at helping us..."

Gulp. What a blow to my superhero therapist's ego! His blatant honesty and lack of guile were disarming. In that moment, I wondered if there was *anything* I could actually do to help him.

But then his eyes lit up. "Can you help me make some friends? Like, teach me some stuff, and...you got groups, right? Can you get me in some groups?"

Finally, some movement!

Even so, I couldn't help but wonder how I was to blame for us all being stuck for so long. I reminded myself this problem existed long before I arrived. All the same, a poignant sense of discomfort set in. I went to my supervisor to complain about the parents. She suggested I sit for awhile with how I was feeling about the case.

With only a half hour before our next session, I shut the door to my office. I could not shake the feeling of helplessness and inadequacy. I was hungry for some perspective. As I went to turn off my computer, this is what popped up on my browser:

> **Be the change you wish to see in the World.**
> **— Gandhi**

I collapsed into my chair and allowed myself to feel the empty pit in my belly as blood rushed to my face, making my head feel squished. *What a terrible failure I was...how inadequate I was at helping them.*

And then I remembered hearing Jake's father telling me how he tackled work problems:

"If it's meant to be, it's up to me."

This had some truth in it, but my mind quickly discarded it, thinking instead: *Change? But I can't change anyone else Least of all these damn parents! Their son is the only one who wishes to change, and he's the one making that happen while they keep doing the same old $@#&!!*

All of a sudden, I felt a jolt of inspiration that made me sit bolt upright in my chair. This time, I heard *Jake's* voice saying in a playful sing-song way—"If it's meant to be, it starts with me!"

Normally, I felt dread when our receptionist announced their arrival. Today, I felt sober and relieved of a terrible burden when they walked into my office. Before they could launch into their usual condemnations, I took the reins and said,

"I get the feeling everyone here feels like a failure. Jake, you keep hearing it everywhere you go."

Looking at Jake's mom and dad, I continued, "You two probably feel like incredible failures when it comes to helping Jake. Being so smart and respected in your work, it must be a terrible blow. I'm guessing my attempts to help you have only made you feel worse. And maybe you've even enjoyed seeing me fail at this all year, at least so I'll really *get* what you go through every single day."

Both parents blushed and nodded.

And then I confessed, "I'm sorry for pushing you to change. I just didn't want to feel like a failure, too."

Being the most passionately verbose family I ever met, it was mesmerizing to see them speechless. The air was clear and silent for what seemed like an eternity— actually, about 2 full minutes of sighing and deep breathing.

The first words spoken were from Jake's mom, thanking me.

Then Jake's dad added, "Yes, it's true. I have felt that way."

"Me, too," said Jake.

It was now me who was lost for words. The path seemed open now, yet I had no clue about our next step.

"Now what?" I asked.

I wish I could report that what followed was a glowing testimonial of my therapeutic prowess, but this is what happened in real life: Jake's mom put herself on anti-anxiety medication, stopped criticizing Jake so much, and began to actually enjoy him. Dad continued to report to me, but only by phone, clarifying that he never really needed my help or any kind of therapy. He said he would continue to ponder Jake's wishes while spending more time with him.

Jake's side of the equation was more transformational and deeply inspiring. Within two weeks, his incidences of violence stopped completely! He continued to see me for another 6 months, getting quite tender and gushy at times—surprising for a feisty, pubescent boy! He also made one good friend and was able to stay in a play group for the first time in his life. What made me nearly fall off my chair was how, in our last session, he unexpectedly praised me for my understanding and help.

I think of Jake whenever I find myself trying too hard to help someone or attempting to move a mountain all by myself. I now try to take a closer, deeper look at how I do help others, asking myself,

"What do *I* have the power to change?"

Because now I know…

If it's meant to be, it has to start with me.

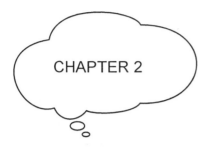

CHAPTER 2

Let Your
Intuition Guide You

by Vtec Janus

T here was a time in my life when I was mostly unhappy, puzzled and lost.

Looking back now, I find it hard to fathom how I could let my life slip away like that. It was just when I was *closest* to realizing my dreams of love and success that things fell apart. The decline began while I was working on a business venture: the desire to make money became so important, it eclipsed all my personal values. The negative effects were terribly obvious. My obsession with wealth ate away at my relationships until I felt I couldn't trust anyone because it seemed like everyone had an ulterior motive or something to hide from me. Friendships were destroyed, love fled the scene, and every day was a series of arguments and confrontations. The situation took a heavy toll on my entire being.

A few years went by like this, and I found myself in a near-constant state of suspicion, feeling irritable and miserable. Then, I hit the wall: One morning, staring at myself in the bathroom mirror, I *knew* I couldn't live this way for one more day. I was so attached to my negative feelings, so enthralled with my preconceptions and convictions, I was at a loss for what to do next. The worst-case scenario was here and now. I found myself on the brink, with thoughts of giving it all up.

Thankfully, Life is rooted in the *miraculous*, so perhaps it's natural that my miracle should appear in the darkest moment of my life. As I continued to stare in the mirror, out of nowhere the loving, wise words of my grandfather echoed loud and clear within me: "Let yourself be guided by your intuition."

This brave man had survived not only months of anguish and deprivation in a prison camp during the war, but also the diagnosis of a terminal disease later on in life. I remembered him telling me it was only by trusting his inner voice that he was able to make it through these devastating experiences. I was blessed to have the spirit of this man's courage and determination with me at the mirror. As memories of him began to surface, I could hear my heart begin calling to me.

I paused, took a deep breath, and listened. With a whole new clarity emerging, I *sensed* the answer. I needed to go in a completely different direction! I couldn't depend on logic this time; I couldn't try to *think* my way out of my current problems. I needed to trust in Grandpa's wisdom. I needed to let go and follow my own inner voice.

The beauty is, we are all blessed with this magical internal guidance system—a knowing and an urging that is deeper and wider than reason. It calls us to embrace who we are and how we are meant to live in this life. As I connected with this Divine wisdom, I could feel the dark clouds dissolve and the weight of the world start to slip off my shoulders. Awakening to this higher awareness, I *knew* that in its own time, Life would bring me the happiness I so longed for in my heart.

I blinked twice at my image in the mirror. Was I already beginning to look different, too?

Moving forward, the more I thought about intuition, the clearer it became that most of the problems in my life were self-imposed. They were exact reflections of my own fears, anger, and desire for revenge. I had cultivated a dangerous habit of blaming my problems on everyone else so I could rationalize my feelings of hopelessness as effects beyond my control. Unfortunately, this propensity served only to make matters worse.

In my moment of truth, I decided to fully *receive* my grandfather's words and turn to my own heart for the hope I needed to keep moving forward. I had to admit it was only <u>me</u> who was making choices that led to my pain and suffering—nobody else. I wanted so desperately to be free of this egoïc tyranny. So, in that moment, I made a new choice: I chose to take responsibility for my life and forgave myself for creating the prison within which I had been living for too long. I also chose to forgive others who I'd felt provoked so much suspicion and dislike from me, for I could see now that it had been <u>my</u> choice to react to them from a perspective of distrust.

I gave myself permission to think and feel in a different way: to simply surrender—deeply, purely, powerfully. Staring at the mirror, I began the practice of looking deep into myself and made a commitment to do it every day, regularly and sincerely. With my unwavering dedication, the fledgling miracle began to unfurl.

New ways of thinking soon produced new ways of acting, which enhanced my adaptability and creativity. By relying on my intuition (instead of rational thought), I went on to accomplish something I'd always wanted to do: I wrote a book. It contained my experiences and insights, interwoven with my grandfather's life story. This never would've happened if I'd remained stuck in my old habitual ways of thinking! My grandfather's wisdom became manifest in my writing—proof that previous experiences of suffering *can* be turned into experiences of joy in the present.

My horizons expanded, and I was able to see life from a different point of view. I no longer feared a lack of money, and I released my desire to have more than I needed. By sharing what I *did* have, instead of pining for what I *didn't* have, that feeling of lack gave way to one of sufficiency and abundance—in many different areas of my life!

I learned to connect with my soul and to synergize my feelings with logical thought. I now know it's up to me how I experience my life. So I choose to follow my heart, and I *genuinely* expect every day to bring love, appreciation, gratitude, honesty and trust.

If the miraculous is at the root of our existence, it follows that nothing that happens can ever be called wholly bad, unpleasant or evil. In fact, nothing happens that is not intended for our greatest good! Life is a process of gaining insight, and insight is dynamic—always expanding. It changes us in ways we do not control, but that always produce benefits. This is what our intuition teaches us. It is the voice of God within, a voice that is always there—that authentic, timeless part of us—refreshing us and renewing our vision. It is intuition that allows us to perform the miracle of turning hopeless moments into joyful possibilities.

Do you find yourself feeling stuck, looking for answers? If you can't find them *out there*, try looking *within*. Follow your intuition. It's that inner voice that says, "Hey, turn right, not left," or "Call your friend today," or "Say yes to this, but no to that." Grant yourself permission to let go of both fear *and* attachment to outcomes. Put yourself in the shoes of others often. You will become more compassionate and forgiving, and you'll also find it easier to release bitterness and resentment. As you connect deeply with your intuition—and follow it—you will find yourself navigating your way through the most difficult trials with greater and greater ease.

Look inside yourself. Do this for five to fifteen minutes a day—regularly and sincerely—and see how your horizons expand, too. By all means, accept yourself and your desires in life! Don't neglect or push them aside. You are worthy of your passions and must embrace them, just as you must embrace your vulnerabilities. Never give up on your dreams.

There are always challenges in life, that's how we grow. It's when we choose to approach our difficulties with an attitude of acceptance and an open mind that we see our world change. By connecting with the soul rather than solely the rational, we can see beyond limitations and conceive more peaceful outcomes and promising eventualities.

What we think of, we become. So bless every moment of your life, no matter how hopeless it may seem. Trust Life and everything that happens. Every person is capable of changing perspective—to look within, to listen to the heart, and to follow intuition. The ultimate choice is yours: it always has been, and always will be, up to you to turn your suffering into joy.

Have faith and courage along the way and prepare to be amazed—not once or twice, but *always*.

CHAPTER 3

My Intention Is For Everyone's Highest and Best Good

by Molly McCord

My Parisian apartment-hunting efforts were not leading anywhere, even after weeks of relentless searching. It didn't have to be a fancy, big or admirable place; I wasn't asking for a suite at Versailles (yet). I just needed to find a decent (safe, bright, cozy!) place so I could get settled for now and begin this exciting new chapter in my life. Somewhere in this huge city, I should be able to unpack my mismatched luggage, hang up my spring-summer-fall-winter clothes, and nestle in with a cup of *Mariage Frères* tea and Vogue *en français*. A much bigger dream was at stake, and my stubborn optimism told me there had to be some little place waiting for me here. There *had* to be.

After days of answering dead-end classified ads, making inconclusive phone calls, standing in crowded viewing lines, and submitting numerous "Please choose me!" applications, nothing changed. No decent (safe, bright, cozy!) place was available, no one was calling me back—no one wanted to rent to an American in Paris. Nothing was moving except my spinning mind and restless, tired feet.

I've been stuck before at key points in my life when the next step was neither obvious, nor encouraging. Stuck in an unfulfilling job with no other desirable options in sight; stuck in emotional spirals over a situation that didn't appear to offer a glowing exit sign; stuck in an apathetic freeze zone with no foreseeable movement on the horizon—even after exerting diligent time and energy in exploring alternate directions. Living in "The Stuck." <u>Yuck</u>. But now time was running out. No doors were opening, and the one thought that kept arising was one of doubt: *Was this lifelong dream ending before it even began?*

One dark evening, as the twinkling lights shone on its steel legs, I stood in my stuck-ness, staring at the Eiffel Tower. Instead of two years earning a Master's degree in the *City of Lights*, I was earning credits in "Unsuccessful House-hunting (101)." Everything I needed to move ahead with my dream rested on finding a place to live. I couldn't fathom leaving before this life adventure had a fair chance to begin! My return airplane ticket to Seattle would have to be moved from a hidden suitcase pocket to the top of my desk. I wasn't ready to acknowledge that ticket existed yet, much less reach for it. After ten short minutes of sparkling magically, the temporary lights on the Eiffel Tower were extinguished. I turned slowly, and feeling a bit like my own light was dimming, walked to the Metro station, just as small May raindrops found me eagerly and easily.

Later that night, as I sat in the darkness of discouragement, a little spark of light slowly began to flicker through my disappointment. Although initially I thought it was the French wine numbing my internal whine, the light became bigger than the power of the shimmering Syrah in my glass. Slowly, the internal shift expanded to a firm knowingness that made my next step clear: I couldn't give up this dream, but I could give up how I was approaching it! I had to change my tactics. I had to change the energy. I had to change my *intention*.

Energy follows intention (as anyone who has sat behind a steering wheel knows). When the intention is bigger, the energy behind it increases exponentially to fill the open space. For the duration of my search so far, I had been motivated by my own immediate need to find shelter, be settled, and begin anew. But focusing on only *my* small personal needs was limiting. I needed to expand, increase and open up my intention—to allow the next steps *I* needed to also answer someone *else's* needs. I needed to stretch beyond the fulfillment of my own wishes to allow something greater to come in and benefit all. I decided, in that moment, to set a higher intention for this home-hunting effort to be for *everyone's* highest good. I also committed, right then and there, to release all expectations of how life might unfold, and to keep going forward with my best efforts. *But would a simple thought even matter or change anything?*

I sat with this idea as my wine glass became lighter and my mind became surprisingly clearer. I sensed a new, elevated inspiration grow with this higher intention. And although alcohol can have that same mind-altering effect, this notion was coming from something bigger and stronger than a bottle. It wasn't time to pull out the return plane ticket yet. The best was yet to come—I *knew* it!

Within 24 hours of putting this expanded intention out into the World, a lovely French acquaintance told me about a woman who was newly desperate for a renter. Her former tenants moved out early and unexpectedly, and she needed money *now* to cover the apartment expenses. She had other properties that were requiring her attention, too, so screening multiple applicants would be time-consuming and less than ideal. It was the 20th of May, and she didn't want to wait until the first of June for a tenant. If I was willing to come by today—*right now*—she would be happy to show me the apartment. I hung up the phone and grabbed my purse in one swift movement.

The studio apartment in the charming 15th *Arrondissement* was bright and *very* cozy at only a mere 200 square feet. I fell in love with it instantly. An exposed wood ceiling beam and bar counter separated the kitchenette from the living and sleeping space. A single floor-to-ceiling window allowed bright light to shine in from the outside courtyard. The bathroom and wall closet were equally compact, but also equally organized and clean. It was one of the best apartments I had toured in the city, and it was available, open and ready—*now*.

I contained my American enthusiasm just enough to tell her *en français* that the apartment was perfect for me.

She replied, "*Je suis heureuse aussi.*" (Translation: I am very happy as well.)

I am American so I smile openly. She is French and smiles discreetly.

We each signed our copies of the rental document, and I handed over the necessary rent. We parted ways at the street entrance 15 minutes later, and I glided back to the Metro stop, ready to officially begin moving into my new Parisian home. I wasn't familiar with this area of Paris, so I made my way up the street, keenly observing every window display, *patisserie* and little dog along the way. Then, I stopped dead in my tracks at an unexpected sight: The Eiffel Tower was straight ahead! My new steel neighbor gleamed in the sunlight, shining brighter than a few nights ago when I was stuck and alone in the dark. It was a new day for both of us!

Back on the Line 10 Metro, I reviewed how easily and quickly this situation turned around once I released a smaller intention and decided to focus on a bigger one. It passed through my mind that this apartment could have shown up anyways, and the outcome would have been the same—regardless of my conscious shift in thought. But there are *always* reasons to be skeptical about esoteric concepts: the rational, logical mind can (and will) find many ways to discount what it can't see, touch, read, *prove* in material form. I find my mind often defaulting to these statements of doubt—it's such a common human trait. But do we *really* have to settle? Or, can we choose something greater? What would happen if I chose to believe in and trust those greater possibilities to show up *whenever I called upon them?* Could it actually work?

Absolutely.

Ever since that first try of setting a higher intention for a solution, a positive outcome has followed *every time* I've been willing to believe in bigger possibilities. Over the years, I've used this system for work situations that appear to be stressful, challenging and seemingly "too big" to solve; for relationships that are changing, ending, separating and growing; for stressful financial scenarios that feel overwhelming and dire; for random, daily life situations where an immediate solution is not clear, but clearly needed. And without fail, without exception, every time I set the intention to benefit *everyone* in a situation in the highest and best possible way, an incredible development takes place. Divine movement occurs. Unseen doors burst open. New possibilities come barreling through. Breakdowns lead to breakthroughs. "Being stuck" becomes just a step, not the story. And then the next steps appear, while I willingly and gratefully walk with higher intention as my guide. It's pretty darn cool to experience.

Consciously opening up the intention for everyone's highest and best good invokes a power greater than the human mind. The highest and best good will *always* come when it is called upon because it's associated with Divine energy—and a willingness to be guided by more than our mere humanness. A higher intention is always there when we are willing to reach for it. This powerful thought was especially significant since finding that Parisian apartment was just the starting point for the time in my life when I truly connected to my soul's highest and best possible path of evolution and service.

But that's a whole other bottle of wine.

CHAPTER 4

I'm Going to Die

by Dr. Annemarie Gockel

Despite the lightning speed propelling our car toward the sheer rock face of the hillside, time slowed to a crawl as the thought *I'm going to die* filled my consciousness. What was so remarkable on that starry December night was this thought was surrounded by a profound peace: an acceptance of what Life was bringing me in that moment and even a burgeoning curiosity about what might lie beyond.

Although I emerged miraculously unscathed from the wreckage to contemplate the flashing lights of the police car and the passing motorists slip-sliding on the icy stretch of blacktop, the near miss sparked a realization I have been unable to shake. It was as though the threadbare veil we usually keep between the intellectual notion of mortality and the deeper awareness of its shocking reality suddenly fell away. *It's true*, I thought, *The one guarantee Life gives us is that none of us is making it out alive We're all going to die.*

Over the following months, working with this activated awareness (or having it work on me) opened a portal inside me. It was like water began to trickle—and then gradually flow—through the mouth of an overgrown fountainhead and into a deeper pool of understanding and appreciation for the wellspring of my life…and the mystery of its unfolding.

This car wreck found me at that most precipitous time our culture recognizes as a "mid-life crisis." It was as if I were being called to build a bridge between what was and what would be in my life. Everything I'd ever wanted, I came to realize, depended on it.

From an early, idealistic intention to *change the World, one self-realized person at a time*, I entered the helping professions in my twenties as a social worker. Over the years, the magic in seeing a spark of awareness in someone's eyes or witnessing the first tentative steps towards a new empowerment gradually gave way to a sense of disillusionment. Apparently our mental health system was oriented toward management and control, rather than healing and transformation.

Optimistic that further studies might help me collaborate with other professionals working together to build a better system, I returned to graduate school only to be swallowed up by the rat race of professionalized education. Whether it's the academic track, the business world or the health profession itself, I discovered the "systems" get us so busy jumping through one hoop after another that our dislocation from ourselves *grows* in proportion to our skill at navigating the complex landscapes of modern professional life.

I could no longer see the forest for the trees. I just wanted to make a meaningful difference in people's lives. Was that too much to ask?

As the hundred mile sprint of graduate school became what felt like a thousand mile marathon of academic life, I found myself falling exhausted at the doorstep of my own closed heart. Just as friends were congratulating me on finding the right man, the right job and having the opportunity to make a real contribution, I felt my interior world crumbling and terror filling the crevices of my being. I made the self-sacrifice so often required in the headlong rush for worldly success in our culture. I put in all the time and effort. Why, then, did I not *feel* successful?

In the months before the car wreck, thoughts of my mortality had been plaguing me. Here I was getting exactly what I had wanted—my PhD, marriage, an assistant professorship at Smith College, and the opportunity to further my research in "Spiritual Coping"—but the process that had brought me here now put me at such a great distance from myself, I could no longer feel the passion that had started my journey. In the open space between me and the next step on my grand path, I stood paralyzed. Daily challenges, small and large, filled me with anxiety. I felt as though an iceberg had taken up residence inside my chest. Nothing was working. All my tried-and-true techniques of focusing on my goals, working harder, and trying to push through in my research and writing were failing. The harder I tried, the slower I progressed. It was like walking through molasses in hip waders. I was utterly stuck and terrified I would face my deathbed without having really shared all I had to give.

In that fateful moment in December, as the car was hurtling through space toward the embankment, suddenly—unexpectedly—I let go. In the face of having absolutely no control, I surrendered to the moment *just as it was*, and I was filled with a deep sense of peace and possibility. It was like nothing else I'd ever felt before.

The experience stayed with me, and despite my characteristic tendency to push hard at all I was doing, I started to have moments of surrender in my everyday movements. I began to experience moments of compassion—simply *being* with the anxiety and the pain of my own struggling to succeed. I stopped running so hard. Instead of trying to overcome the great disaster of my life, I turned *into* it, and began to see it for what it really was—a calling for me to awaken.

As I started to open to a more gentle heart-centred way of being, the iceberg in my chest began to melt. Initially, I noticed small rivulets of relief in the tender embrace of a listening friend. Over time, the "letting go" became rivers and sometimes floods of grief for all of the disappointments, missed opportunities, broken relationships, and lack of love and caring for myself and many dear ones—all casualties of my battle within myself and aspects of my life gone by.

As I listened—really listened—to the flow of grief in my heart, I realized I had been striving to prove myself my entire life in all the ways our culture measures success: accomplishments, money, possessions, marriage and family. I thought these external accomplishments would help me feel loved and valued on the inside. The small ego self that serves to protect our developing consciousness had been ever-vigilant: I was always working to be better, to be liked, to be needed, to be useful, to anticipate and prepare for challenges, to build intelligent plans and control outcomes so as to guarantee my desired result. I approached life like one long obstacle course I was determined to conquer and win—to prove my worth, once and for all. My sense of self rose and fell in tandem with my successes and my failures.

As I opened to my new realization, it became obvious to me I had been going in the wrong direction. Nothing I accomplished on the outside was ever going to make me more than I already was on the inside! The price of all this ego-striving was turning out to be nothing less than abandoning my own heart. The now melting iceberg was a clear reflection of my renewed commitment to myself: either I change now or risk missing the best parts of my life! It was time to let go of some of the ego's protections and step into my life from the heart-based, professional vision I had once been so passionate about.

This mid-life course correction continues. I wish I could say it was easy or that it was over, but it continues to unfold masterfully with all its joys and sorrows. It involves daily surrender to the reality of being with myself openly and honestly, just as I am—without trying to overcome, control, manage, transform or improve. I now get to embrace myself whole-heartedly, right here and now because this is where the action is!

It's an ongoing process of death and rebirth. I'm continually dying to the ego: releasing the compulsion to strive to be more, to be the architect of all my plans, desires, fears and worries. I choose instead to be reborn in the moment—I choose to be with my heart, mind and body as fully, consciously and completely as I can. It's exquisitely vulnerable and surprisingly powerful! I am allowing myself to feel everything in my life deeply, in a way I once thought I couldn't stand. It's what I call *full-contact living*!

As my mind slowed during those critical seconds of my accident, it demonstrated the power of slowing down itself—yet it led to a quickening of my spiritual evolution. Slowing down to be with myself in a new way is allowing me to hear more of the messages Life has for me. There really is significant guidance available from within when I'm willing to engage with my immediate experience. Life is starting to flow through me in a new way because I'm more available in the moment. It's alive and exciting—who knows what will happen?

I no longer know how it's supposed to go, nor do I need to. I'm beginning to sense the unfolding mystery of existence making Life the adventure it's meant to be. Dying to the ego has been a real developmental milestone for me—the fortunate result of a mid-life wake-up call and an ongoing practice of surrender. It takes regular meditation practice, truth-telling, and moment-by-moment diligence to keep letting go of the habits of a lifetime. The more I'm willing to enter the void of not knowing, the more I am finding a sense of love, joy and a renewed excitement about my plain old ordinary life—just as it is.

Who ever thought facing death could bring me so fully back to life?

CHAPTER 5

The Only Way to BE Is ME!

by Pilar Stella

Today you are You, that is truer than true.
There is no one alive who is you-er than You.
— Dr. Seuss

spent much of my life trying to be what I thought others wanted me to be.

I often did things to please, trying to be perfect for *them*. But it didn't get me very far. I just ended up getting more and more lost, until one day, I woke up wondering who I was and how I had gotten so off-course. I was sick physically, exhausted mentally, and struggling to find myself in a challenging marriage. While my life may have seemed OK to others, I was waging a war with myself on the inside. I had created a prison of my own making and couldn't find a way out.

Then it hit me. It was not one distinct event or something specific somebody said to me that triggered the thought. It just hit me. On the verge of a divorce, struggling to get up out of bed every day, angry at myself and the World, I realized the *only* thing standing in the way of me and happiness was…ME. I could continue to go on trying to be someone others thought I should be, do what they thought I should do, think what people thought I should think—or I could just be…ME!

Sounds simple, right?

Wrong.

For some people, this may seem as obvious as day. But somehow it had escaped me for much of my life, taking 30-odd years to figure it out. The bad news is I had to endure a lot of pain, suffering and drama to come to that realization. The good news is it *only* took me that long. I consider myself one of the lucky ones. Some never get there at all.

At first, this thought seemed quite daunting and unnatural for me. I had to un-learn many years of living the opposite way. As a child, I was raised in what I call the "post-Depression Era mentality." That is, rather than being taught to be ourselves, to follow our hearts and trust our own inner guidance (as we cultivate our career and families), we are taught to look outside ourselves for security in money, success and things. Then we are told that someday down the road—if we are lucky enough—we will have the time and money that will allow us to figure out *who we really are* and what makes our hearts sing. But for so many people, that time of self-discovery and self-expression never comes, and happiness seems to slip away a little more each day.

Although it always seemed so backward to me, I too had fallen into that pattern and succumbed to those beliefs. In doing so, I created so much suffering for myself that I was actually on the verge of choosing out of this thing called Life altogether.

What a drastic contrast to the child I once was—so full of spunk, sass and sparkle! I remember an article written about me by an elementary grade teacher that started, "Perky Pilar sat bright eyed…"

Back then, I didn't know how to be anything *other* than ME! I exuded ME with laugher, joy and confidence. I walked around saying, "One day I'll be the head of the United Nations…or the World Health Organization…or the first woman President of the United States!" However bold my proclamations, they were always met with the same response from the adults around me: "That's wonderful, Pilar— but what are you *really* going to do?"

Even though it hurt, I realize they were doing the best they could. They were simply doing what *they* knew to be true, trying to guide me based on what *they* were taught. But in the process, they were stamping out the light, hope and possibility of the real, unlimited ME! As a little girl, I didn't know any better; I allowed the bright light within me to start dimming.

Yet this is what ultimately led to discovering the beauty in all we are learning today about our human potential and evolution. Many people around us are (consciously or unconsciously) just projecting their own limitations upon us. The magic about this thing called Life is we do not have to take on other people's perceptions or beliefs. We do not have to please them. We do not have to worry about what other people think. We do not have to limit our possibilities because other people limit theirs. We do not have to dim our lights because other people dim theirs. We do not have to hide our greatness for fear of what others think. In fact, it's just the opposite.

As Marianne Williamson so beautifully expressed in *A Return To Love: Reflections on the Principles of A Course in Miracles* (HarperCollins, 1992):

> **Our deepest fear is not that we are inadequate.**
> **Our deepest fear is that we are powerful beyond measure.**
> **It is our light, not our darkness that most frightens us.**
> **We are all meant to shine…**
> **…And as we let our own light shine,**
> **We unconsciously give other people permission to do the same.**
> **As we are liberated from our own fear,**
> **Our presence automatically liberates others.**

I finally realized it is my responsibility—even my duty—to shine *my* light, to be *my* most bold self, to courageously be ME! I've come to know it as "choosing in" or "choosing out." I agree with Morgan Freeman's character in the movie *"Shawshank Redemption,"* when he says, "You can either get busy living or get busy dying." I know it sounds pretty black and white, but that's the truth of it.

Fortunately, I've come to embrace the power of personal choice. I realize I am the only one who can make choices for ME. And I choose <u>in</u>. I choose to live life fully, completely and wholeheartedly. With that choice, I know it means being ME—no excuses or apologies! I now know that the <u>only</u> way to be is ME—audaciously, vivaciously, authentically and outrageously—even if it means an on-going journey of figuring out who ME is. And, most importantly, no matter what anyone else thinks!

Be who you are and say what you feel,
Because those who mind don't matter,
and those who matter don't mind.
— Dr. Seuss

The minute I committed to being ME, my life started to turn around. I started to make new choices for myself: I started to dress how I wanted to dress, I started to act how I wanted to act, and I started to say what I wanted to say. I started to let go of what others thought or what others told me. Although I respected what others wanted (from me), I started listening to my own inner voice and respected it *more*.

Every day I got a little more courageous and reclaimed that little skip in my step. I had a smile on my face I hadn't experienced since I was a little girl—splashing in puddles, dancing in the rain, running around barefoot, and proclaiming my dreams to anyone and everyone who would listen. I realized I was finally learning who I really was, and I actually *liked* ME.

> *It takes courage to grow up*
> *And turn out to be who you really are.*
> — e.e. cummings

I had finally found the key to unlock the door to the prison I'd created: it was as simple as *being* me and learning to *love* me. And, as a result, I also learned how to better love others.

The bolder I got, the more different I felt—yet the more ME I knew I was! We are so often trained to be "normal" or to "fit in" and to conform that many of us forget what we actually like, desire or prefer. Roses or lilies? Chocolate or vanilla? Night owl or early riser? When we've been taught by the adults, teachers and media around us that we "shouldn't" or "can't," we allow their limiting beliefs to become our own. The reality is that, with every breath and every decision, we can choose something else. We can choose to BE who we are, DO what we want, and ENJOY the happiness, abundance, love, health and peace that come with those liberating choices.

The incredible thing is that the more I dress, act, speak and breathe who I truly am, the more I get stopped and told by others how unique and amazing I am! The more I step out of my comfort zone and stretch beyond my own limitations, the more I see the possibilities and opportunities open up around me. The more I love, accept and embrace who I am, the more I reflect that light out to others and allow them to be who they are, too. The more I am who I AM, the more I accept others for who they are.

This is the beauty, grace and simplicity I found as a result of choosing to be ME. That's all I have, but it's also all I ever want—for the rest of my life. And I wish this powerful, beautiful experience for everyone—starting today. How might a commitment to being YOU—fully and completely—change *your* life forever?

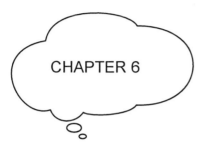

CHAPTER 6

I *Will* Walk Again.

by Catherine Kozuch

Just before I attempted to swing my legs over the side of the hospital bed and stand up, I heard the doctor say to me, "You will never walk again."

The previous 36 hours of my life immediately rushed back to me in one huge wave of shock and emotion: First, I remembered jumping joyfully into our truck for the drive down to Mexico with my boyfriend, thinking how crazy my parents had been all these years to advise me against traveling to this paradise destination! Next, I lamented about how a simple "no thanks" could have saved me so much pain and suffering—instead of giving in and warily accepting a ride back to my hotel in a "friend's" dune buggy on the very first afternoon. Finally, my mind flashed back to the accident.

Repeating the event all over again in my mind was almost as painful as the actual experience. Fear gripped my entire being, and I felt myself clenching my teeth and fists as I recalled being the helpless passenger as the buggy flipped end over end down that steep dune—for what seemed like an eternity. Sand was flying everywhere; I felt it hit my face like a blast of shotgun pellets. My body was lifted multiple times from the seat up against the now torturous seatbelt, then slammed violently back down, knocking the wind out of me—crushing two bones in my thoracic spine. The vehicle finally came to a stop, my body lying painfully limp in the wreckage at the bottom of the hill.

I looked over to see if my driver was okay, but he was gone. I was afraid he had been thrown from the buggy, but I'd later learn he had already fled the scene—leaving me alone in the desert without saying a word or doing anything to help me. I made several breathless, painful attempts to cry for help. I have no idea how long I actually lay there, but luckily I had good friends with me in Mexico who finally came to my rescue, bringing an emergency medical team with them.

Memories of the ambulance ride back to the Mexican hospital were just as terrifying. The pain was unbearable and my chest felt on fire. I begged repeatedly for the EMT to help me, to do something to alleviate the pain—but he simply sat at the other end of the ambulance listening to his mariachi music, staring blankly back at me.

It may sound strange, but I now fondly acknowledge those memories as the defining moments of my entire life. My path had taken a very sudden and quite unexpected turn, but I would not accept my suggested fate. In fact, the doctor telling me I would never walk again sounded so ludicrous, I *could not* accept it.

Instead, a life-changing thought emerged. I remember silently screaming these defiant words back at that doctor: *Who are you to tell me I'll never be able to do something again?*

In that one moment, it became my *mission* to walk out of that hospital by my own power. The thought of being paralyzed for the rest of my life was simply unacceptable. I would force myself to be positive and optimistic. My daily affirmation, "*I will walk again,*" was emblazoned in my heart and mind.

Many expressed disbelief, saying it was "impossible." After all, it was only a few short hours ago the doctors were pulling bone fragments out of my spinal cord from 2 crushed vertebrae. According to them, I was "just lucky to be alive" and shouldn't think such crazy thoughts or get my hopes up. After-all, I was paralyzed!

But here's what I knew: Some of the most respected sources of scientific research provide evidence that we can heal miraculously from any number of life-threatening conditions. Although this can provide hope for those who survive the most horrific disasters, statistics (as presented by our doctors) can also leave many of us contemplating only the darkest of possible outcomes. Why are we not encouraged by those "experts" to believe we're all created to be different—in body, mind and soul—and that each one of us is born with the ability to perform medical miracles? Why is this not the *first* suggested outcome?

Ultimately, we need to look within ourselves to define our own destiny. Someone else's diagnosis (or opinion of us) does not have to become our reality. In truth, we are superior to our circumstances, yet only those who dare believe this to be true are best equipped to change their thoughts and manifest their desires.

My beliefs alone, however, did not guarantee the immediate fulfillment of my prediction. Four weeks after my confident declaration that I would walk again, I found myself *very* frustrated. My legs still felt dipped in concrete, and I simply couldn't take any more failure. So, focusing on my toe with all the brainpower I could muster, I started to yell, "BIG TOE MOVE! BIG TOE MOVE!" A sudden burst of energy shot through me, and I witnessed the first of many miracles. My big toe actually…*moved!*

Some doctors did not believe me, saying it must have just been a twitch. Unbelievably, there I was again in my white-walled hospital room, frustrated by the faithless all around me. *I will simply have to do this myself,* I thought. Right then and there, I created a mantra: "I will prove them wrong. I will prove them wrong…" I spent *hours* focusing on my toes, telling them to move. As if answering my command, all my left toes obediently started to wiggle, one by one! A couple days later my left ankle moved…then a few days after that, my left knee joined in…then my whole left leg was getting in the game!

With much diligence, in a few short weeks my right toes woke up, and slowly the rest of my right leg started to move, too. A mere three months later, I walked out of that hospital barely leaning on a walker. Exiting the hospital doors, I looked back at the staff who doubted me, and I grinned ear-to-ear. I couldn't help but think (and I may have even whispered it under my breath), *I told you so.*

What was the key factor to embodying this miracle? I believed in myself and my "inner superior circumstance"—and I'm sure this is what allowed me to walk again.

You see, we can either dwell on a bad situation or show the World how powerful our thoughts are to make it better. When I was told I was paralyzed, I blocked *that* thought out of my mind and immediately focused on walking again. I continuously reminded myself my life was more deserving of freedom than the prison-sentence a wheelchair offered me. This belief, combined with the image of walking down the catwalk in stilettos, created a more positive and exciting mindset!

Looking back, I can see how my thoughts actually created a *self-fulfilling prophecy:* Fueled by my courage to believe in the unbelievable—that I would walk again—I *compelled* my desire to manifest in an experience others couldn't even fathom. I never lost sight of my goal.

It's my belief that every adverse, life-changing event occurs for a reason. We all face difficulties from time to time; but each one passes and can even lead to some of our most unexpected, breathtaking victories. Where would I be now if I didn't stay focused on my dream? What would have happened if I hadn't believed in myself and done whatever it took to keep moving forward?

No one can tell us how to accept what happens in our lives. We all have the power to interpret and recreate our thoughts in a positive light! All we need is to motivate ourselves to search deeper than the surface of our current circumstance and find meaning behind every obstacle.

Be patient. We cannot rush things just because we're frustrated or think time's running out. There may be times we come so close to our goals, yet can't see how close we are because we're focused instead on an unexpected difficulty that shows up. We must *trust* that everything will fall into place when the time is right, remembering to embrace the beautiful, *blooming* stages in between. If we're too critical of ourselves or our situation, we may miss the wonderful gift in each and every present moment.

The Universe is always conspiring to give us everything we need so we may grow and expand. When "obstacles" appear, it may be the Universe's way of checking in to see how badly we really want what we say we want—or it could be a sign pointing us in a new direction. When we walk in the dark and encounter mysterious challenges, we are meant to keep facing forward, heading toward the light of a brand new day—perhaps one that is even greater than we could ever imagine.

Those who persist with faith and determination *will* realize their dreams. The glorious thing about dreams is they don't have deadlines—or limits. No matter what has happened to you in the past, use today to start fresh. You can create your own miracles, too. Believe in yourself—the rest will follow.

CHAPTER 7

Success in Business & Adventure in Life *Can* Unite

by Natalie Sisson

When I tell people I live out of a suitcase—travelling the world while running my business—most people stare at me in disbelief. They either think it's funny, crazy or one of the best things they've ever heard!

I laugh to myself when I hear comments like, "Ohhh, I'd love to be able to do that. It sounds magical." Then the kicker: "It's just not possible for *me*. I have {*insert excuse here*} to look after and manage. So I have to stay put."

Really?

Who told you that having your ideal lifestyle, a successful business, and healthy relationships meant you have to stay put? If anything, it's the *last* thing in the world you should be doing if your heart longs for adventure. Haven't you heard? The only constant in life is change, and the only way to grow is by learning through new experiences. This requires you to take *action*.

The key question is, "Do you *really* want to give this lifestyle a whirl…and…are you ready to take that first step?"

A Life-changing Moment

I decided *I* was ready in 2006.

This is when I left behind the country I fondly call Paradise—New Zealand. Many wondered why I'd leave the shores of this beautiful country to find adventure somewhere else. But it wasn't really anything new for me: I was lucky to have two wonderful European parents who travelled with me all over the World since I was two. As a result, I got to experience many other cultures, learning their value systems and their languages. This not only opened my eyes to the very nature of humanity, but it has also helped shape me into the well-rounded, tolerant and worldly person I am today.

Although the choice to travel was made for me originally, this is probably why I feel so at home wherever I go. In fact, wherever my heart is, *that's* my home. And in 2006, my heart was calling for me to hit the road again. This time, I was taking my business with me!

The Suitcase Entrepreneur Lifestyle

When people think of owning a business, most visualize it as a *location*. In our truly global marketplace of today, the Internet and other ubiquitous technologies make distance and borders more and more obsolete. We have the ability to work from anywhere, at any time—even with a virtual team. This allows all of us the opportunity to transcend time-zones and cultures. We can even operate in the "cloud!" The truth is, the dream of combining work and travel is *entirely* possible, no matter where you are! You simply have to believe in yourself and your vision.

None of us needs work that feels like a J.O.B.—working *more* (and more) hours for *less* money. You definitely don't need the mortgage, the expensive car payments and all that furniture in your house either. What you *do* need is work that is fulfilling and to feel like you're not alone in the World! You also need to feel like you're making a valuable difference—a genuine and positive impact. So do I. Living the *Suitcase Entrepreneur* lifestyle allows me to do this by aligning my personal and professional efforts with my heart and my dreams. In my work as a Business Coach and Social Media Personal Trainer, I even get to support others to do the same. When I focus on these things, I feel like the luckiest woman in the world. Rich beyond words.

Don't buy *stuff*. Invest instead in experiences, adventure and yourself. At the end of the day, all those material assets can be lost, but your experiences and memories are forever yours. Wouldn't it make sense to have as many of them as you can during your time on this planet? If you agree, then pack up the right mindset, choose a direction, and go! Be open to new experiences. Be open to change. Know that while life will not always be easy, it will certainly be an adventure.

You have a unique reason for being on this Earth. Call it what you want: your calling, your destiny, your true purpose. Acknowledge that if you're feeling unhappy, limited or caged in right now, then it may be the Universe's way of telling you you're not living your purpose. Perhaps it's time to hit the road!

The Universe can only give you so many signs or inspiring "A-ha!" moments before you need to recognize them as the powerful, *personal* messages they are—and act on them! If you feel energized or scared on a daily basis—like you're constantly pushing yourself and battling non-believers—then you're probably on the right track. Remember, if you're trying to change the World, it may get tough at times. Dream big anyway! Desire great things and empower yourself to take action in your own life and business. This is where infinite possibility begins.

Inspire (and Hire) Your Dream CEO

Somewhere along the way, about the time you left your childhood, you probably hired the same full-time advisor the rest of us did, called "The Inner Critic." This inner voice probably convinced you to doubt yourself and your dream, arguing that you're not good enough, you're never going to be a success, you can't have it all or you can't be the beautiful, happy, grounded, free person you were meant to be. I think this was the lousiest hire we've ever made!

Instead, why not hire "Mr. or Ms. Incredibly Supportive" as your (inner) Dream CEO? Like the best boss you could ever imagine, your Dream CEO's job is to give you that little whisper in your ear each morning telling you how amazing you are when you wake up. Or, to provide you with that helpful nudge off the couch, reminding you how capable you actually are of changing your world today—if you'd just take those couple small, measurable action steps. This is the voice you want to listen to!

So when I hear people say, "I'd love to try that some day!" or (better yet) "I wish I could do that!" I encourage them to ban these words from their vocabulary. I think it's actually language invented by the Inner Critic, and it only serves to hold us back—keeping us on the couch or chained to a storefront. What would your Dream

CEO say instead? We're all familiar with what happens when we want something badly enough: we somehow find the courage, the energy and the will to move heaven and earth to make it happen. Why not want *this* badly enough to make it your new reality?

Keep in mind nothing ever came from *talking* about building a great business, sailing around the world, being the best piano player or becoming the best cupcake-maker ever. Everything comes from having a vision and taking action. The first action I advise you to take is to silence your Inner Critic. Tell him to just shut up and bugger off! Then hire your Dream CEO and get on with planning your next great adventure.

The Road Awaits You

Most of the time, things go according to a well thought-out plan. But if you hop on the wrong ferry…take a bus going east instead of west…or simply accept an offer to travel with new friends off the beaten path…it could very well be the coolest, life-changing experience *you never saw coming*! This sometimes makes all the difference in the world, but likely won't ever happen in your living room or boardroom! This is *your* life to fall in love with each day. That is, if you want to make every day an adventure.

I often remind myself, "I *can* have the lifestyle of my dreams!" And, I get messages from women around the World every day, expressing how amazed they are at how I live my life—travelling to different countries and going on adventures, all while running my business. Not surprisingly, they want to know how they can do it, too. If you're one of these women—or men—perhaps you think you need to have it all together first? Well, *I* certainly don't. I do, however, know what I want and where I'm going. It hasn't always been that way, but I think that's part of life's journey.

I've dragon-boated across the English Channel, smashing a World Record in the process. I've played Ultimate Frisbee on the beaches of Brazil and won a gold medal in the World Championships. I've coached budding women entrepreneurs from trains and boats, and had the opportunity to stay with complete strangers on my travels thanks to Twitter and my blogs. I've launched digital products and programs by the side of the pool at my apartment in Buenos Aires and been interviewed on radio shows and tele-seminars while on the move to a new destination.

In the realm of possibility and global enterprise, there really are no limits. From these experiences of success and adventure as a Suitcase Entrepreneur, I know there's nothing but my very best life—and yours—waiting on the road up ahead.

CHAPTER 8

Given the choice, most people would choose the certainty of misery over the misery of uncertainty.

by Lee Johnson

I first encountered this concept[6] many years ago as an advertising copywriter working on a campaign for a major bank in South Africa. Their research suggested people were more likely to change their spouses than change their bank accounts! This led us to develop campaigns for banking products targeting alternative markets (i.e. teenagers and youths).

But it didn't end there for me.

The whole idea shocked me to the core. Were people really that resistant to change? Would they *really* choose the certainty of misery over the misery of uncertainty? As I began to look around me through these lenses of insight, I had to agree with Henry David Thoreau that most people seemed content to "lead lives of quiet desperation." Remember, this was a country in the last days of Apartheid. White people were terrified a Black government would mean revenge, disaster and death. Black people were terrified the White Man would never relinquish power without massive bloodshed.

---

6   The origin of this phrase is uncertain. Most sources credit therapist Virginia Satir from her book *Your Many Faces* (Celestial Arts, 1978). However, others attribute it to cartoonist Walt Kelly who drew the "Pogo" comic strip in the '60s.

The whole population was nervous and afraid. Threats and violence were an ever-present fact of life. Almost every house had eight-foot high security walls with barbed wire and a battery of spotlights, not to mention a brace of guard dogs. Though I chose not to own a firearm myself, almost everyone I knew carried a gun. I recall vividly the sounds of police and army helicopters flying overhead almost every night; the sharp rattle of automatic weapons from the neighbouring Black townships; the progressive chorus of dogs barking through the night, prompting me to incessantly feel for the baseball bat I kept beside my bed and the Samurai sword hidden under the mattress.

If the situation was considered terrible for White people, it was far worse for the Black population. Most lived in shanty towns with little or no sanitation, running water or electricity. Crime was endemic: it was said a human life was worth no more than a pair of sneakers. Passengers on crammed commuter trains ran the risk of a sharpened bicycle spoke forced into their spine if they were reluctant to surrender their meager wage packet to a criminal. Children walking to school might have to bypass a charred body, the gasoline-soaked car tyre still smoldering around its neck.

Looking back, it seems incredible there was not a mass exodus. And yet, like the frog that doesn't jump out of the water as the temperature is being raised only one degree at a time, we were all virtually at our boiling point without being aware of it.

I was one of the lucky ones. Overall, I can say I was actually pretty happy and comfortable. I was a highly successful businessman with my own award-winning advertising agency, travelling the World and winning international awards. I had a wonderful family, and lived in a dream home with a bar and formal lounge cantilevered over a swimming pool. It would be pretty easy to assume I was just one of those racist bastards who chose to be oblivious to what was happening around me; yet the reverse was true. We had sent our children to a multi-racial school from Grade 0 at a time when it was a huge risk to do so. Our advertising agency was completely colour- and gender-blind. My wife and I ran a promotions company and our biggest client was the Kaizer Chiefs soccer team, the most successful in Africa. We would go to games at FNB Stadium (later the main venue for the Soccer World Cup in 2010) and be the only two white people in a sea of 90,000 Blacks. After Nelson Mandela was released, he would walk past us, smile and nod pleasantly, then go out onto the field to a deafening chant of "Mandela—President! Mandela—President!" Even thinking about it now, it sends chills down my spine.

In my country, the imminence of change was palpable, like some giant sword of Damocles. But part of me was still blind to it. I kept telling myself how happy I was—

even pretty proud of my racial impartiality—yet I couldn't escape the facts of what was happening around me. With the multitudes of various crimes in our country occurring all the time, we were forced to implement a ridiculous level of security in our homes. The stories of people being killed in broad daylight in downtown Johannesburg were mind-numbing and appalling at the same time. Bribery and corruption at every level of business and everyday life were commonplace. The dubious future for my wife and sons loomed ominously over my head like a dark cloud, and our weariness from the anxiety of living perpetually on a knife's edge was becoming something we could no longer ignore.

I couldn't help returning to the phrase produced by the bank's research: *Given the choice, most people would choose the certainty of misery over the misery of uncertainty.*

Could that actually be true of ME?

It was humbling to consider this a possibility. I had always regarded myself as someone at the very forefront of innovation and change. A client's wife once said I reminded her of a lone man in a white casual suit walking through an army of businessmen in charcoal pin-striped suits going the other way (a popular TV commercial at the time). Me? Afraid of change? Impossible!

Yet, the more I stepped back and took an honest look at myself, the more I had to confront the truth. As if years of grime were slowly being wiped away from my window to the World, I began to see things in a different light. I began to read everything I could find about the process of change in an attempt to understand why people were so resistant to it. I kept asking myself, *Isn't it natural to live in a state of optimism? Isn't that a good thing? Or was my <u>optimism</u> just my way of expressing an unconscious <u>denial</u>?*

Everything in the entire Universe is in a constant process of movement, progress and growth. Even decay and death are not only valid parts of this eternal and ubiquitous process, but they are indeed essential aspects of it. For only through decay and death can new birth begin. Only humans with our rational minds capable of contemplating our own destiny have the misguided desire and ability to consciously suspend, delay or manipulate this process.

Just as medical science prolongs an often fatally diseased physical life, and social mores around the institution of marriage often prolong fatally diseased relationships, so too can psychological hang-ups and defense mechanisms such as denial and rationalization often perpetuate and prolong diseased emotional, material and spiritual wastelands—those most insidious of traps which we call *comfort zones.*

Dr. Jill Murray once proposed it's only when people eventually make up their minds to risk the misery of uncertainty that they will be ready to make changes—and that's when we can become creators of our own destiny. Or, as Neale Donald Walsh would later say, "Life begins at the end of your comfort zone."

I think Morris West expressed it perfectly in his book, *The Shoes of the Fisherman* (HarperCollins, 1976):

> **It costs so much to be a full human being that there are very few who have the enlightenment or the courage to pay the price...one has to abandon altogether the search for security and reach out to the risk of living with both arms.**

If we're not prepared to do that; if we prefer to keep our security bubble of rationalizations and illusions and self-deceptions intact rather than confront truth and our own honesty; if we're not prepared to take the risks and face the consequences, then we are doomed to forever remain un-naturally trapped.

But once we've begun the journey—once we have taken off the blinders—we will never be able to fool ourselves again; we will either have to continue the journey or live forever with the knowledge that we are living a *compromise*.

And that is the most uncomfortable comfort zone of all.

Determined to examine all sides of the subject, I sat up many a night with friends, discussing the matter until the sun rose. Like dominoes, my blocks of oblivion were falling and revealing insights into things like honesty and authenticity, showing how critical it is to make every action and behaviour an expression of who we truly are inside. I was changing before my own eyes.

Change was now an imperative. I was being driven by a sense of urgency I had never experienced before. Within a few months, I had applied for my family to emigrate to Canada. While I was waiting, I decided I'd write a book on the topic called *How to Escape Your Comfort Zones* (The Penguin Group [SA] Ltd, 1995). It was published without a single edit and became an immediate hit, topping the bestseller charts for eight consecutive weeks.

These thoughts became my book. That book has become my life.

I guess one could say it's my way of making my contribution; walking my talk—with beautiful certainty.

CHAPTER 9

Forgiveness Is A Gift You Give Yourself

by Dr. Christian Guenette

As a child, life was not easy for me.

My parents separated when I was only two years old, and my mother did her best to raise three kids on her own, without any support from my father. This "best she could do" unfortunately included bringing unstable relationships with men into our home. I not-so-affectionately remember them as my "substitute fathers." One of these men—the person we spent most of our childhood with—was a raging alcoholic.

Although there were times when life at home was not a scary or negative experience, there were other moments when I would literally fear for my life.

It was like having a fear of roller coasters, and finding yourself on one without ever having the option of getting off. No exit, no emergency brake. No choosing a softer or gentler ride. There is only the living, breathing roller coaster with its gut-wrenching peaks, valleys and hairpin curves that leave you wondering where the fear stops and the fun begins.

Of course, there were those blessedly peaceful periods, too—those times when the cars would simply coast along a relatively flat portion of the track, teasing the rider (me) into a false sense of security. I was even naïve enough, once or twice, to believe the scary parts were over. But then, with jarring unpredictability, the cars would suddenly lurch forward, throwing me into yet another frighteningly steep slope, barreling toward a blind curve that left me wondering whether *this* would be that one time the safety mechanisms would fail...

Eventually, I stopped hoping the ride would end.

Instead, I made the best of a bad situation and discovered ways of coping. Since I was good at both school and sports, I knew I could create stability in my environment by excelling in either of these arenas. With a string of straight-A's on my report cards and a fist-full of first place ribbons to hang on my wall, I could be practically invisible—escaping the outbursts of irrational violence associated with yet another weekend binge. My brother and sister weren't quite as fortunate.

However, even though I was the wheel that *didn't* need the grease, good behavior couldn't always grant me immunity from the sheer and utter madness...

I remember one winter in particular when I was twelve years old. Like many other kids my age, my excitement grew as the Christmas season approached. The tree was decorated, the presents were piling up underneath, and the stockings were hung, just begging to be stuffed. The present with my name on it (the biggest one under the tree) looked *exactly* the same size as the item I'd put on the very top of my wish-list!

Then, just before the BIG DAY, I came home to find the seemingly unimaginable: in the magical spot where the tree and presents used to be, there was only emptiness. All it took was one little smart alec remark from a 12-year old to take him over the edge; as a result, my step-dad decided if *he* wasn't happy, *nobody* would be happy— at least not anyone in *my* family. All our presents were given away to others. I hope whoever got my "biggest wish" that year appreciated my wrong turn.

Weirder still, sometimes even the best of intentions *led* to the most trouble.

One night, not so long after the Christmas incident, I remember a "discussion" between my mother and step-father at the dinner table. It started innocently enough, but soon it escalated into a full-blown, beer-fueled argument. Before we knew what was happening, the dinner table was flipped on its side, dishes and food flying everywhere. My brother and sister raced to their bedrooms to find refuge from the yelling and the airborne objects. I didn't. I sensed his anger could easily turn into violence directed at my mother, and for the first time, I became truly concerned for her safety.

In a mindless act of bravado, I decided it was time somebody stood up to this bully, and that somebody was going to be *me*. Standing between the two of them, I tried to rationalize with the wide-eyed man full of rage. Apparently it's dangerous to rationalize with someone who is being irrational (especially one more than twice your size), for the next thing I knew, I was picked up by my throat, feet dangling, choking and fighting for air. I'm just thankful I was able to turn my head ever-so-slightly from side to side, for this meant I was able to answer him when he asked if I would ever do *that* again?! Nope. Not me. Can you imagine what effect that might have on the little boy from that point on?

I can.

I spent many sleepless nights imagining the countless ways that man should suffer for what he did to me. However, no matter how firm I held onto the belief that he should be made to pay, my wishes for retribution remained unfulfilled.

Since then, I've done my best to lessen my fears and anger with understanding. I've studied human psychology in attempt to make sense of it all. I've learned how we humans sometimes lash out at those we care about as an unconscious expression of our own pain, and I've often wondered what kind of torture this man must have endured in *his* life to not see the tremendous amount of collateral damage he was causing *us* in the form of pain and suffering.

Then it hit me. It was many years later and occurred while I was randomly ruminating about my uncomfortable past (yet again). I experienced a flash of insight that I now consider one of my favorite "a-ha" moments. It was just a *thought,* but one that would lead to the greatest sense of liberation I have ever known. In that one moment, what I realized was that by holding onto anger, *I was perpetuating my own pain and suffering*! The accused, on the other hand, was not being punished by my angry thoughts at all—nor would he *ever* be!

He and my mom had long since separated, and he was going on with his life, probably completely ignorant of my pain—yet going on, nonetheless. On the other hand, I was carrying this burden, and it was causing *me* a tremendous amount of grief. Every time I thought of him with anger and resentment, I brought the old hurt into my present moment, causing me suffering *today*, even though the acts had been committed many years before.

The Buddha was once quoted as saying,

Holding onto anger is like grasping a hot coal
with the intent of throwing it at someone else;
you are the one who gets burned.

This was me!

I was finally aware of my wrongful attitude and so incredibly grateful for the insight! But how could I turn this knowledge into relief? I longed to be released from the pain, but I couldn't grasp how I could let this person get away with such atrocious acts!

Suddenly, another revolutionary thought occurred to me. I used to think if I forgave him it was the same as saying, "The abuse was okay." But this simply wasn't true. By forgiving him, I would *not* be condoning the offensive act; instead, I would be *surrendering* to the imperfect nature of human existence. You see, I've always believed in my God as an unconditionally loving and forgiving God. And, if His love can be unconditional, couldn't mine be as well? If anyone deserves forgiveness in the eyes of God, this person deserved forgiveness, too.

Holding onto the ideas of resentment and revenge instead of love and forgiveness was simply maintaining my feelings of anger and hurt, allowing *me* to suffer. My past pain was at the hands of another, but my choice to suffer (or not) in the present moment, now lay solely, beautifully, powerfully—in *my own hands*.

I finally surrendered to this idea of unconditional love. I decided to forgive for forgiveness' sake. Instead of cursing my step-father, I decided to feel pity for him. Whatever he said and did in the past was obviously a reflection of his ignorance or simply an expression of his own pain and suffering. Holding him accountable for my feelings now—and for all these years—was not serving anyone, least of all me.

I decided this act of forgiveness would include everyone involved: I forgave *him* for the senseless violence. I forgave *my mother* for putting me in harm's way, time and again. I forgave *myself* for holding onto these hurt feelings for so long. I let go of any wish that my past could have been different than it was. I released all silent desires that my perpetrator should pay for what he did.

Over time, as I continued to think differently about this situation, I also began to feel different. I truly let go.

I live today free of my past. I am free of old pain. I am free of the feelings of betrayal, and I am free to experience my present moment without the negative influence of these painful experiences. I am truly free. The joy I deserved when I was a kid is the same joy I now claim. When I think back to those times, the story has lost its hold on me. As an evolved and evolv*ing* human being, I recognize I have the power to choose *joy* over pain, *freedom* over suffering, *forgiveness* over anger.

Hot coals? Not for me anymore! What about you?

Next time you find yourself thinking about the painful memories of *your* past, see if you can exercise the right to choose—and choose forgiveness. It's a gift you can give yourself, at any time of year.

CHAPTER 10

The Greatest Insights Sometimes Come From Our Darkest Despair

by Dr. Dena Churchill

The year is 1996, and I've just graduated from Chiropractic College. I'm now studying acupuncture in China with a group of other North Americans, and we're working at a Traditional Chinese Medicine (TCM) hospital just outside Beijing. I'm in awe of the healing wisdom infused in the very walls of this building, as well as in the souls of the doctors—all versed in the "magic" of Eastern healing philosophies. Perhaps it is this magic that's leading me to the depth of personal healing and understanding I need—for my whole perspective about Life itself is about to be turned inside out.

Three days before our international group of student doctors is to return to Los Angeles, I'm robbed. I find it quite ironic, actually, that it's happening to me, as I'm the kind of person who does not trust leaving my belongings in the hotel room. So I carry <u>all</u> my valuables with me in a money belt around my waist. My precautions are to my detriment, apparently, as a rather effortless acquisition of the belt is made with a quick slit of the strap on a crowded bus. Included amongst the lost items: my overseas ticket, my working visa, my jewelry, all my cash and personal identification.

In my moment of realization, I'm feeling rather shocked, but I'm also confident I can work out a solution. The local police are stoic while listening to my entire translated story, but offer not much more than brief condolences before being on their way. Lucky for me, our Chinese group leader takes the initiative to speak with the airline representative; he reassures me the insurance I purchased will reimburse the cost of the ticket. So I breathe a sigh of relief, borrow some cash to get me through the next few days and look forward to my trip home.

When travel day arrives, we pack everything up. The group leaves together on the shuttle for the airport, luggage in tow. All except for me, that is. I still need to take a slight detour to pick up my new plane ticket. I grab my Chinese-English dictionary and hop in a taxi to the travel agent headquarters in Beijing. Arriving at the ticket agent, I fully expect to be in and out of the office quickly, then on my way to the airport. Imagine my shock and dismay when I discover I had actually purchased a non-refundable ticket! And, even if I had the $800USD required to purchase another, I'm told I cannot fly without ID or a passport.

My heart falls into my shoes as I face the stark reality that the rest of my group is boarding the plane (with <u>my</u> luggage), and I am here in Beijing, with nothing but my dictionary and the clothes on my back. So I do what any mature healthcare professional would do in that situation—I go outside, straighten my skirt, sit on the sidewalk and start to cry...sending out wishes into the Universe for a friend, a bag of money, a place to stay or a ticket back home.

Little do I know it, but sometimes *the greatest insights come from times of darkest despair.* In this moment of utter loneliness, feeling vulnerable and scared, what I witness next would change my life forever.

Totally self-absorbed in pity, I don't notice the vagrant lady nearby. She sees me crying and takes it upon herself to come over as a friend, to comfort me. Between my tears, I manage to point to the Chinese translation in my dictionary for, "I was robbed." My newfound friend's eyes immediately widen, and she begins calling out to anyone in the street who will listen. To this day, I'm not sure what she said, but within minutes there is a crowd of locals standing around me handing me money and flashing me smiles of comfort. Looking back now, she could have been yelling, "Come smile at this Canadian lady! The more money you give her the more of her leg she will show you!" But in this moment, their display of kindness in my weakest moment makes me cry even more. The vagrant lady isn't exactly a *sweet-smelling* friend, but she <u>does</u> offer me her hand in friendship and a shoulder to cry on—and I am so grateful for her.

Four or five hours pass, and although I now have some money, it is not *nearly* enough to pay for my flight home or a night at the hotel. My thoughts begin to drift to which cardboard box or park bench I might be sharing that evening. And this is when the most astounding thing happens. A doctor from the hospital where I worked arrives outside the travel agency holding a brown paper bag. Apparently the tour leader had contacted the acupuncture Department Head and shared my story with him before the plane took off without me. When I see the gentleman, he motions for me to come over. When I do, he opens the bag to reveal 8000 Yuan, or about $800USD at the time. That might not sound like a lot to you, but this is a full year's salary for a doctor in his hospital! To think they collected this money so quickly and are now giving it to me for a ticket—it's too much for me. The flood-gates to my heart and eyes open once again. I mouth the words "thank you", but I cannot make a sound. I am utterly speechless.

Somewhere amidst the endless tears and sobs, I hear the acupuncture doctor reassuring me in broken English, "No, no cry. You go home...no be sad, you go home...here is money for ticket." The Chinese-English dictionary I am carrying doesn't contain the phrase "tears of gratitude," but when I force a smile and point to the phrase "I am happy," he relaxes enough to smile with me. I rest for just a moment in grace and then rush back into the travel agency to purchase an airplane ticket for the next day. With ticket in hand and hope back in my heart, I point to the word "passport," and the doctor arranges a ride to the Canadian embassy so I can be issued a temporary passport.

By this time it's dark. The taxi driver asks me where I will sleep, and I think about my cardboard box friends, who probably would not be so willing to share their bed if I arrive in a taxi. I have no more money, and I cannot remember the Chinese name for the hotel where I last stayed. Fortunately, rummaging through my pockets produces a napkin with the hotel name on it. It's the only place I know, so I give it to the taxi driver. Approaching the hotel, I wonder if perhaps I might be forced to sleep outside in the garden. At least I will feel safer there—the staff might recognize me and not call the police.

Before I settle down in my "bed" of flowers, I decide to go inside and share my story first. This way they will be less shocked when they find me in their garden. To my disbelief, they immediately show me to a room, completely ignoring me as I show them my empty pockets. As if this isn't already the most incredible of fortunes, their smiles and generosity continue the following morning. I wake up to discover them offering me breakfast and a ride to the airport, with hugs and blessings for a safe trip back to North America!

The rest is history. I make it back home safely to my small fishing village in Portugal Cove, Newfoundland in Canada with a gift of gratitude and a renewed trust in the Universe that now forever lives in my heart.

Once my thoughts were clear, focused and specific to what I valued and needed, I voiced them out loud, and they appeared: the friend, the money, the passport *and* the ticket. It's often difficult to see that loving matrix all around us, supporting us through our greatest challenges *when we're still experiencing them*. But whenever we look back on our lives, it's easy to see we're never alone. That loving, nurturing, infinite force is ever-present.

My experience in China has reinforced my faith in the Universe—that I'm supported, guided and protected in all manners of abundance, and that these beautiful gifts sometimes come from unexpected sources! But I now know they are given freely, and I can use my thoughts and intentions to call in everything I need to build my dreams.

What if you assume the Universe is transpiring to bring you all that you love? Imagine holding this thought for a day, a week, a lifetime. Everything that is handed to you is material for you to build your dreams. Trust there are no mistakes, no extra pieces and no "return-to-sender" stamps on your wishes—just potential adventures in the World! All simply miraculous rides on the breeze, as we each learn to truly love.

CHAPTER 11

My Happiness — *My Problem*

by Dixie Gillaspie

This thought not only changed my life—it saved my life.

A thought can do that.

It was the year I got my driver's permit, and the year I looked at a boy and for the first time thought, *Wow, so that's what all the fuss is about!*

The same year my father was diagnosed with cancer and his "anger management problem" turned into uncontrollable rage. The year I went to worship and school with black eyes and a broken nose—and no one said a word.

I was fourteen years old.

That year, I would also read a line in a book that placed me firmly, inarguably, in the driver's seat of my own destiny.

A thought can do that.

I was almost glad for the damage to my face. This wasn't like the welts on my back and my legs; it wasn't easily hidden or ignored. For the first time, I knew I would have to talk about what had been happening since I was five years old.

It started on a Friday night when I got out the old sewing machine to finish a skirt I was making.

"What do you think you're doing?" my father demanded.

"I'm going to sew."

"Don't tell me what you're going to do or I'll knock you right down on the floor!" he fired back.

I took a stand in front of the wood-burning stove. With more desperation and bravado than wisdom, I answered, "I know you will."

He did.

He pinned me against the wall behind the stove, and when he was finished, my eyes were already swelling shut. No one would be able to look away this time. Adults would undoubtedly intervene. This would be the year that everything changed.

But Saturday I boarded a school bus and traveled with my classmates and coach to a speech competition for schools in the area. Sunday I went to worship. Monday I went to school. No one looked me in the eye. No one said a thing.

Monday before lunchtime, I was called to the Principal's office and introduced to two ladies from Social Services. They gave me three options: 1) they could place me in foster care *if* they could find a place for me, 2) they could have a talk with my father, or 3) they asked me, "Do you think you can handle it alone?" I'd been handling it alone for years. I said I could and walked away.

Well, I thought, *that's that, no one cares. If no one loves me enough to intervene even when my face is black and blue, why do I bother to live?*

That year I concluded there *was* no reason for me to continue living.

A thought can do that.

The first thing that saved my life was my nearly comical naiveté about the resilience of the human body. *My* body anyway. I was young, strong, and, apparently, bouncy. After a swan dive off the highest point of a pole barn didn't break any bones (let alone my neck), but only left me more bruised than my father had on a bad day, I had to think again.

Our medicine cabinet wasn't much help. We were a "healthy family"—no prescription medications there. Swallowing the contents of the aspirin bottle did no more than give me the "flu" for a day. Guns were a mystery to me; if I'd known *where* to get a handgun I wouldn't have known how to load one or how to take the safety off. I was never any good at tying knots. A razor blade looked like the most viable option for ending my life, but I hated to leave such a mess!

I don't remember where I found it or how it found me, but in the midst of this dilemma, I came upon a book entitled *Illusions: The Adventures of a Reluctant Messiah* by Richard Bach (Dell, 1989).

The cover didn't say, "This book will save your life." No, it simply sported a neon blue feather floating on a black-as-midnight background with a few dots that were *maybe* supposed to be stars. Underneath the feather it said, "The glorious bestseller by Richard Bach, author of *Jonathan Livingston Seagull*." That's all it said.

I've always been a voracious reader. I swallow books whole, then often reread them like a cow chewing her cud. I was zipping right along on my first pass when, on page 96, one character says to the other, "Well, you asked for it… If your happiness depends on what somebody else does, I guess you do have a problem."

Suddenly, I *was* Donald. That remark was addressed to *me*! I felt my head jerk and my eyes blaze just as his did. I knew why he smiled when he said, "You…are… *right*!"

How many times had I lain in the Kansas grass just as he lay in the Illinois grass? I could feel that grass underneath me, connecting me to that mystical, *possibly* fictional character as the thought flowed through my brain, into my heart, and washed over the spirit that I had barely begun to acknowledge as my own.

I guess you do have a problem.

You have a problem.

Your problem.

Yours!

If making my happiness dependent on what *other* people chose to do was "asking for it," then could I ask for something different by making my happiness dependent on what I chose to do?

I had been making my happiness dependent on my father and my mother and all those people who saw my face but looked the other way after that fateful night. I had been letting myself believe that if no one would *stop* the abuse or cared enough to try, then my life was worthless.

I had *thought* my problem was that other people did things to make me unhappy or didn't do things to make me happy. Now I realized that my *problem* was that I was making my happiness dependent on other people.

Goodness knows I had plenty to be happy about: I had love. I had friends and family who cared for me. I had an uncle who took off work every year on my birthday to take me to the zoo. I had grandmothers who taught me to crochet and play the piano. I had a mother who read to me so much that I learned to read when I was not yet five years old from following her finger as it moved across the page. I had friends who rode horse-back with me—racing up and down the dirt roads, bareback, hair flying, whooping like savages; something I never would have been able to do if my father hadn't given me horses and encouraged me to ride them.

Most of all, I had me. There was a reason I had been nicknamed "Sunshine" and "Dynamite." I had light and energy, and I had the power to live.

I thought, *As long as I can be happy, I can be creative, I can be productive, and I can fulfill a purpose! And as long as I can fulfill a purpose, I can be happy. My happiness is my right, and my responsibility.*

Like Donald, I smiled.

A thought can do that.

That thought has brought me back to *me* many times. It has kept me grounded as I wrestled with finding my passion and purpose, and as I transformed them into the Blast Thru Coaching™ platform I work from today.

I still have that book—tattered now—and I read it at least once a year. Every time I come to page 96, I pause and think, *My happiness, my problem—solved!*

On a recent trip to Florida, I walked the beach with a friend and colleague who said she couldn't understand why, although I feel no need to hold my father accountable for my suffering, I *do* feel the need to give my thanks to Richard Bach for saving my life—a man I do not know and will likely never meet.

"Who would I hold accountable?" I asked. "My parents? Their parents? The community? How wide a net and how far back in time would I have to throw it to find the beginning of the pain and the fear?"

On the other hand, I *do* know who to thank. I say a prayer of gratitude for my father, dead more than 24 years, because through all his fear and anger he showed me more love than he showed himself; for friends and family, who may not have known how to reach out to me with my battered face, but have since reached out to share in the healing of a bruised spirit.

I say a prayer of gratitude for every dreamer, every writer, every reluctant messiah, everyone who has shared a thought, like a bird winging into the night sky. You don't know whose heart those feathers might touch, whose spirit they might heal or whose life they might save.

A thought can do that.

CHAPTER 12

Who Am I?

by Lynn Sumida

"**Y**ou've got cancer."

Although those unthinkable words flooded my entire system with chaotic surges of disbelief, fear and dread, they are *not* the words that changed my life.

With my hysterectomy a barely-passed milestone, the doctor matter-of-factly proceeded with his description of my upcoming fate: chemotherapy, nausea, drugs, hair-loss at three weeks, complete baldness at four weeks, twenty-five subsequent radiation treatments, etc. I was numb with shock. It was surreal.

An eternity of overwhelm passed in a matter of seconds. And then I heard the words that *did* change my life:

Stop. You are exactly the same as you were twenty minutes ago, when you didn't know you had cancer.

What? Who said that?

But then, in an instant, I "got it." The panic began to melt away and a great calm spread over me. I felt like I had just woken up, and the World was quiet and peaceful. Cancer was an external thing that was happening to me, but *I* hadn't changed: my essential self, my authentic identity, "who I Am" was still exactly the same as it had been just moments before. The simplicity and impact of this truth washed through me and grounded me in an extraordinary and profound way. No matter what's happening around me, I can always return to the thought, *I Am*. This was the beginning of my amazing journey navigating the tempestuous waters of "cancer treatment."

What do I believe?

Let me back-track for a few moments to give a bit of context. Over the decades, I have been a close acquaintance of the "power of positive thinking," but I was about to catapult this relationship to a whole new level. Although I definitely believed thoughts can change things, I wouldn't have bet my paycheque on thoughts doing something as significant as changing water into medicine. That would have been the equivalent of turning water into wine—definitely a miracle!

Dr. Masarau Emoto, a Japanese scientist, brought widespread awareness to the power of our thoughts in his groundbreaking book *Hidden Messages in Water* (Beyond Words Publishing, 2004). His work with jars of water (featured in the movie *"What the Bleep Do We Know!?"*) showed that different words written on jar labels could actually change the molecular structure of the water in those jars. This was fascinating to me as an intellectual idea, but that was as far as it went until suddenly I really *needed* water to change—and in a big way.

Am I bleeding to death?

While waiting for my hysterectomy, but before my cancer had become an unequivocal fact, I was hemorrhaging so severely I couldn't be away from a washroom for more than 30 minutes at a time. A very strong prescription was the only thing that worked to control the hemorrhaging: that is, until a week before surgery, when I was required to stop all medications. I reminded the doctor that I couldn't function without the medication, but he informed me there was no choice. I had to be medication-free for the surgery.

Not liking this at all, I phoned a pharmacist to see how long the medication would remain active in my system, trying to predict how many days of severe bleeding I would have to endure. I wondered how much blood a person could lose before being in real danger. But, despite my misgivings, I followed the doctor's orders. I stopped taking my medication on Monday and estimated I would be okay until Thursday. Sure enough, as predicted, Thursday night the bleeding started again, and by Friday morning, I was in serious trouble. I had been up all night, and it wouldn't stop. There were three more days to go! I didn't know how I could bleed this much and still be *alive* for the surgery on Monday.

I called my homeopath immediately to see if there was any natural remedy that would control the hemorrhaging without interfering with the surgery. She recommended a remedy for *exactly what I was experiencing*. I took a deep breath—and felt a sense of relief. But wait: she went on to say she didn't have the remedy, nor was it likely that anyone else would. I was stunned. What now?

How can this be?

"Well," she said, "we do a paper remedy."

"What's that?" I asked.

"Do you remember Dr. Emoto's work?"

"Yes," I replied, somewhat confused.

"Well, we're going to do the same thing."

She gave me the name of the remedy and told me to write it on a piece of paper. Numbly, as instructed, I wrote it down. Then we checked to see what strength of remedy I needed, and I wrote that on the paper, too. She asked me to fill a clean glass jar with water and screw on a lid. Trancelike, my mind could make no sense of this, so I just surrendered. Next she told me to put the paper with the remedy written on it onto the counter, place my hands on the top and bottom of the jar, and tap it up and down on the paper 100 times.

This is crazy! How can this possibly work?

When I finished the tapping, she instructed me to take a tablespoon of the water. I swallowed the water, hung up the phone, and waited. Nothing remarkable happened, and I sat there thinking, *What now?* Thirty minutes later, I realized I was still sitting there, and I wasn't rushing to the bathroom. An hour passed and then another. Nothing. No bleeding. It had stopped! It was like a faucet had been turned off, and it remained so until the morning of the surgery—three days later. How could this happen? How does a *word* written on a piece of paper—just a thought, really—have so much power? I didn't understand, but gratitude filled me as I recognized the opportunity I'd been given to experience a different reality—a world of unseen possibilities where miracles happen.

What *is* a miracle?

Four weeks after my hysterectomy, my chemotherapy began. It was a bright sunny day in early May, and I was "ready" for the chemo. Despite choosing this path intentionally and fully believing in my treatments, old movie images of people being dreadfully sick from chemo still floated just below the surface of my mind. But when I consciously remembered the thought that changed my life—*I am exactly the same as I was twenty minutes ago*—a calm, grounded peace returned and sustained me from within.

Filled with gratitude for the wonderful support and care I was receiving on all fronts, I sat in the hospital Waiting Room before my first chemo treatment. I felt deep appreciation for all those who had taken this path before me, as well as all the time and dedication of the scientists, doctors, nurses and other practitioners who created the foundation for me to have the best care available. Overflowing with love, I walked into the treatment room. Two dear friends accompanied me, and we spent the time catching up with each other and sharing our plans for the future.

The five hours of that first treatment passed in a warm, swift and loving blur. I had no anxiety and no adverse reactions! We were amazed when the nurse came in and said it was finished. Walking out of the room, I felt victorious and deeply moved—in awe. The incredible session I had just experienced—one that could have been so horrible—was instead filled with the kind of wonder I felt while bathed in the sacred beauty of the Notre Dame Cathedral in Paris. I was shocked to realize that my chemotherapy treatment had become a spiritual experience for me. Another miracle!

Who Am I?

In that moment, I knew with complete clarity this experience with cancer was not about the disease, but about *who I Am and what I believe.* Who we are can be defined in so many ways: what we do, how we look, who we are married to (or not), and the list goes on. It seems almost impossible not to fall into the trap of defining ourselves in some kind of tangible, external way. But if we define ourselves by whom or what we are attached to, it can all come crashing down, and sometimes instantly. So, what do we hold onto, if it isn't all those tangible realities "out there?"

For me, the answer to this question continues to shift my focus from "the concrete" to the intangible, from what I can "grasp" to who "I Am" on the inside. When I focus on the outside world, it is easy to feel anxiety and fear. When I let my thoughts run away with me, I forget who I am—and I am lost. As soon as I come back to myself—my "I Am"—I connect to the present moment, to a feeling of calm, and a sense of peace. This is the key: *Being fully present makes the past and the future disappear.*

Regardless of circumstance—whether I'm leading a workshop or facing treatment for cancer, when I am living fully in each moment and choosing to remember *I am exactly the same as I was twenty minutes ago,* I know exactly *who I Am.* And that is the most powerful miracle there *is.*

CHAPTER 13

Time Is Relative

by Stephen Thompson

There I sat, on the side of the mountain, watching the paramedics—at a twenty foot distance—race to keep my body alive. This odd, third-person perspective was an entirely new sensation. It was as if I were viewing the World through a fuzzy, white lens where everything glowed and the concept of linear time as I understood it, ceased.

My senses were heightened, and I understood what was going on—including the events leading up to this moment—but it just didn't seem relevant to me anymore.

Just a few hours prior, I left my hometown of Chico, California with the goal of meeting up with my Boy Scout troop in Salmon Falls, Idaho. Other Scout Masters and troop members had left days earlier for the Western States tour, but I could only leave my interior design firm for the kayaking portion of the adventure.

On that June afternoon in 1990, my big, yuppie Kawasaki motorcycle—which many would have viewed as a mid-life crisis purchase—was packed and ready for the long, three-state trek. It had been six years since I'd had a "man's trip," and I wanted to take my time. The soundtrack for the movie *"Easy Rider"* played through my quadraphonic stereo helmet, matching my laid back mood as the long, valley highways stretched into windy, mountain roads.

Traveling up the canyon, a large motor home slowed my pace around the curving turns. I wasn't in a hurry though. The view of the pristine Feather River, the bold mountain peaks, and the soaring hawks engulfed my senses. Time was also a gracious companion.

Little did I know, but a recent rockslide covered the road with gravel and shale. I hit the brakes as I approached the debris, but it was too late. Even at the slower speed of thirty miles per hour, I could not keep the bike steady. I slid out of control and impacted the guardrail. My knee was nearly torn off when my effort to jump the rail was inhibited by a large post. Nonetheless, forward momentum carried me away from the road and down a vertical slope towards the rushing water below.

The final damage assessment when my body came to a halt included: a cracked helmet, broken sunglasses, facial lacerations, and—with the help of an x-ray confirmation later on—a punctured stomach and broken bones in over 110 places.

Lying on the side of the mountain, I drifted in and out of consciousness. When my awareness became more constant, I realized my condition was dire. Fear was my new attendant, and I was soon consumed with thoughts of being eaten alive by coyotes, known to populate the canyon I found myself in.

I somehow managed to replace my fright with a calm understanding, and I began to pray. My pain magically disappeared as I transitioned into a near-death experience. As I sat on a lichen-covered rock, my life started playing like a fast-forward movie. Everything I had done, including all my hopes and aspirations, was revealed in an orderly fashion.

Like a dream emerging from my subconscious, I also saw a huge book written in my own handwriting that had recorded my every move. Yet surprisingly, some pieces of my life were missing. Some of the sentences were incomplete. When I looked closer, the pages were blank during those times in my past when I was not on my path. Negative experiences I remembered having, marked by guilt or sadness, caught my attention by their lighter font. It was as though the empty space or the change in writing provided a new awareness and the opportunity to make changes to my own history. I saw how the way I often chose to live my life was not consistent with my own personal values.

While this truth serum flowed into my body-less being, linear time stood still. I could have been there minutes, hours or simply nanoseconds according to the highest-tech clock. It suddenly became clear to me: if I wanted to right *any* wrongdoings or correct my lifestyle as a workaholic, I had to come back into my physical body.

In this timeless space, there was no way to fully understand the extent of my decision. Little did I know my body would undergo 28 reconstructive surgeries or that I would spend two years in a hospital bed, sometimes going weeks at a time without someone washing my hair. There was no way to express the humility of having to rely on another individual's help to go to the bathroom or the inevitability of wetting the bed when no one was able to be present. Nor was there any way to measure the effects of six years without walking or the loneliness of losing connection with the outside world.

The thoughts and concerns about the future did not arise while outside of my body. But with a (soul-full) decision to live, I was immediately transported back into the bloody mess of a body that was lying beneath the rescuers' hands. Pain quickly returned, and the underlying fear of the unknown with it.

Yet, the moments, minutes or hours I spent in a timeless, near-death space changed my life forever.

It did take several years for a full physical recovery. My interior design firm closed and my profession changed with the new insights about my life's purpose. Now, instead of redecorating people's homes, I'd help them reconstruct their entire lives from the inside out. I also delved into learning many of the healing techniques that helped save my life, and I was ready to share them with others in the hopes they too could experience the same transformation I did (without needing to fall off the side of a mountain first).

Admittedly, it was never easy. There were many challenging times throughout my recovery, including financial ruin and a divorce. However, throughout it all, I chose to maintain a broader perspective of Life.

Time is relative. It provides the framework within which we experience all of our life lessons, and it's not good or bad—it just *is*. It is our perception of time that affects our emotional responses, creating feelings of stress and anxiety or ease and excitement.

In years past, I was impulsive and impatient. Many nights were filled with wariness about the business projects that lacked completion or the family issues left unresolved. Often I was overwhelmed and frustrated.

But now, I view time through a much larger scope. I understand there is a Divine timing that allows events, people and circumstances to come together with a purpose far greater than what the eye can see. If a project doesn't get done today, my world isn't going to collapse. With a more lenient viewpoint of time, I can relax and enjoy the process of doing just as much as the end result I am aiming towards.

I also understand the amount of personal responsibility involved in making the most out of each moment I am alive. I now take the time to speak more honestly and kindly to those around me. I am able to be more patient, open-minded and loving. Ultimately, I know how to utilize my relationship with time to create the best human experience possible, both for myself and others.

Thanks to my time spent on the mountainside, and the many years it took to fully recover, I finally understand the concept of time:

The past is a cancelled check—the future is a promissory note—and the current moment is a gift, which is why it is called *the present.*

SECTION II

BY ME

The ancestor of every action is a thought.

— Ralph Waldo Emerson

CHAPTER 14

I Can Re-Invent My Life!

Reflections On the Price We Pay to Live in Resignation

by Dr. Joe Rubino

I remember the moment clearly. It was 1991, and I was sitting in a personal development "intensive" seminar.

At that time, my life was characterized by apathy, sadness, anger and resignation. Just like most people mired in the old "work ethic" paradigm, I was deeply embedded in the typical "9 to 5" J-O-B mentality. For me, that job was dentistry. Although financially rewarding and successful by society's standards (my practice grossed nearly $1 million annually and attracted 250 new patients a month), there still seemed to be an important part missing—a desire for something more meaningful. It seemed to call to me from just out of reach, begging the question,

"Is this really all there is to life?"

For one thing, despite the money, I had no time freedom. I had to work day in and day out just to feed the "overhead monster." Though I loved to travel, I barely managed to get away for a week or two each year with my family. Even when I did, I found myself worrying constantly about the practice, my patients, and the constant headaches that go along with a staff of fifteen!

This says nothing of my day-to-day reality of being bent over looking into people's dark (and sometimes smelly) mouths, often causing them discomfort—if not actual pain—while they were wishing they were somewhere else, too! I often thought, *Did I actually choose this occupation?*

Despite the fact that everything inside me longed to escape from my self-imposed professional prison, I had created a solid, unending series of justifications that kept the status quo firmly in place: *How can I walk away from such a lucrative practice? How can I throw away seven years of advanced schooling and the huge financial investment? How can I let down my patients when they depend on me? How can I ever provide for my family and replace my significant six-figure income?* More to the point, *How could I even consider asking any of these questions when all I thought I was capable of was "drilling and filling?"*

If there was a way out of the resigned rut I had created for myself, it was surely unknown to me then. The whole concept of taking responsibility for my life in a way that supported my happiness and honored my core values was entirely foreign to me.

To make matters worse, I thought of myself as an extreme introvert! In my mind, I was so socially incompetent that I consistently chose to do my continuing education credits by mail to avoid the frightening possibility of actually talking to my colleagues at professional seminars! Not only was my sense of insecurity and resignation creating a barrier to reinventing my life, but it was also hindering my connection with others and leaving me feeling wholly insignificant in the grand scheme of things! I had accumulated literally *thousands* of pieces of evidence since the age of five that convinced me, "It's just the way I am!" So there was little I or anyone else could do about these "facts," right?

So there I sat, that fine day in my first "intensive" seminar, intrigued by the concept of personal development, but arrogantly confident that my "unique situation" was so far beyond hope there was little anyone could do to help me out of my dilemma. Love and belonging, contribution, creativity, inspiration, fun and adventure (the core values forming the basis of my life today) were concepts that worked for all those *other* people. The notion I might possess unrealized gifts was preposterous!

I was convinced my life was totally devoid of any significant purpose beyond survival and getting through my daily struggles. I clung to the vague hope that perhaps I could one day enjoy life. And to me, "one day" meant waiting for retirement in 30 years!

My resignation was so pronounced, in fact, I was prepared to do battle with anyone who might even suggest there was a better way because I *knew* there was no hope.

Or so I told myself.

This is when my coach Mike Smith had the audacity to ask me the question, "Joe, have you ever considered what it's *costing* you to live with the belief that you have no other options for creating an empowered and fulfilling life?"

Costs?

It would be silly of me to attempt to deny their existence. But given their sheer numbers, how could I give them the attention they deserved without being completely overwhelmed? As I began to consider the question asked of me, the list in my head seemed endless: the cost to my mental health from living in daily resignation, anger and sadness; the cost to my relationships—avoiding others because I believed I did not belong or have anything significant to contribute; the cost to my happiness—refusing to step into an empowered and fulfilling life; the cost of sacrificing my most important values; the cost of not allowing myself to have fun and pursue my passions—which were, at the time, undiscovered for the most part; the cost of not enjoying the present moment, but waiting until I could retire to start living; and finally, the cost of not stepping into a life of true giving and service to others, rather than one focused solely on my own petty concerns and grievances.

I sat there dazed—as if stricken by an unseen force of nature. The impact from this tsunami-sized collection of costs thrust me into my breakthrough experience head-on. I immediately sensed how the convenient and distorted interpretations I had constructed all around my life kept me stuck and suffering. In that moment, I *knew* my suffering was a function of believing my life was filled with things I did not want and plagued by wanting things I thought were beyond my reach.

What if I simply "let go?"

In an instant, hope replaced despair. I felt there was actually a chance I could reinterpret my life and my potential! I saw how I could choose to live from a declaration of who I wanted to be, rather than from the "default me" constructed with evidence I'd amassed over the first 35 years of my life. I sensed the freedom in creating a *new* vision for my life—in harmony with the essential values at the core of my very being. In the moment of this realization, my life changed forever!

In a flash, I understood how my resignation was costing me my life in *every significant way*. As Norman Cousins once said, "The tragedy of life is not death, but that which dies inside us while we are still living." When I focused on the thought that *I could create any reality I wanted—simply by having the courage to believe in myself and to pursue my dreams*—my entire world appeared anew to me, never to be the same again.

With the support of my coaches, I committed to a rigorous personal development program that would end up manifesting these changes into my life. I took on the task of re-inventing myself to be the person I declared myself to be. For nine years, I relentlessly pursued my new commitment, step-by-step, putting into action ideas that previously felt destined only for others:

- I studied to become an inspirational life-coach and leader;
- I sought out the key success principles that would allow me to be optimally effective;
- I applied these secrets to my life and gave up my right to be invalidated;
- I decided to focus on contributing to others rather than looking good or being liked;
- I completely dedicated my life to acquiring and implementing the skills needed to help people elevate their self-esteem, just as I had done for myself;
- I decided to make choices that clearly reflected my decision to be an inspiration to myself and others, gratefully letting go of those that had kept me stuck and suffering.

By following my heart and trusting my intuition, I cultivated a personal approach to my life from which I was able to pursue my passions, honor my essence, and attract even greater abundance into my life than I ever had as a dentist. Literally in an instant, the sudden realization of the tremendous price I was paying to live in resignation thrust me from my self-imposed prison. No longer was I tied to beliefs of "I should do this" or "I shouldn't do that." By developing an unwavering belief in myself and using that as my solid foundation, I now know anything is possible for me.

Of course, like all of us, my life is a work in process. But what a difference to be *enjoying* it now! The realization of what it was costing me to play small and stay resigned to my life of apathy continues to inspire me every day. I remind myself to remain open to possibilities and to remember the Universe provides us all with an endless series of opportunities to make a difference and live our best lives. I relish each day for the chance to play full-out and pursue a life of no regrets. I not only wish this for you, I challenge you to know it for yourself—for you, too, possess the ability to reinterpret your life and potential!

What is the alternative costing you?

CHAPTER 15

I'm Here For A Special Reason After All:

A Caribbean Food Revolution?

by Maureen Cubbon

Though I don't subscribe to any particular faith, I've always believed deep down that my life has an unforeseen purpose. I've come to notice over the years that (for some reason) people respond positively to me when I serve in a teaching capacity. It's made me wonder if I've been put here as a messenger of sorts. This curiosity has led me down several very different paths, a journey culminating in the belief that we *all* have a special purpose in this lifetime—even me!

I started to gain clarity and momentum in uncovering my purpose when I moved back to the Cayman Islands in 2005. I went to work as the Marketing Manager for the largest food distribution company on the island. As much as I enjoyed the creative and social aspects of the job, I found that implementing community programs and connecting with people about food and nutrition lit me up. In fact, after helping create a children's health and wellness program for one of our community partners (a global health insurance company), I ended up going to work for *them* instead!

My new job opened my eyes to the dynamic world of health insurance. The learning curve was quite steep, but I was granted a lot of freedom to message the company's philosophy (and strategy) to the public in innovative ways. I took this to heart and worked hard to make sure their mission to support better health in the islands was well-received.

With my scientific background, I regarded this humanitarian approach as simply a "feel good" touch we offered that no one else was. But as I did my work every day, I grew to realize we actually had a *responsibility* to make sure people were empowered around their health and wellness. As I began to connect my work to my own desire to help others, I came to understand our corporate responsibility was also my *personal duty*!

Because I've always been someone who loves good food and great wine, I'm pretty conscious of what goes on my plate and into my system. I knew this could work in my favour professionally at some point, but I wasn't quite sure how. Though I have no formal chef training, I do have loads of hands-on experience in some of the World's greatest dining establishments. This had to count for something, right?

Well, it has! About a year ago, a woman came up to me in a grocery store and asked me why I didn't do my healthy cooking show anymore (part of my original marketing job with the distribution company). As humble as her family was, she said she was always so grateful to learn small, practical solutions to make her family's life healthier. She encouraged me to go on TV again, as she knew many others who'd taken our message to heart and were making healthier choices.

The very next day, another interesting thing happened: I was running a Children's Fun Day on our sister island, Cayman Brac. After it was all said and done, three little kids ran up and hugged me, telling me they'd learned a lot from us being there. This made me feel like maybe I was on the right path! Upon returning one year later, the very same kids not only remembered us, but also recited what we'd taught them over twelve months earlier! These moments kept repeating again and again, each time we went into the schools. I felt so gratified knowing we were making a difference—even if it was just a few children at a time.

This program has now been running successfully in Cayman since 2006 and officially went "international" when we launched it in the Bahamas in 2010!

Now my next creation is on-track to take our community to the next level. In April, 2011, we launched an exciting school garden project for the schools in the Cayman Islands. The requirements were simple: each school's principal must submit an application for us to come in, and we would then do an on-site assessment for suitability. As it stands, fourteen schools want the program in 2012! It'll be lot of work, but the overwhelmingly positive response has given me confirmation that it's the best thing we could have done here. We are ready!

To me, this is a critical initiative, illuminating the concept of "from seed to table" for the youth of the country. In our World of packaged, processed, "convenience" foods, most of us have really lost touch with what's in our food, how it is made, and where it really comes from. I believe this is a big reason we've turned into a largely unhealthy society, out of touch with such a basic idea—how we nourish and sustain ourselves. My passion was to design the program with children in mind, to help them understand at a young age where all food comes from, and most importantly, that they can make healthy food *choices*. A healthy body and healthy mind can open the World up for a lot of people, especially children. It's a dream come true for me.

Inspired by Jamie Oliver, I first did an informal experiment in a few schools: With fruits and vegetables on a table, I simply asked the kids what each one was. Some knew, but most didn't. I then held up a ketchup bottle and asked, "How is this made?" This produced many wide eyes and whispers. It was only when I picked up a bunch of tomatoes and put the two together that I saw the realization in their eyes. How do they not know what goes in their favorite burger condiment? *Was this a bigger problem that I thought?* After a couple more schools—many unnamed bunches of broccoli and bananas later—this proved to be a rather serious issue.

What could I do to generate a really powerful, "out of the box" call to action? How could we avoid the usual information overload and trite (albeit important) message that no one really listens to? We all know we need to eat more fruits and veggies (and why), but how could we make this hit home in a different way—especially for the children?

I strongly believe having school gardens provides the answer. It restores that lost connection to food, gets children outside, and helps them learn how to grow and cultivate food while enjoying the end result. They come to understand how food is made along the way, and this can teach them how to make healthier choices every day. But I not only want to change how children (and the rest of our islanders) think about food, I want to expand this project to include *all* the Caribbean communities.

If Jamie Oliver (truly one of the best people on the face of the earth, in my opinion) can start a "Food Revolution"—why can't I create a "*Cayman* Food Revolution?" Since I haven't been able to come up with a solid reason why not, it's pretty clear to me that it's now my purpose to do it.

If someone like me—just an average person—can become so clear about what I'm supposed to do in this life (after so much searching), I truly believe we all have this potential inside us. It turns out it was right in front of me after-all; what finally made me see it was shifting my perspective—letting my passions and life experience illuminate that sweet spot where I connected with my purpose to help others in a whole new way.

Amid all the wonderful developments in my special projects, an opportunity to appear on television has recently presented itself again. Although the thought of being in the media spotlight doesn't really excite the more private side of me, I realize it's a powerful avenue to expand my reach—to help those who can't always help themselves. Knowledge is power, and I know I must accept that my knowledge around food and nutrition can help empower others in a meaningful way.

No matter where my work path has taken me so far—waiting on tables in a hip downtown restaurant, resolving a health crisis for an insurance client, showing a family new ways to make healthy inexpensive meals or simply playing dodge-ball with a bunch of kids—I needed to open my eyes and my heart to see that I *am* special. I have the desire and power to guide, teach and influence others in a positive way—to share an important message—and it has made me a better person.

I feel I've only glimpsed my potential to really make a difference in this World. My most recent opportunity has been to tell you this story—so perhaps you might uncover that purpose you've always believed deep down was there. I know you are special, too—with something inside you the planet needs right now. It doesn't have to be grandiose. It just has to honour your heart.

CHAPTER 16

The Present Moment Is the Best Moment of My Life

by Jonathan Yudis

I've been a "spiritual seeker" my whole life. This term might be unfamiliar to some and "out there" to others, but it's been true for me as far back as I can remember. My heart has always longed for something deeper than my daily experience—something *eternal*, something Divine. In grade school, I began by learning to meditate. By high school, I sought to commune with Spirit by immersing myself in nature and through running. As I ran with every ounce of my energy focused upon the running itself, everything else disappeared, and it felt like I was getting closer to the answer. Later, I used this same tremendous concentration to climb some of my country's highest peaks, where I found moments of pure peace, awe and exhilaration. I even traveled to India and spent time with great masters, mystics and saints—seeking to learn their every secret to Life's greatest calling. Yet it was all to no avail. My deep-rooted longing persisted.

You see, I wanted more than mere *glimpses* of God. I wanted *pure bliss* and *true enlightenment*.

I dreamed that one day I would simply be touched by someone and become completely awake. In *yoga vedanta*, this is called *nivikalpa samadhi* or "ever-existent, conscious and new bliss." The Buddhists often refer to this as *nirvana or* "perfect peace in the mind"; in Judaism, *moksha* or "liberation." Every religion and mystical tradition seems to have some name for this blessed state of consciousness. The problem is there's an enormous gap between reading or fantasizing about this and *becoming* it. While I seemed to understand enlightenment intellectually and pursued it with passion, it always remained just out of my reach.

Then one day in my reflections, I had a thought that forever changed my life! Perhaps describing it as a thought does not fully capture the scope of the experience; in that moment, I came to better understand the truth of what I'd been seeking my whole life.

I was sitting in perfect stillness when the realization finally surfaced: my lifelong goal of becoming enlightened one day was *never* going to happen. In fact, it was impossible the way I was conceptualizing it! I'd always envisioned enlightenment occurring "one day"—that is, in the future. But *being* in the future itself is a literal impossibility! Our minds conceive ideas, images and visions which we see and project into the future, but the future never actually happens. Even when our previously imagined ideas actually manifest, they can only truly be experienced in the (new) present moment.

I took this line of thinking one step further, concluding that since nothing could actually occur in the future—including achieving enlightenment—it was not possible for *any* given moment to be "better" than the one I'm currently in. And since this can never change, it must mean that if *any* moment is valuable at all, then *this* moment—right now—is the best moment of my life. In fact, it's the only one I truly ever have!

So I pause and take notice of the current moment. I focus on my breath: inhale, exhale. As I breathe, I mentally repeat the thought: *This moment is the best moment of my life*. At once, something utterly ordinary becomes instantaneously extraordinary.

Everything just seems to melt away before me and within me. No longer am I sitting in a room or a country or a body. No longer am I just me. Everything I see appears to my eyes as solid and yet, in my new state of consciousness, also as a dance of light. Outwardly, nothing has changed, but I'm suddenly able to perceive every proton, electron, neutron—*lifetron*—of vibrating light. Each sparkles brilliantly before me, within me, *as me*! The long-awaited goal is suddenly real in this now moment. Enlightenment is happening! Beyond all striving and seeking, this is it: the present moment is God. This is Bliss right now!

My heart cracks like a glacier in the Arctic, melting into an all-pervasive ocean of love. I've gone nowhere. I've done nothing. And yet, this simple, seemingly ordinary moment is everything! Beyond words, beyond thought, almost beyond comprehension!

Tears of love and humility flow down my cheeks from the far corners of my eyes, like a trickling waterfall of devotion. How can I accurately describe the present moment? Simply, as *perfect*. Everything is, always has been and always will be, perfect. Time evaporates—minutes, seconds, hours. Nothing earth-bound seems to compute in the present awareness of the moment.

Compassion enfolds me. I am a witness to all the perceived daily stresses of life which prevail, but I am no longer obliged to identify with them.

For the first time, I completely understand the notion of surrender. This is not my fight—I *choose* to fight it. This is not my story—I've just *made* it my own! This is not my movie—I'm simply a *player* in it. Surrender is nothing more than acceptance, yet I've been living in denial my entire life. I've been resisting the present moment. Surrender doesn't mean *giving up*, it means *giving in*. Giving up is when I stop giving of myself because it's challenging—even though I know there is more inside me to give. Giving in is when I accept what is, stop resisting it, and give anyway. This is the gift of being present.

But don't take my word for it. Try a simple experiment: sit quietly and relax by taking several deep breaths. Begin to observe your breath as you focus on your inhale and exhale. Mentally say to yourself, "*I open my heart to accepting this present moment exactly as it is.*"

What happens?

You will see, I promise—resistance is futile! No matter how much we deny the present moment, we can never escape it. The moment we begin to recognize and accept our resistance is the moment it begins to dissipate and fade away. By recognizing it, we can choose to release it. This is the nature of the statement, "Let go and let God." Stop holding on to what is desired and allow exactly *what is true right now* to carry you into the natural flow of your own existence.

The act of thinking itself can keep us resisting being present in the moment. But because it's so natural, we often don't recognize the nature of our thoughts. If our mind registers an itch, we scratch it. We do not consciously ponder it, we simply react. In the same way, as we think, we do not typically recognize that the thinking process itself is keeping us busy and occupied instead of being present. Just like a glass of agitated, muddy water (brown and opaque), only when it has settled does the mud sink to the bottom so we can see clearly through the glass.

The same goes for our mind. As long as it remains agitated with a constant and seemingly limitless stream of thoughts, it's difficult to see it clearly. Only once our thoughts have settled a bit are we given the opportunity to become a witness to the act of thinking itself. Then we can recognize that identifying with the thoughts we've been busy thinking is an act of resistance itself. The solution lies not in attempting to stop the thinking process altogether, but rather simply in observing it happen.

When we are honest with ourselves, almost everything we do can be seen as an act of resistance to—or defiance against—the present moment. The sooner we get this, the sooner our walls can come down so present moment awareness can emerge naturally.

If enlightenment is something you've been seeking too, how about becoming it right now? Of course, our minds might rail against the thought of this, saying, "I can't just become enlightened right now because I'm not enlightened right now! I'm just an ordinary person who's got issues and troubles and is reading this book and meditating because I want to be enlightened one day."

Are you sure? What if this simple, mundane and utterly ordinary moment is actually enlightened? What if enlightenment is accessible right now? What if enlightenment *is* present moment awareness? What if as you read these words—inhaling and exhaling—this moment *is* the greatest moment of your life? What if you knew and understood that your life can never get any "better" than it is right now? What if this awareness *is* the enlightenment you've been seeking for so long?

Instead of being mysterious and glamorous, your moments of enlightenment can be genuinely experienced when you simply accept this moment in its fullness. Once we let go of the fantasy of enlightenment and the illusion of it only happening sometime in the future, we will recognize that enlightenment is possible right now. With this insight, my longing has been transformed forever, and my gratitude is complete because I have awakened to the divine truth:

My life can never become more perfect than it is right now because *this present moment is the BEST moment of my life!*

CHAPTER 17

I Need to Start Health

by Scott Simons

I guess we all have a story to tell about growing up.

I was born into one of the most successful business families in Quebec City, and so my last name made me stick out at a very young age. I felt judged everywhere I went, by pretty much everybody I met. Life became even more challenging when I was sent to a French high school. Being one of the only English-speaking kids only added to my awkward feelings, and once again I felt like an outsider. Of course, being a Simons didn't help matters either. With the language barrier, I could not communicate easily with my peers, and over time, I felt more and more disconnected—unable to make any friends. I just couldn't seem to find my place. I was lost.

That all changed the day I picked up a basketball. The game came naturally to me, and on the court, I came alive! I felt more confident and started actually connecting with the other kids. Suddenly, I felt like I belonged after all! Being the only English kid and a Simons didn't seem to matter anymore. At last, it seemed I was beginning to be accepted for just being *me*.

As high school progressed, other new experiences came. At the age of fifteen, I smoked hash for the first time. I found it brought me very close to the same feelings I experienced on the basketball court, infusing me with an incredible sense of freedom. Whether I was shooting hoops or smoking up, I didn't feel like an outsider. I was found!

Before long, I'd become very good at both my extra-curricular activities: I loved to play ball *and* I loved to party. Nothing else really interested me. Academic subjects certainly didn't grab my attention, so I started failing my way through high school. Somehow I still made it into college though, where I continued to excel on the basketball court. Even while I continued to party hard, my natural athletic abilities and talent for the game kept me on the starting five. But that wouldn't last for long.

In second year, everything started to spiral downwards. My parents divorced and all kinds of hidden family issues came to light—making me retreat into the darkness. I was no longer drinking and smoking simply to have fun. I needed to *forget* what was going on around me. The weed began slowly taking over my life, creating a whole new layer of problems for me—and my skills on the basketball court steadily weakened. I went from League Rookie of the Year to barely being able to score. As I continued the downward slide and with my talent dimming, I gradually let go of my interest in the very game I loved the most.

Once again, I was lost. My smile faded. My fire was out.

Then came the ultimate low point for me: I invited over a hundred people to my family home for a (unsanctioned) Christmas party. It was going to be a blast! The previous year, we'd had a "magic mushroom" soiree. This year was a year to forget, so I decided to take it up a notch. This year, my party favour of choice was acid. My friends warned me not to take an entire "hit" all in one go, but I did. The result: fourteen of the scariest hours of my entire life. Terrifying thoughts mixed with deadly hallucinations took over my psyche. I tried desperately to get the drug out of my system, but it was too late. There was no escape and no turning back. I awoke from my "trip" to a house that was completely destroyed, and a mind in a state of utter ruin.

I had officially hit rock-bottom.

At that point, I knew I needed help. I didn't <u>ever</u> want to go back into such darkness. Fortunately, after a brief search I found a program designed to help young adults with drug and alcohol problems, and I somehow mustered the courage to sign myself up.

I spent the entire three months of the summer fully immersed in nature with 15 other youths. Being out in the wilderness and fresh air like that was a first for me (running, fishing, group hikes and activities) and it offered an experience of health I'd never tasted before. At first, I didn't know what was happening to me. I was detoxifying on so many levels—letting my body clear from the effects of heavy smoking and drinking. I was also connecting more deeply with others during our group sessions where we got to share our thoughts and feelings. All I knew was my smile was coming back. My eyes sparkled with renewed inspiration. Most surprising to me, this experience provided access to a level of well-being that made me feel better than any drug I'd ever tried.

It wasn't until I returned to the city that I got to see the contrast between how I'd been when I'd left for camp and how I was now. I seemed to be sourcing something within me that I never had before. I was pitching health to my party friends and new wisdom was coming out of me that I didn't know was there. While the program was a step in the right direction, I soon came to realize I had a long way to go. No matter where I went, I still seemed to attract the opportunity to party, and I quickly discovered weed continued to have a firm grasp on me. I succumbed. Even though it gave me paranoid thoughts, heart palpitations and cold sweats, I couldn't seem to stop myself from lighting up joint after joint. I felt like a fraud—so guilty—as if I was cheating on myself and my potential.

It became painfully clear to me that quitting drugs was going to be too difficult. If I wanted my life to change, I would have to switch my strategy. A healthy seed had been planted within me, but the ground it was planted in was still unhealthy. I had to do something more to get to where I wanted to be. Then it came back to me— how I felt in the woods, surrounded by nature and breathing in healthy, fresh air. I thought: *Instead of stopping drugs, I need to start health!* Thankfully, I immediately acted on my new idea, and very quickly, it took root. The more disciplined I was, the more freedom I felt. The more healthy I *got*, the more healthy I wanted to *get*. The more addicted I became to health, the less addicted I was to drugs. It was official: I was turning into a *health* addict!

I began to feel the same inspiration I'd felt when I first picked up a basketball—yet this provided a feeling of exhilaration stronger than any experience I'd ever had— including any drug I'd ever taken. I didn't want to stop—my newfound, long-lost sense of authenticity brought with it a whole new range of opportunities for self-discovery. It was intoxicating, but I was actually sober; I was no longer a puddle of health (easy to pollute), I was now a river in motion on my way to becoming an ocean of health!

It was at that point I knew I wanted to give back the gift I'd received. My new life's mission became to inspire others to attain (or regain) mastery of their own health! This led me to spearhead a number of exciting, local initiatives, including a community wellness center in the heart of Montreal, and an outreach program for marginalized young adults. I took my own health and chosen profession to another level, too. I became certified as a personal trainer, yoga teacher and life coach. All this experience and passion culminated in the creation of my own company— Organik Santé Corporative—dedicated to providing on-site health and wellness services to corporations.

I now like to call myself an "eco-preneur," which means "putting people, purpose and the planet before profit." Every day, I feel I move closer and closer to my own authentic purpose and potential—the very same gifts I came so close to throwing away. Like everyone else, my life still has its ups and downs. However, health offers me an amazing sense of stability and freedom. I continue to fill my life with this health and vitality, and stay laser-focused on my mission to inspire others to do the same. My daily meditation and yoga practices keep my inner fire burning strong, and I love being able to share the warmth and power of this fire—reminding others how simple and accessible health is as a foundation for happiness and authentic connection.

The summer spent in the woods saved my life. I found the strength to face my negative addictions and learned to channel my energy into building my *own* authentic foundation of health. It also paved the way to a career filled with opportunities to help transform the lives of many. "Starting health" has totally redefined my life, and it's a life I now love every day!

Cancer Is *Not* Your Enemy—
It Is Your Teacher

by Brenda Michaels

When the thought, *Cancer is <u>not</u> your enemy—It is your teacher* came to me, I couldn't believe it. *Everyone* knows cancer is "the enemy." After all, we've been waging war with cancer on this planet for decades. Oh, did I forget to mention? When this thought came to me, I was entrenched in my very own battle with the disease. That is, until this thought revealed itself to me—and proceeded to change my life forever.

My first diagnosis of cancer came when I was 26. It was at that time cancer had infiltrated my cervix.

Like any good soldier that follows orders, I did what my doctor recommended and had a hysterectomy. Luckily, no additional treatments were necessary then, and I went on with my life as if nothing had happened. That is, with the exception of no longer being able to have children.

Thirteen years later, cancer came calling again. Only this time, I was diagnosed with cancer in my left breast.

It took three specialists nearly two years to diagnose my condition properly. By then, the cancer covered most of my nipple area, necessitating the removal of my entire left breast. One year later, during a routine mammogram, cancer was at work again in my right breast; this time, my lymph nodes were involved, forcing the removal of that breast as well.

After my surgeries, when my oncologist strongly suggested I take chemotherapy treatments, everything in me screamed, "No!" I'd had many chances to consider this option previously, and I came to the conclusion it didn't make sense to have treatments that would tax my body more than it was already being taxed, with no guarantee of a cure.

After lots of prayer, meditation, discussions with my doctor and my (then) husband—along with a very strong intuitive sense to move in another direction—I finally opted out of traditional medical treatments.

On the heels of this decision, my oncologist gave me a very grim prognosis. He told me matter-of-factly that within a year, the cancer would metastasize (because it was systemic in my body), and there would be little, if anything, they could do for me. In other words, according to him—and the statistics—I had about a year to live, give or take.

This prognosis, and everything I'd heard about cancer up to this point, crystallized in me the belief that I was in for the fight of my life. It was then the thought, *Cancer is not your enemy* floated through my mind. At first, I rejected these words. I thought, *How preposterous!* Quickly followed by, *Where the heck did that come from?*

I tried to put this seemingly crazy thought out of my mind. Thankfully it haunted me like a playful ghost wanting to be validated for its existence. "I'm a *thought*, and therefore I *am*," it seemed to be saying to me.

As I continued to wrestle with how this notion might be possible, I did my best to move through feelings of fear and trepidation, until one day I decided to open myself to the possibility there may be some truth in what the thought was offering up.

This was a moment of real surrender for me, and soon after, I began to download further information about why my cancer was presenting itself. It was inviting me to awaken to the deeper issues that needed healing, and to let the situation teach me what I needed to know about myself so I could regain not just my health, but my *vitality*. This insight, coupled with the initial message I'd received earlier, made it apparent to me that even more surrender would be necessary, especially around a much older belief—one that says, "*Cancer kills. The only way to deal with it is to walk the traditional medical path and hope for the best.*"

I realized it was this older belief that would be the most difficult to release, and I then found myself fighting not only the cancer, but the medical institutions as well. I was David and traditional medicine was my Goliath.

Passionately, I began to explore the emotional blocks and negative patterns I intuitively felt were the source of the physical manifestation of my cancer. Although this was critical for my progress, all the while I was still dealing with my fear of moving in this direction. My mind kept questioning: *Wouldn't an easier route be to accept my cancer as only a physical problem, turn myself over to my doctors, and be done with it?* But my intuition, like the unassuming presence of David's sling, was reminding me of what I *knew* was possible. I just had to trust it.

Thankfully, the Universe offered an answer during one of my more intense meditations. While I sat quietly, focusing my mind on illuminating the direction that would be best for me, I felt a beautiful energy move through my body. As I brought my awareness to it, I knew instantly that my Spirit was asking me to make peace with myself—and to make peace with my cancer. I had a feeling that if I were able to maintain this state of peace, a deep healing would ensue. I immediately felt encouraged. Unfortunately, that feeling didn't last long, as it was closely followed by the belief that *I am not a very capable person*—causing me even more uncertainty about myself than before.

Sadly, I realized this belief was tied to even deeper core beliefs, such as: *I don't deserve to be healthy*, and *I'm not good enough to have a life of health and well-being.* So I thought I might as well just give in and walk the path many others had walked before me, and hope for the best. Luckily for me, shortly after I began this downward spiral, the energy I felt in my earlier meditation once again began moving through me, this time roaring up like a lion and coursing through me in such a way it almost took my breath away! As I steadied myself and continued to breathe, soon an inner strength in me began to emerge as never before, giving me the courage to continue on.

To say the rest of my journey was a walk in the park after this wouldn't be the truth. Even with my newfound strength and feelings of empowerment, I had many challenging days and weeks as I continued to deepen spiritually, working on healing my emotional wounds and the negative beliefs and patterns that had influenced my choices—and health—up to that point. At the same time, I continued to hold true to the possibility that by making peace with myself—and my cancer—I was going to heal the disease that was threatening to rob me of my life.

What was interesting, in spite of the everyday challenges I found myself working through, was that my life began to take on a magical quality. Although I was not in a financial position to receive therapy, the ideal books and spiritual teachers began to appear in my life, further helping me to release my toxic thoughts, beliefs and negative patterning.

As one example of this magic, I found out that Marianne Williamson was speaking at a church only two blocks from where I was living. Once a week, I planted myself in the front row and drank in every word she said. In addition to soaking up *her* message, I also began to immerse myself in reading *A Course In Miracles* (Foundation for Inner Peace, 1976), one of the great spiritual textbooks of our time. This helped me immensely during some of my darkest days.

Soon after I discovered Marianne and this treasured book, I was told about a doctor of immunology in New York whose work with cancer was having phenomenal results. Around this same time, my husband was hired onto a film project. With money now available, I was able to fly to New York and meet with Dr. Gonzalez. As I listened to his holistic approach, I knew without a doubt his program would be perfect to help me heal my physical body. So with all the gusto I could conjure up, I jumped in with both feet. Meanwhile, I continued my inner work and spiritual growth, and as a result of all my efforts, I was finally healed!

That was twenty-one years ago.

This incredible journey occurred because of one simple thought: *Cancer is __not__ your enemy—It's your teacher*. Since that time, I've learned to embrace the (sometimes) radical, yet powerful thoughts that come to me, and in doing so, I've come to recognize that thoughts can *truly* open us up to transformation and healing. These thoughts come from the higher mind—the part of us that is directly connected to the Divine—the *God presence* expressing itself in human form. To discover this has been a great blessing in my life, in more ways than I can count.

Today, I am dedicated to sharing this insight with those who are ready to choose *vitality* over *disease*, to help them truly heal their lives and become a beacon of healing light in the lives of others. As my story illuminates, our thoughts can truly be our teachers, if we listen well and allow them to deliver their infinite wisdom.

CHAPTER 19

Learning to Really LIVE May Be the Best Cure For Illness

by Dr. Bernie Siegel

Over my years as a medical professional, I've become known for my mind-body approach to health and healing. I've been blessed to witness (even play a role in) countless healing "miracles." But it was only after a series of inspirational thoughts—gifts, really—that I came to understand the key to living a truly healthy life. I'm so grateful for the difference these thoughts made for me and my patients.

It all began many years ago with a single comment from one patient. We both happened to attend the same meeting run by Dr. Carl Simonton—an information session about empowering cancer patients to get well and *stay* well. I had presumed it was just for medical doctors, but upon my arrival, I was surprised to find myself surrounded by two psychotherapists and 122 cancer patients, but not another MD in sight! In the group, I saw a familiar face—a young female patient of mine who was experiencing breast cancer. As we greeted one another and exchanged small-talk, I asked her why she was there. Her response was simple enough, but it launched me into a profound state of self-reflection. She politely turned to me and said,

"You're a nice guy. I feel better when I'm in the office with you, but I can't take you home with me. So I need to know how to live between office visits."

This comment instantly pressed on one of my most painful vulnerabilities as a doctor: *Even with the latest and greatest tools at my disposal, technology and expertise can ultimately fall short of finding a cure to illness—and my patient dies anyway, despite my best efforts.*

Her words brought me to a thought—*the* thought—that changed the direction of my career and my entire life from that moment on: *If I can help people learn to <u>live</u>, I will never have to feel like a failure for not curing their illness.*

The truth is, doctors are not usually educated about caring for their patients (or themselves), especially when it comes to the tough process of handling loss. They get information about treating disease. The frustrating reality of dealing with death (a.k.a. "failed attempts at keeping patients alive") is incredibly stressful for most doctors. The suicide rate for surgeons is much higher than you'd think.

So for me, this amazing thought gave me renewed hope! I decided then and there I would begin offering patients special programs and support groups to help them live a longer and *better* life—no matter what. Excited for what was in store for my patients (and me), I promptly sent out one hundred letters announcing an information session on my new approach. I expected several hundred responses *at least* because I forgot to say the invitation was only for the people receiving the letter (i.e. my patients). I waited in panic for that first meeting. When only a dozen women showed up, it was a humbling sign that I didn't really *know* the people I was caring for or about their will (or lack thereof) to live.

Despite that slow start, the meetings continued to grow over the years, and I've come to learn how critical loving one's life and body contributes to a patient's survival. This led to another thought: *Our bodies love us, but if we do not love our bodies and the way we live our lives, our body will not see death as the worst outcome—often freeing us from our problem by putting an end to the life of our body.*

Monday morning is a dramatic illustration of this point: more heart attacks, strokes, suicides and illnesses strike on Mondays than any other day of the week. If what we do doesn't *bring us to life*, it can potentially take it away. It's *that* vital to understand the importance of doing what makes us happy.

Those of us who grow up feeling loved by our parents tend to feel greater self-worth and take better care of ourselves in this way. One study revealed that by mid-life, only one quarter of subjects who felt loved by their parents experienced a serious illness. In contrast, almost 100% of those who felt unloved growing up experienced dis-ease of some sort! To illustrate this point, a young suicidal patient I was helping approached me once and called me her "CD". When I asked her what she was talking about, she answered, "You're my Chosen Dad." So the next thought that changed my life—and the lives of many others—was: *I should start to re-parent people and help them to re-birth themselves into a new and authentic life.*

I began to "adopt" others in need, helping them to feel loved until they truly wanted to live. The result was nothing less than remarkable. As I continued to help patients be born again into a new life, we witnessed how their bodies got the message and would do all it took to keep them alive. This is not what you might call a spontaneous remission or unexplained miracle, it is *self-induced healing.* I sincerely feel doctors need to understand that! The difficult thing for many people, however, is they have to confront their mortality and surrender to Life in order to become the person they were meant to be.

> **When I let go of what I am, I become what I might be.**
> **— Lao Tzu**

Too often, I see people become focused on guilt, shame and blame when taking responsibility for their health. This blocks their true recovery! I like to ask people what is going on in their lives that may be making them vulnerable to illness in their bodies. This is not about blaming them, but seeking to discover why they may be vulnerable to disease at that particular time. I encourage them to look at their personal healing potential versus what they did "wrong" that got them feeling sick in the first place. The truth is, each one of us is capable of miraculous, self-induced healing.

If we want to be healthy in the life we have, we need to understand our genes don't make decisions for us. Even eating perfectly, getting loads of sleep, and drinking plenty of water will not make us immortal. It's considering all aspects of being human—the mind, body *and* spirit—that determines whether we are healthy or sick. Studies of twin siblings have confirmed this: a submissive twin who internalizes anger and tries to please everyone is more likely to develop breast cancer then her devilish identical twin sister who is doing her thing and not worrying about what her parents think. In addition, when actors were studied for similar effects, researchers found that immune function and stress hormone levels were changed by the role they were playing: a comedy enhanced their health and ability to resist infections while a tragedy had the opposite consequences.

So do what makes you happy and let your heart make up your mind. Your body will follow suit!

I try to teach people to live in the moment; to heal their *lives,* not just the disease. At all times, we get our patients to work *with* the body, not against it. When patients focus on killing their disease, fighting the war just ends up empowering the enemy. But when they see their bodies as expressive life-forms telling a sad or angry story, they are able to embrace hope for their future instead of fearing their mortality.

Most physicians criticize alternative forms of healing, making claims that the only reason people get well using these forms of treatment is due to the placebo effect. The *only* reason? I say this is the most powerful and therapeutic reason! Even if this is true, this would be yet another example of how the power of the mind—directing our thoughts toward health and healing—can have profound, positive effects! Wordswordswords can become swordsswordsswords which kill or cure also.

In my practice, I have seen patients have absolutely no side-effects from radiation and chemotherapy when they saw it as a gift for their bodies. Studies have also shown, time and time again, how the power of laughter and faith can help people live longer, healthier lives. I know many people who have left their troubles to God and are alive and well today when most doctors would have given up hope on them.

> *Be content with what you have. Rejoice in the way things are.*
> *When you realize nothing is lacking, the whole world belongs to you.*
> — **Lao Tzu**

My last thought is: *It's time to end this chapter now.*

Remember, when you have to make a decision, do what makes you happy. Say "no" to things you don't want to do. Realize problems are God's redirections from which something good will come.

Yesterday is dead and gone and tomorrow is out of sight, so enjoy *this* moment. Love your life and let your body serve and be served in this healing vibration! Trust in the incredible healing power of your thoughts and eliminate any desire for something you do not have—for everything is perfect just the way it is, right here and now. This is the way to truly LIVE your life and enjoy vibrant health.

CHAPTER 20

What If My Deepest Fear Is My Greatest Gift?

by Daniel Mauro

Around the World, public speaking is feared by many people. In fact, this phobia is so common it is often ranked <u>above</u> the fear of death. Jerry Seinfeld even joked about public speaking when he quipped, "...if you go to a funeral, you're better off in the casket than doing the eulogy!" It may sound ridiculous when described that way, but for those of us who have experienced this fear, it's not all that far-fetched. For the longest time, I was one of those individuals who'd rather die than get up on stage.

If you also find yourself shuddering at the thought of speaking in front of an audience, fear not, for there is hope! Hope not only that you can overcome your challenges around speaking in public, but hope you can successfully transform virtually any fear you may be carrying around with you.

The message I wish to share with you is simple yet powerful: FEAR, in all its myriad forms, can be consciously used as a potent catalyst of self-mastery. When we realize some of our deepest fears are there for a reason—that they may actually contain special gifts inside—we can hold those vulnerable aspects of ourselves in a radically different light and take our personal evolution to the next level.

My story begins in early grade school with that innocent little elementary school ritual known as "Show-and-Tell." Once a week, we would gather in a circle and take turns sharing about our weekend activities or showing off our favourite "cool" object. Invariably, the same sorts of stressful thoughts went through my mind each time: *Why do I have to do this? I have absolutely nothing to talk about. I feel so embarrassed sitting here.* I could hardly pay attention to what any of my grade one buddies were saying, so loud and incessant was that scared little voice in my head. As my turn to speak steadily approached, a dreadful, panicky feeling grew within the pit of my stomach, and a wave of anxiety swept through me.

This heightened physical-emotional state would become an unwelcome yet all-too-familiar companion throughout my educational journey. In high school, college and university, I avoided public speaking situations like the plague. Occasionally, when I had no choice but to get up on stage for those compulsory speaking assignments, I simply coped the best way I knew how. I'd agonize for days and days, overcompensating with tremendous amounts of preparation, memorizing my speech word for word—even gulping sedatives to calm my nerves just before I went on! I learned how to survive those academic presentations, but after awhile, my "coping rituals" became tedious and tiresome.

Just when I thought I'd become pretty good at managing my stage fright, I enrolled in graduate school, and my fears suddenly escalated to a whole new level. It was bad enough having to participate in mandatory seminars on a regular basis, but now I would be forced to express myself in front of the most knowledgeable and articulate individuals I'd ever met! At times, the anguish over these graduate presentations became unbearable. My apprehension over an upcoming seminar was often worse than giving the talk itself. Days before, my heart would begin racing, my throat would constrict, and my stomach would twist into knots at the mere thought of it all.

It was during a particularly agitated moment preparing for one of those early graduate seminars that I experienced a pivotal turning point in my life. In a sudden flash of inspiration, I had a self-actualizing thought: *If I'm to be successful as a professional academic, I really need to tackle this debilitating fear of public speaking, once and for all!* From this thought followed a series of self-directed questions that shifted the way I perceived my fears and myself from that moment on:

What if, rather than just overcoming this all-consuming fear, I could transcend it entirely? What if I'm meant to become a decent speaker, perhaps even a great speaker? What if the thing I fear most is actually a hidden gift, waiting to be explored, nurtured and fully developed?

The possibilities intrigued and excited me all at once! A wave of mental images streamed through my mind in which I imagined myself in future scenes delivering inspiring and eloquent presentations to captivated audiences. For the first time in my life, I experienced a tangible spark of positive, hopeful energy around the idea of having to speak in public.

Fuelled by the epiphany that my anxiety around speaking might actually be hiding a mysterious inner gift, I searched eagerly for new ways to transform it—to bring forth that confident, fearless speaker I now believed was concealed within me. What happened next was nothing short of miraculous. All the techniques I would ever need for mastering public speaking—specifically those that seemed tailored just for me—became immediately "obvious." It was as if by simply imagining myself with an entirely new professional identity and believing I could succeed, I opened the door to the previously unimaginable: I *can* be a comfortable, polished speaker after all!

Fast forward several years, and I am now that person. I do public speaking "gigs" regularly, not because I have to (as in the past), but because I choose to. I thoroughly enjoy addressing groups of any size in all sorts of contexts. There are no longer any traces of that once familiar tension that used to reside in the pit of my stomach or the incessant mental chatter that would sneak into my consciousness uninvited. The self-perpetuating "worry movies" have stopped, replaced instead by "success movies."

I find I'm so comfortable speaking to groups that I often no longer need to prepare formalized presentations in advance. I embrace the challenge of being (relatively) unstructured, in the moment, improvising as I go. Every time I speak without a script, I marvel at the fact I once found the very idea so daunting, so intimidating, so terrifying. I'm amazed that, once upon a time, it was next to impossible for me to imagine myself doing what I now do with such ease.

An important aspect of self-mastery is to dig deep down into your most vulnerable areas and face them head on. Being courageous is not about behaving in a foolhardy or reckless manner; it is about taking action, despite your fear. It is about moving consciously through fear-based emotions even while the experiences are unpleasant or the outcome is uncertain. It's about being okay with being judged, misunderstood or rejected. Indeed, it's this fear of rejection that is at the very heart of performance anxiety for most people.

To be human is to experience fear at one time or another. We all carry our own unique repertoire of fears in assorted shapes and sizes. We can gloss superficially over them, minimize them or pretend they don't even exist. For a time, coping serves its purpose, but after a while the coping rituals become exhausting and even ridiculous (as I discovered). Feeling either tired or silly around your fear(s) is a good thing because it can motivate you to initiate some much needed changes in your life!

Whenever you catch yourself immersed in a fear, try to remind yourself of the following truth: each and every challenge in your life was meant as a powerful opportunity for growth. You can choose to move through it consciously, confidently and courageously—or you can choose to cling to the uncomfortably familiar. The greater the challenge you transcend, the greater the potential for your personal growth and fulfillment. As you begin to transform your vulnerabilities into sources of power—your fears into gifts—you will begin to look forward to each opportunity of transformation!

Such is the power of that single, inquisitive thought that appeared in my mind several years ago. A thought that grew in power and momentum until it became manifest in concrete action and ultimately changed the course of my life from that point onward! This priceless process has afforded me the opportunity to surpass all my wildest expectations, even teaching others how to transform their fear of public speaking, too!

Any and all fears, no matter how great or small, can be consciously transformed—whether it's public speaking, spiders or taxes. The next time you're faced with a deep-seated fear, ask yourself these three questions: What if this fear which I experience as threatening is actually masking a powerful, inborn gift? What if I've got this amazing gift within me just waiting to be explored, but I've dared not look inside because its outer wrapping makes me feel uncomfortable? How might my life change for the better if I suddenly shifted my thoughts around the fear and chose instead to courageously open up my gift for the World to see?

Give it a try. Your greatest fear could very well be your greatest gift.

CHAPTER 21

Your Heart Always Knows the Way to Go

by Michael Robins

A dream is a wish your heart makes.
— **Cinderella**

I stood on the brink of completing a journey that included ten long years of very hard work. As a final requirement for my PhD in English literature, I handed in my dissertation on "The Function of the Knight in Chaucer's *Canterbury Tales.*" I was more than ready for a break from the incessant responsibilities of classes, exams, writing papers and fulfilling my assistantship duties, and I eagerly anticipated being able to take a well-deserved rest from it all.

So when I received notice that my dissertation needed significant revisions, the shock that hit me was two-fold: 1) I felt I had done everything I already could, and 2) I knew everything I had worked for over the last ten years hinged upon answering this request.

What was I to do?

In a flash of impulsivity, my whole life shifted as I heard myself speak these four radically defiant, yet simple words: "That's it, I quit." I decided in that moment to walk away from a ten-year commitment and the promise of a certain, seemingly desirable future into an unknown, yet suddenly compelling world. My heart cried out for freedom, and I embarked on a journey to discover it.

From a logical vantage point, there is no doubt I was doing something quite irrational. Many years later, when I did go back to teaching, I definitely realized the loss of many prestigious and lucrative opportunities because I did not have my doctorate. And, it was not like me to give up on anything. I had always been a diligent student. I made SP (Special Progress) and completed three years of junior high school in two. I never slacked off in any of my studies, and after going to Brooklyn College and making the Dean's List, I won an assistantship at Ohio University. This was followed by another at the University of Wisconsin, where I taught Freshman Composition and took courses for my Masters' and Doctorate degrees. I put in the demanding hours faithfully. Why then would I waste all that effort? Why not just dig a few feet deeper to reach my goal?

I don't really remember all the thoughts and feelings I experienced leading up to that fateful decision to walk away. That all happened over 45 years ago. What I do know is that by taking actions that honored the call of my heart and reflected my passion for freedom, I made the most valuable choice of my entire life. I found the courage to take the road less-traveled and discovered a path of wonder.

Our educational systems do not teach us how to hear the communication of our hearts, and our society does not usually encourage us to follow that voice. In fact, our social mind is very rigid and protective; it embraces the familiar even when the familiar is less than fulfilling.

Back then, when I made the decision to abandon *my* familiar, I knew to be free, I needed to cut all ties and simply trust in whatever the unfolding adventure promised me. The fact that I had recently inherited $60,000 (a whole lot of money in those days) certainly made the decision easier, but I quickly spent it, giving a lot of it away to people who crossed my path.

For the vast majority of time spent on my 12-year journey of discovering true liberation, I lived without a home, without money, and without working. This provided a very different education than the one I got from ten years in college! While it required no financial investment, the rewards were infinitely valuable. It fostered within me a great trust in Life and taught me things I never could have learned in school or in a more "conventional" lifestyle.

Periodically, I'd hitchhike to places where I found old friends who were established and successful in the World—but they didn't seem to have the happiness, energy and joy I did. They would often remark about their eagerness to join me on my adventure, only to find one excuse or another that would keep them plugged into the comfortable familiarity of their daily routines. After our visit, I would just stick my thumb out and continue on my way. Their fancy homes, cars and prestigious jobs held no lure for my joyous heart, which vastly treasured freedom and discovery over material security.

Although I have since settled in one place and adopted a more normative lifestyle, my heart's quest for freedom continues to be strong and serves as the driving force behind my life's ambition—to observe, discover and grow. We can and do get stuck in our journey at times. Our conditioning and the chattering of our minds can block us from hearing the still, small voice of our heart. But a greater Intelligence moves the cycles of Life, and our ultimate destiny is wondrous and certain when we let it move us. However closed off we may feel at times, the good news is nothing can permanently stop us from realizing the potential of this ever-expanding, magnificent journey of the heart.

Ironically, I once again have become a diligent student. I continuously scour writings on religion, philosophy, spirituality, psychology and the art of living— seeking understanding and guidance. I consider all perspectives, wanting to *know*, not just believe. I have learned to embrace any experience that resonates with both mind and heart, and I now use this resonance as an indicator of what is right for me.

The freedom I ultimately discovered—and am still discovering—is deeply rooted in my heart's desire for happiness. It's an inner reality. No matter how deeply buried this happiness is or how non-existent it may seem to be at times, it resides at the core of *every* heart. It will find you, but you can actually bend time by *actively seeking it*. The passionate pursuit of your joy is what makes it personally transformational.

I encourage you to dig down deeply below the wounds, frustrations, resistance or disbeliefs. Ask yourself what you really want. A joyful heart leads us into the adventures of Life because it's in touch with Source; but a dis-satisfied heart can drive us forward also. Sometimes, your heart is dis-satisfied because it recognizes there is more. And there is always more! Take the time to ask your heart what it wants, then follow it. Though the road may be bumpy, it will eventually take you where you really want to go. That's the Divine design!

Summon the courage to follow your heart even if what your heart is calling for does not make sense to your logical mind, for *your heart always knows the way to go*. It holds the key to realizing the greatest dreams you can ever imagine.

I celebrate that irrational moment when I threw away ten years of work because my heart spoke to me in a way it never had before. It felt so undeniably right for me at the time, and the invaluable life lessons I received on my journey of self-discovery verified the heart's calling as the true path I should follow. That one choice grounded me in a *lifetime* of seeking true happiness, with no regrets—and I continue to embrace the calling of my heart with each and every opportunity. I may lose sight of that wisdom at times, but when I do, it's not long before I return to my inner guidance—my heart—trusting it will lead me back to where I should be. In reconnecting with this trust, it propels me, again and again, up the spiral of an ever-expanding, better life.

The same happiness and fulfillment await you. Each one of us possesses a unique gift to give the World—one it is currently incomplete without. My hope is that in this story, you find a heartfelt nudge of inspiration and encouragement to find which way your heart wants you to go. It is speaking to you right now. It's hoping you can hear it and you will not only listen, but take action. It's never too late to improve the quality of your life and to realize your dreams. Listen to your heart, for it only wants the very best for you—now and forever.

CHAPTER 22

I Believe in the Freedom That Is Me

by Cathy Matarazzo

D o you believe freedom is only attained when everything is perfect and you are achieving the goals you set out for yourself? Do you need to have everything in-hand and tangible before you can see freedom alive in your world? Or, might you begin to imagine a freedom that is *inherently* yours by mere virtue of your existence here on this Earth plane? One whose very nature is alive deep inside and independent of any outside circumstance or situation, just waiting to be embraced by an awakened soul?

Of all the many brilliant people I've had the wonderful privilege of interviewing over the years, the vast majority have spoken of freedom as something external and separate from them—that is, <u>not</u> an inherent human characteristic. This I find quite fascinating! So to pose a wild idea, might I suggest here that *freedom* and *you* are one and the same?! To embrace this concept will involve opening your mind and heart to experiencing the totality of your existence—adopting a mindset of knowing with complete and utter certainty that indeed we *are* freedom within our deepest, most sacred heart expression.

I was just like those I interviewed until I had my own spiritual breakthrough many years ago (what some might call a near-nervous breakdown). I will never forget this experience for as long as I live because it was the *ultimate* turning point that brought me face-to-face with my illusion-filled mind…and then my truthful heart! My entire world stopped dead as I faced the decision to either continue on a road that was leading me directly into the hospital OR take one that would set me free to live a life on purpose.

I was plagued with a depression so deep I could not escape the sense of confinement I felt in every aspect of my world. I was utterly lifeless. My responsibilities for kids, a husband, extended family—even getting up in the morning—all became too much for me to handle. I was so overwhelmed, desperate for space to breathe and the simple PEACE to feel alive again! Prayers for this peace became my moment-to-moment mantra! Then one day, I found myself locked in my bedroom, on my knees and praying for *salvation*. "Take me now or use me!" These were the words that ultimately saved my life, opening a path that instantly ushered my YES into the arms of Spirit! It was at that fork in the road I finally chose a path of surrender and service, and my life has never been the same since.

Have you found yourself at a similar crossroads in your life, wanting to choose the right path—one that has deep meaning and substance? I believe in order to move forward and to stay connected to a life filled with a sense of purpose, it's important to at least begin this process by looking at how YOU personally define freedom in your heart. Is it a concept or a reality? And, similarly, how would you define *you*?

In order to *believe in the freedom that is you*, you must draw your awareness (and pay careful attention) to your personal beliefs and choices, including the clarity about who you *really* are! I cannot stress this enough. For if you neglect to really awaken to the gift of your precious life, you will simply become a hidden treasure, never actualized. I did this for almost 45 years!

You see, it's very easy to get caught up in our daily and worldly events—most of which do not align in the slightest with what I am attempting to describe to you here. I now find it so ironic that a great majority of us choose to believe that freedom is *outside* our current circumstances; that it is something we need to *attain*, as opposed to simply believing, receiving and being true to who and what is already *within* us!

What we choose to *believe* is really the key determining factor of our experiences. The spiritual Law of Attraction says "like attracts like." What we believe as being Truth will attract to us the corresponding energy to bring forth that very experience—be it good, bad or indifferent! It is so very important for our human race to understand just how much power resides behind the words that express our beliefs—this is the *cause* behind every *effect* we experience.

But let's play a little game and create a new equation for you about freedom. Let's say you need only believe this one thing I say to you: "*You are freedom!*" Imagine receiving these words in your mind and heart the very same as me saying, "You are *beautiful!*" or, "You are *smart!*" or, "You are *great!*"

Do you realize what happens and can happen when you actually believe this to be true? If who and what you are is inherently freedom, then this simply means you are the divine reflection of everything this word encompasses, effortlessly. Freedom is not only an energetic vibration; it is your very essence and cosmic blueprint! So every goal you have been seeking to achieve is already in you: you are "the *peace*", "the *abundance*", "the *joy*", "the *love*", "the *compassion*" and more! You are all of these things when you choose to tap into what lies beneath the surface of your everyday life—the freedom that is your birthright.

The life path we humans travel is really about figuring out how to best get from the *outside* (the playground of fear where most of us live) to being on the *inside* of this heart-felt truth of freedom. I will lovingly repeat: this *is* our truest essence and the source of *who we really are*. But in order to take this trip—to get aboard the freedom train—you must first have a ticket! In this case, it's to simply make a choice and just say YES to the heart-tug!

When you say YES, what you are doing is making a verbal agreement to the heart (which is in direct communication with the soul): "Here I come! I'm ready to celebrate and be the truth of all that I am!" It is an agreement you make with yourself to let "**Your Essence Shine**"…get it? **Y.E.S.**! Should you decide on the other hand to say NO, you are choosing instead to make a verbal agreement that says to the heart: "I am not coming in. I am 'Not Open' to this heart trip…**N.O.** way, José!" In my case, a NO would have meant I'd never surrendered. If *that* had happened, well, God knows where I'd be—*if* I'd be! Having faith and surrendering to the divine order of things are essential ingredients if we want to align with freedom!

Many of you reading this may wonder how a simple YES/NO exercise can lead us to living the life we are meant to live; how can assessing opportunities with a YES/NO (or maybe even a simple "I don't know") be so powerful? Well, it really *is* simple because when you say YES to your heart you are inevitably uniting with your heart *song*; that place deep within that is uniquely you—the complete union of your heart and soul that allows your spirit to fully communicate love! You are allowing your truth, essence and the *holiness* within you to shine through you, as you, for the entire Universe's benefit. You are being *you* to the fullest, which is *freedom* in its greatest expression!

When you say NO, you are stating to your deeper self that you're not choosing your awesomeness (*who you really are*) to emerge and shine forth in this World. You are dis-connecting, denying the ticket to get aboard the freedom train, skipping the ride, refusing to align with the gift of your magnificence and authenticity that's ultimately been waiting patiently at *Heart & Soul Station*! By saying NO, you have volunteered to remain on the outside—to be unceremoniously removed from your sacredness and all of your dreams, passions and life purpose! Instead of opting to experience the effortless flow of love in the diverse landscapes of your heart (by saying YES), you will experience a life that is safe, normal and separate...but perfectly mirroring the ego—an ego that keeps you chasing the illusion of "perfection before freedom." An ego that keeps you desiring everything you're not; an ego that requires you to believe the only way to truly stay safe is to follow its lead.

Do me (and the World) a huge favor and allow yourself to rise up to your full potential! You have nothing to lose and everything to gain, my friends! If you must do it "your own way," like good ole Frank Sinatra suggests, then by all means do so—but just <u>do</u> it!

All we have is now, this very sacred moment! It doesn't matter what you believed about yourself—even two minutes ago—for all that is gone except the memory. Use the gift of the present and make the choice to take hold of your ticket, step forward, and say YES to your highest purpose, your greatest expression, your holy essence, your divine destiny...the freedom and truth of who you really are! I see it, I feel it, and my heart knows it...now it is time for <u>you</u> to also *believe it*!

CHAPTER 23

No Mud, No Lotus

by Jacob Nordby

"**H**ere, take a look at this. It might help."

My wise old friend had been scribbling something on his napkin and now slid it across the coffee-shop table. I turned it around so the writing was right-side up and tried to decipher his shaky scrawl. It was one short sentence—incomplete at that:

No mud, no lotus
— Thich Nhat Hanh

I squinted at the words and then up at Mark, who was regarding me with quiet eyes over the rim of his coffee mug.

"What does it mean...and who is this Thitch Nut guy?"

He shook his tangle of gray hair and laughed out loud. "Whoa there, camper. You called this meeting. Before I explain anything, think back to why we're here today."

I drew a deep breath and let my gaze slide out through the big window next to our table. It was a rainy day and cars swished past in the street, flinging sheets of water from their tires. My mind wandered several years back in time and conjured up

128

memories of the events which had shattered my old life and unlocked the door of a powerful spiritual breakthrough.

I lost everything I once valued so highly: my business, my reputation, my emotional equilibrium. At the same time though, I was drawn into the exhilarating high country of my spirit. I saw the World through new eyes and entered a realm of peace, beauty and inspiration which long-bearded mystics and poets forever rave about from their mountaintop perches. Every day was filled with amazing revelations and a flow of information which nourished my new-born soul like manna from heaven. I wrote a book and began to feel a fresh purpose in life emerging from the ashes of my former self. People gathered around to enjoy my ecstatic dance of realization. I often thought, *This is it! I'm fully alive and connected again. I have finally found my grand reason for being here!*

Then something changed.

Like a pilgrim who falls asleep at night in a leafy oasis and awakens the next morning in a parched, sun-blasted desert, I was stunned to find that as quickly as it had appeared, my artesian spring had vanished. I looked frantically for it—this juicy inspiration I loved so much—but no amount of reading, meditating or writing seemed to work. I would fall asleep at night with the desperate hope that some radiant dream would set things right, but morning would find me dragging myself out of bed like a gritty-eyed crocodile. I would growl quite un-spiritually at my children and curse at the idiot in traffic who just couldn't seem to pick up the pace fast enough through the green light.

Something felt very wrong, but I couldn't put my finger on what it was. I knew better than all of this chaos and worked very hard to push my un-saintly feelings out of sight. But they always came creeping back and lay in wait to pounce on me like a shadow wolf outside my door.

The problem was I felt I needed to get the *magic* back. Everything which was emerging in my new life depended upon a constant stream of beauty and wisdom— or so I thought. That's when I called my sage friend and asked to meet for coffee. Mark had put in many years as a healer and traveling teacher. I was hoping he could pull some trick out of his bag and plug me back into whatever I was missing.

I stirred from these memories and glanced over to see him sitting across from me like a living Sphinx in overalls. He had a *stillness* about his presence—a balance and wholeness I was hungry to assimilate. He caught me looking and waggled his eyebrows.

"Well," he said, "You got anything?"

"I know why I'm here—with you today, I mean."

"And why is that?"

"Because I'm afraid I got off track somewhere. I've made so much rapid progress in my journey, you know? But now I keep getting tangled up in the everyday, unspiritual stuff. I'm questioning what I believe and if I actually have anything of value to share with others. Where did all my joy and inspiration go?"

Mark scratched his head and stared at his fingers for awhile. Finally, he roused and said, "Read it again. The note I gave you."

I didn't need to look. I quoted it from memory, "No mud, no lotus."

"Mmhmm," he said, "That's it right there."

I shook my head. "What's 'it'? Please tell me what you mean."

"Well, let's remember what Dr. Carl Jung once wrote. Similar thing, different words: 'Enlightenment is not imagining figures of light but making the darkness conscious.' Does that make any sense to you?" he asked.

I shrugged and gave a little nod.

"Okay, think of it this way," he continued, "A lotus flower is an ancient symbol. You see it everywhere in Buddhist art. The bloom is so beautiful, and if you walk near a pond full of them, the scent is heavenly. In fact, if you sit down on the bank and meditate with this aroma all around, you might imagine you're floating away into a realm where only sweetness and light exist."

I snickered. "Yes, I've been there before."

"Oh," he said, "I know you have. But there's a problem here; it's a common rookie mistake, too. Know what it is?"

"What?"

"You're ignoring reality. You get focused on the high feelings of love and oneness and all that wonderful blossomy stuff, but you forget how a lotus comes to be in the first place. When you're knocked out of your trance by the muddy parts of life, you get terrified that maybe you'll never find your happy place again."

"You just described me, Mark," I said, "That's exactly where I've been for awhile now. But I didn't want to admit it to anyone, either."

He smiled and took a sip of coffee. "I know. Don't be hard on yourself. What you're going through is normal. Let's follow the story a little further, shall we?"

I nodded.

"So, imagine the shimmering lotus flower sticking out of the pond. Can a blossom survive without its stem? Of course not. Follow that stem down into the water where all the pollywogs and turtles and dead leaves are. Keep going all the way into the thick, black, stinking mud at the bottom. Down in all that mess is exactly where the lotus roots are anchored. That's where they dig their little fingers in and draw out the nutrients the whole plant needs if it's going to grow, expand, and become fully itself."

A tingle ran up my spine as the realization unfolded. "Oh! So you're saying if I don't pay attention to the muddy parts, I can't continue to grow?"

"It goes beyond that, actually," he said. "The problem with lots of us spiritual types is when we finally notice a blossom opening in our lives, we get all excited. 'This is what it's all about,' we say. Then we snip the stem and put the blossom in a crystal vase. We're so proud of our beautiful flower we put it on display for all to see. We even sit and stare at it for hours. For awhile it's perfect—everything looks great. But because we've separated the flower from its source, the petals soon fall off and we're just left with a dead stick."

The truth of his words washed me with relief. I started to speak, but Mark held up his hand.

"Wait a minute. I want to be sure you get this part. Life isn't found in the mud or in the blossom. Life is *all of it*. It is the process of becoming. The mud is our unconscious. It's full of unanswered questions, old wounds, predispositions and beliefs. But it's also rich with creativity and powerful wisdom. The stem is our human consciousness which draws all of that upward—transforms it into useful energy. The lotus flower is just the manifestation which reminds us that we are beings of beauty and radiance. We are more than mud, but we are not only flower, either. We are all of it and so much more than any of us can imagine."

"Mark, this is exactly what I needed to hear right now. I don't know how to say thank you."

My old guru friend just smirked and nudged my leg with his boot. "Does this mean you're buying my breakfast?"

○ ○ ○

As much as any other teaching I've received along my journey, this lesson helps me understand the unique and powerful alchemy of being human. We are called to the wholeness and radiance of the angels but have been given this living stem of a body with roots deep in the earth. No other beings on the planet process and transmute consciousness in exactly the way we do by our presence here. Truly, we are the very looms upon which heaven and earth are woven together.

CHAPTER 24

Greatness Follows Excellence

by Dr. L. Jon Porman

Are any of us destined for *Greatness*?

All my life, I have been inspired to reach for the stars, to go that extra mile. When I was asked to write a chapter for this book, to provide motivation for those out there seeking guidance and inspiration, the first thing I could think of was to tell each and every one of you, "YOU have the potential to be *great*. Not just ordinary, but *Great!*"

I'm not talking about achieving fame, wealth, and to be the most popular amongst your peers, colleagues or in your community. I'm talking about connecting with the knowledge you are *inherently* great. And to cultivate and nurture that *Greatness,* you simply need to develop those natural qualities that bring about your greatest good.

But what is *Greatness*?

As far as I can remember, my first exposure to *Greatness* and how I've come to define it came to me when I was only nine years old. This is when my grandfather taught me how to achieve *Greatness* through *Excellence*.

We were going to go for lunch as soon as I restocked the oil cans in the back of his gas station's garage. I had placed all the cans on the old greasy shelves, but all the labels were not facing outward. When I told him I was done, he came to inspect the job right before we left for our mid-day snack. I cherished those times with him because I had my favorite person all to myself in one of two small town restaurants across the street from the gas station. Most times we could only take 30 minutes from my grandpa's busy schedule, but it was worth it.

As he stood towering beside me, inspecting the work I had just accomplished for him, I looked up and eagerly awaited his approval. To me, he was a *Great* man. And, I wanted to be seen as *Great* in his eyes, too.

After what seemed like an eternity to a little kid (probably no more than ten seconds), he turned away from the shelves and toward me, asking if I saw anything wrong with what I had done. Matter-of-factly, I replied, "No, sir." He then asked if all the cans' labels were facing forward. I stated, "Nope. Not *all* of them." I tossed him a confused look and added, "But why does it matter, Grandpa? Nobody can see them anyway."

He paused and scratched his head, as grandpas often do. Then, he looked me straight in the eyes, and with one hand resting firmly but comfortably on my shoulder, he stated, "If *you* can see they're not all facing forward, then that's all that matters." Next came the words that have echoed in my mind ever since: "Jonnie," he said, "a job worth doing is a job worth doing right. If it's not worth doing right, it's not worth doing at all."

These words spoken on any other day or by any other person probably would not have garnered a second's hesitation from me. But, it was my grandpa after all, and somehow I understood quite clearly he wasn't just talking about the cans. He was talking about my *character*. I knew, from that moment forward, I would dedicate my every action to proving I understood his message. The love and respect I had for my grandpa would ensure it.

I immediately set my dedication in motion and returned to the shelves. One by one, I turned the labels outward, perfectly aligned for all to see. With a quick nod of approval, my grandfather reached for my hand, and we took off for lunch.

Never again did we talk about that day, nor did we ever have to. In that brief exchange with my grandpa, I learned why he was so successful, and why everyone in town trusted him to care for their cars and trucks. Whenever they brought their vehicles in to him, they knew they would get his very best effort, each and every time. He did not perform work that was *good enough*, he performed work that reflected *Excellence*. Every job was a masterpiece for all to see, not just a task accomplished as a means to support his family.

That experience was a valuable lesson, and taught me the meaning of *Excellence*, and how it contributes to one's *Greatness*. But when I was 15 years old, I came to know *Greatness*.

It was perhaps one of the most painful moments in my life, but it is a memory that will forever reinforce in me the principles of *Greatness* and *Excellence*... through *Compassion*.

That moment was the night my sister died.

By the time the hospital reached my parents on the telephone to tell us there had been a terrible car accident, my sister was no longer with us. In utter disbelief, we all immediately rushed to the hospital, hoping that somehow, in some way, they had made a mistake. They must have got it wrong. But when we arrived at the hospital, the torturous reality of the situation sank in as we were asked by the staff in Emergency to go down to the morgue to identify her body. I'm certain I will never experience anything as difficult as following those instructions.

If I ever felt disconnected from God at any point in my life, it was then.

The next few days remain a blurred memory for me, as my mind was clouded in emotional disbelief and a tremendous sense of loss. The multitudes of friends and family members sending their condolences, combined with the constant reminders of her absence almost everywhere I turned, were almost too much to bear. As the dutiful son and faithful brother, however, I tried my best to remain "strong for the family."

The night of my sister's "viewing" was accompanied by the worst weather you could ever imagine. It was not only bone-chilling cold, but was pouring down freezing rain and the wind was blowing the rain sideways.

Nobody appeared to mind. People came out in *droves* to pay their last respects. This included all the troubled people my sister had lent a helping hand to: from drug addicts to alcoholics and even the homeless, nothing seemed to hinder their path to the funeral home.

Once there, one by one they flowed past us and told my family about how my sister, Cindy Sue, had reached out to help them in their desperate time of need. They were there to let us know what an amazing person she was, how they appreciated her love and attention, and how she always went above and beyond the call of duty to help them when they needed her most. She did not judge or criticize them for their decisions or situations in their lives. She just focused on what she could do to help solve their problems. She was a true "giver," in every sense of the word.

As I sat through story after story of how compassionate and caring she was, there was a point when I remember feeling a very sudden, perceptible shift deep inside me. It was then that everything changed forever. I knew in that moment my sister's death would not be in vain. I made a conscious decision I would carry the torch she had so generously lit for me. It has become my mission to care for others' pain and suffering just like my sister had done. Like Cindy Sue, I don't ask what they can do for me in return. I just do what I know I can, and let go of the rest. I give them the *Excellence* that my grandfather taught me by paying attention to every detail, and I show them *Compassion* as a loving human being. Every time I do, I feel my sister's presence, and I know <u>this</u> is the true expression of my *Greatness*.

From the very core of my being, I know that *Excellence* is the driving force in ALL great achievers. Once you've set the bar each day at *Excellence*, you do not need to settle for anything less. Keep in mind that *Excellence* is not *what* you achieve, but it is the love and attention you put *into* your achievements.

Although my commitment to the principles of *Excellence* has helped me become a sought-after specialist in the field of sports injury and performance, often working with some of the world's best Olympic and professional athletes, my own personal *Greatness* is only truly realized when I bring this same level of dedication and care to every single patient. So, whether I'm helping a gold medal track athlete shave tenths of a second off his personal best or a local youth just wanting to be able to "get back in the game" with his buddies on the football team, I show them both *Excellence* and *Compassion* <u>every time</u>.

We ALL have "defining moments" that help shape our lives. They often arrive at seemingly the most inopportune times, and sometimes within the most painful of experiences. But they always lead us toward our *Greatness*. If we allow these thoughts to take wings and soar, then a light will shine in the place where darkness used to be, our focus will shift to things bigger than ourselves, and then, and only then, will we realize that *true Greatness* is attainable for each and every one of us.

CHAPTER 25

Asking *What If?*
Challenges *What Is*

by Dr. Caroline P. Mueller

The war had ended, and the victors occupied my father's hometown. His family had survived, but battles raged on. Skirmishes were won on the sidelines and via underground railways ferrying people to safety. Determined, resilient youth, (including my father) slipped past enemy sentries to return home with supplies on their strong backs. These were the indomitable few, displaying acts of bravery within chaos and destruction. Still, the bullet that pierced my father's hand one night inspired the need for even more courageous thinking and an openness to more radical solutions.

What if a beloved house in a well-known neighborhood and the familiar hills and valleys were no longer home? *What if* a well-respected business built through hard work and determination was now less valuable than the search for freedom? *What if* friends and family needed to be left behind when imprisonment became a veritable certainty? *What if* this new reality—occupied, dangerous and oppressive—would eventually suffocate their spirits?

Despite the victory of their escape, their newfound "freedom" was difficult in ways they had not anticipated. Survival in cramped quarters alongside a population of people shamed and barely subsisting became their new reality. Certain they had made the right decision, however, they did not look back. Things improved steadily, and new thoughts of *What if* shone a light on even greater possibilities:

What if after generations of unshakable patriotism, rebuilding in his homeland no longer made sense to my father on a profoundly personal level? *What if* after years of effort, it made more sense to start over? *What if* taking a precious $200 gamble on a ticket to Canada became both a leap of faith and the most compelling idea? Eventually, my father did take the leap across the Atlantic, emigrating to a country filled with new opportunities and potential.

I did not understand initially that my tendency to embrace *What if* questions had found its origins in the genetic make-up and environmental imperatives of these courageous freedom fighters. I realize now my father lovingly honed that inclination as he sought to help me manage my adolescent anxieties. "*What if* the worst thing happens and your deepest fears are realized?" he would often ask. Somehow, facing my subconscious fears *together* lessened the drama; the mental exercise served to evoke more constructive thoughts of what could be done to deal with each potential eventuality. The ensuing explorations—rich with possibility—laid the foundation for a life of curiosity, problem solving and system shifting, while deepening my appreciation for Life's bounty.

The potential of *What if* has since become fundamental to my every quandary, new road taken, and significant life shift. At times, a friendly reminder to rethink a seemingly impossible situation. At other times, the fire that fuels a new awakening. *What if* ignites the courage to step outside the box of societal constructs that might otherwise remain the boundaries of a proscribed reality— the *What Is* box.

The people in my family were merchants, builders and thinkers—so it made sense for me to start my university studies in the Faculty of Commerce. But, over time, *What ifs* began whispering from the depths of my heart and soul and soon became impossible to ignore. Eventually, I set aside the accounting and economics books and turned my attention to my spirit's calling—to become a medical doctor. By listening and responding to that calling, I discovered a passion to help others find answers to their own profoundly personal *What ifs*.

Persevering on this journey seemed so daunting; however, I feared at times I might not survive the challenge. Thankfully, as it had on so many other occasions, the trusted *What if* came to the rescue, offering its unbiased wisdom: "*What if* I <u>don't</u> follow my calling?" Because book learning did not come easily to me, I found myself often despairing of my ability to adequately serve my patients. This is why I was so grateful when a gentler Universe responded and sent me to the Obstetrics case room where I knew I'd found my place.

The unpredictability of childbirth, coupled with a lifetime of guaranteed long hours (mostly at night), made Obstetrics exceptionally undesirable for my med-school chums, yet it filled me with joy! Their *What ifs* went something like, "*What if* things don't go according to the textbook and a baby dies? *What if* a woman starts bleeding and won't stop?" My *What ifs* were quite the opposite: "*What if* I found the very thing that would make each long hour meaningful? *What if* my life were to be blessed with a multitude of shared journeys—each one more remarkable than the last? *What if* counting the number of deliveries made no sense to me because each one seemed entirely unique? *What if* five years of ninety-six hour work weeks being witness to countless individual birthing experiences helped me to hone the skills and discern basic patterns that would, during some critical event, point the way to solving a wholly unique circumstance in the complex fabric of human birth?"

As I established my medical practice, I welcomed a series of new *What ifs* in developing collaborative relationships with my colleagues. Some questions were simply fun to play with, while others required considerable courage to voice while being immersed in the patriarchal world of western medicine. My "audacity" often seemed to leave them flabbergasted: "*What if* we no longer made office decisions facing the men's urinal where I could not ably participate? *What if* operating room time was apportioned by committee rather than by seniority? *What if* there were no waiting times for patients?"

As I matured in my craft, the patients referred to my care, at times, inspired profoundly unsettling, self-directed *What ifs*: *What if* a hysterectomy could not solve the "problem?" *What if* a patient's pelvic pain actually had nothing to do with her pelvic organs? *What if*, in truly hearing a patient's story, I came to understand that nothing in my tool kit would heal her? *What if* listening deeply was enough? *What if* doing so empowered her to *heal herself*?

Even more boldly, I began to ask myself, *What if* western medicine is failing its patients when managing problems other than those that require immediate, life-saving interventions? *What if*, in its certainty, western medicine has stopped asking questions? *What if* a continued attachment to antiquated beliefs about healing and a focus on *illness* has disconnected us from our *wellness*?

These are dangerous *What ifs* to pose in a community of practitioners faithful to the teachings of their professors and loyal to the tenets of a well-constructed, double-blind study. The risks for giving them voice are expulsion from the hallowed hallways and ivory towers of learning and rejection from colleagues. The rewards: limitless. Because asking questions is fundamental to creating the possibility for change.

My own *What ifs* have led me to embrace possibilities for healing inherent in cleansing and detoxifying the body. This has given me a renewed hope for the prevention and treatment of many chronic conditions that are, even now, threatening to bankrupt our healthcare systems. *What if* detoxifying our bodies made some medical treatments obsolete? *What if* prevention really is the cure?

I've been fortunate to embrace the dance of *What ifs*. It remains my valiant, trusted and playful companion through transition and countless challenges. *What if* is the first thing I pack for a new adventure. Together, we have done the impossible and served the World in ways I might not have otherwise conceived.

I invite you to participate in your own dance of *What if*. At first, you may ask, "*What if…I'm wrong?*" Let this qualm be your first indication you're embarking on a journey of limitless potential—for that question is never answerable inside the *What Is* box. *What if* in the asking you were to uncover your best self and discover a new world that's yours to create? *What if* the unique gift you bring to that world is unwrapped beautifully and simply, through a process of enquiry, where each question leads you to the next crucial question?

What if together, we envision a World so remarkable that it transforms each fear, each challenge, and each apparent boundary into a powerful new possibility? *What if* that were enough to change this planet in ways we have not yet imagined? If the power of a single *What if* is astounding, then the potential of combining our *What ifs* is immeasurable!

CHAPTER 26

Perception
Changes Everything

by Gwenn Henkel

My life changed on June 21, 1995 at 4:45pm.

For sixteen years, I worked at the Stanford University Medical Center as a unit coordinator in the Coronary Care Unit (CCU) and Cardiac Surveillance Unit (CSU). That night was slated to be full, with eight admits expected during the shift. Early on, however, the patient count was low for the two units. So, my counterpart was sent to a busier area, leaving me to oversee both the CCU and CSU. I left momentarily as well to deliver blood samples to the lab.

I was gone not even a minute.

When I returned to the CSU, the phone was ringing with no one answering it. I hurried over to my desk, and just as I had done hundreds of times before, dropped myself into my chair and simultaneously reached for the ringing phone. In one surreal instant, I was airborne. My body violently jack-knifed, and I saw my black suede shoes at eye level at the same time my tailbone was smashing down on the chair—the same one some joker had rigged just one foot from the ground, mere moments before. Electric pain shot up my spine, struck the base of my skull, and set aflame a million stars in a field of blackness right before my eyes. The crushing pain in my head silenced everything around me.

In a matter of seconds, my life was dramatically changed forever.

What happened to the young man working on our unit who thought it would be amusing to set all the chairs to their lowest positions? He received only a minor scolding. I, on the other hand, went straight to the emergency room—never to see that man again. In fact, I never saw my units again, nor was I able to do anything remotely "normal" for the next *3½ years.*

In that time, I went from a 112 lb. runner to a nearly 200 lb. professional patient—at only 5'2"!

When I thought it couldn't get any worse, it <u>did</u>. One evening after a long, therapeutic bath, I reached for our bathtub soap dish to help pull myself up. Just as I was almost upright, it suddenly popped out of the wall, sending me backwards once again onto my tailbone, compounding all the previous injuries. Although I didn't believe it possible, this fall felt even more painful than the first. My husband had to give me a massive dose of pain medication before he could even think about helping me out of the tub.

My symptoms expanded beyond the physical boundaries of my injuries. Every inch of my body *hurt.* My skin was painful to the touch, and my cognitive abilities were noticeably impaired. I started to get lost driving in my own neighborhood. And, to my ultimate disbelief, I experienced two *more* "accidents." One where I slipped on an orange peel, landing in the splits, followed soon after by my car being rear-ended on a major highway.

I had moments when I begged God to take me.

All my injuries and symptoms brought me to the Sequoia Pain Clinic, where a team of doctors attempted to find the root cause of my intense, near-continuous pain. It took some time and a lot of different tests and treatments (one nearly killed me due to a serious allergic reaction), but eventually they presented me with the best solution they could find for my problems. I remember very clearly hearing the neurologist saying,

"Do you want the good news or the bad news first?"

I was so thrilled to know I wasn't crazy for feeling the way I did, the part about there being bad news didn't even register. I opted for the good news.

He said, "You have Fibromyalgia, Myofascial Pain Syndrome and Chronic Fatigue Syndrome." Yes! I had actual reasons for my pain! With no real time to celebrate this incredible discovery, the doctor continued, "The bad news is there are no cures for these conditions. Your doctor's very difficult job will be to find out what your 'normal' is for the rest of your life. You will need to learn to live with your conditions."

I remember those words floating right over my head as I asked my next question, "But you have a pill for this, right?"

As it turned out, there was no single pill, but many—many pills that may or may not help. I remember him walking me out and saying, "I feel like a really horrible thing has happened to a very nice lady."

My doctors and I tried for a long time to find "normal" in my life—to no avail. Drug therapy was most challenging because I'm very drug-sensitive. Physical therapy made the pain worse. My doctors decided since these two things were not working, I should try hypnosis. *Hypnosis?* I thought they were crazy and must have given up on me! After all, my primary physician was head of the anesthesia department. If he couldn't fix me, no one could! Apparently my assumption was wrong. As they explained the mind-body connection to me, I saw how they were truly hopeful I may do well with this type of treatment.

My cognitive abilities were challenged, but I wasn't about to let just *anyone* mess with my brain! Since my doctors did not actually do hypnosis, I decided to learn it myself. My first step was to sign up for Hypnosis 101. (Really.) There, I learned that our minds are more powerful than I'd ever imagined! I became intrigued by the possibilities hypnotherapy presented, and a glimmer of hope presented itself to me for the first time in many months. I realized if I continued with school and became a Medical and Master Hypnotherapist, not only might I be able to pursue my passion for helping people (as I'd been doing at Stanford Medical Center originally), I may also learn how to control my own debilitating conditions.

And that's exactly what I did.

Dr. Wayne Dyer once said, "When you change the way you look at things, the things you look at change." I had an "a-ha!" moment when I heard this because I was starting to do exactly that! And, it was making me *feel better*. To complete my healing journey, I knew I needed to change my perception of the incident that had grounded my life for 3½ years. I needed to stop blaming the young man for my maladies and allow myself to grow into the person I am now—someone who can completely understand the pain and suffering of others while applying new skills and knowledge that really help people!

"Everything happens for a reason," I've heard the experts and gurus say.

At the time, I couldn't think of one good reason why all of this was happening to me, but I decided to surrender to this spiritual principle and prayed to God for understanding. Shortly after, the answer appeared to me in a meditation—*if the young man hadn't played his prank, I wouldn't have gone to hypnotherapy school! If I didn't experience all that suffering, I probably would have remained tied to a job that had grown more and more unfulfilling.* So I committed to this new shift in perspective, and let that simple, yet monumental thought create all the difference for how I've lived my life ever since.

You might wonder if I was ever bitter about what happened to me that dreadful night at work. YOU BET I WAS! I was furious with that young man for having ruined my healthy, active life! He was in college getting his life started while I was an invalid with a handicap sticker on my car. I was in pain 24/7 and had nothing to look forward to other than my next doctor's appointment, not to mention I'd had to file for bankruptcy.

However, even though I wanted that man to PAY for what he did, I decided to bless the young man for his mistake anyway. As a result, I let go of all the bitterness and blame. I accepted my newly realized gift and claimed my purpose. I was free.

Dr. Dyer, thank you so much for helping me to see the light. Perception really *can* change everything! I share this wisdom almost daily. I love seeing the light dawn in my client's eyes when they shift their perspective and begin to see their situation differently. I am a perfect example of how change accompanies a new way of thinking: even when my situation seemed truly bad, it was transformed into goodness when I changed the way I looked at it! By the time I finished hypnotherapy school, I had remarkably transformed all my conditions and reduced my pain by at least 85%! I stopped all medications, and best of all, started my own practice—reconnecting with my dream of helping people every day. With hypnotherapy, my patients get to experience new levels of awareness and well-being—and new ways of seeing themselves and their lives.

Why not try it for yourself? The pain of today can become the triumph of tomorrow. It's really all how you look at it.

I'm living proof.

SECTION III

THROUGH ME

The marble not yet carved can hold the form of
every thought the greatest artist has.

— Michelangelo

CHAPTER 27

How Did I Know?

by Marlyse Carroll
(alias Gabrielle)

"Can you tell me in which ways your baby's death was a blessing?"

Gabrielle's heart missed a beat even before she intellectually understood the question. She also felt a little stirring in her lower belly, as if her ovaries were attached by invisible strings to these words, pulling ever so lightly. It wasn't painful, just a little reminder of the body-mind connection.

Gabrielle was standing in front of a group of people who had come for the launch of her first book, *Am I going Mad? The Unsettling Phenomena of Spiritual Evolution* (Inner Peace Publishing, 2007). She had been talking about her belief that the most painful events in one's life always hide a gift. "It might seem paradoxical that we are the most likely to find inner light when we willingly enter into the darkness of our deepest pain," she said. She had then hesitated for a split second before revealing that she spoke from personal experience, having lost her first son to cot death many years earlier.

This is when a man she had never met before asked her to clarify what she meant. "Can you tell me in which ways your baby's death was a blessing?" he asked.

This direct question took Gabrielle by surprise—as had her spontaneous disclosure—because she hadn't planned to touch on this event. In fact, it was a subject she consistently avoided. Yet, she knew that whenever she followed her intuition and took an emotional risk, the rewards were always greater than any temporary discomfort. As she opened her heart, it seemed others in the audience did the same.

A young woman sitting in the first row started to cry. Maybe she was just imagining what it would be like to wake up one morning and find her youngest child dead without any warnings. No obvious reasons—no crying, no fever, no doctor's visits, no dramas—just death silently collecting an infant's soul whilst everyone slept, leaving a lifeless, pale little body in a cot.

In the second it took Gabrielle to collect her thoughts and start answering the question, she relived in a timeless instant that fateful Boxing Day morning.

She was 25 years of age, very much in love with her husband. They had two beautiful children—a two and a half year old little girl named Annick and a baby boy whose name was Ivan. They still lived in Switzerland, but not for much longer, as they were due to move to Australia a week later. With their belongings and furniture packed in a container already on its way to the new land, the young family was spending the month of December with Gabrielle's parents.

Their life over the previous year had been joyfully exciting, with more and more of their desires becoming reality. One of them had been the birth of a healthy baby boy. The latest happy event was that Gabrielle's husband had been appointed to a managerial position in Melbourne, and they were both looking forward to a new adventure. At that time, they thought that living in Australia would be like a long, although temporary, working holiday. Little did they know that they would love it so much they would choose to stay!

Ever since she was a child, Gabrielle had always been an optimist. She welcomed change, especially when she was part of the planning, and rarely experienced anxiety. Yet, during that month of December, she had started to feel uneasy and to worry about their little boy.

Ivan was seven months old. He had always been a quiet, easy child who rarely cried, and he was still just as content as he had always been. Had she been asked to describe him in two words, she would have said "little philosopher." Wherever he was, he seemed to observe the World with interest. He participated in nondemanding ways and welcomed attention with equanimity. Some people called him "a dream baby."

Externally nothing had changed, but as the day of the big move came closer, Gabrielle felt more and more anxious. Her feelings of impending doom didn't make sense to her until one day the nature of her fear became fully conscious.

Gabrielle woke up early one morning with the realisation that she couldn't imagine their life in Australia with Ivan. Sobbing uncontrollably, she told her husband that she feared their infant son would never live there. In her mind's eye, as she projected her thoughts into the future, she could see Annick growing up, she got glimpses of another child, but Ivan wasn't part of any of these scenes. It was as if the little boy who had received so much of their love, time and attention ever since his conception was slowly becoming invisible. Energetically, he was withdrawing from their life. Day after day, the young mother became more distressed without any obvious external reasons. Her family explained away these irrational feelings as some unconscious fear of the unknown.

Shortly before Christmas, Gabrielle's father suggested she take Ivan to a pediatrician for a full check-up. They all hoped it would ease her mind. So a consultation was promptly organised and, after numerous tests, the baby received a clean bill of health. The middle-aged doctor who examined him was thorough, friendly, and very compassionate. He spent much time reassuring Gabrielle that her fears were unfounded, although somehow understandable.

She wanted very much to believe him, and so she stopped talking about her private nightmare. It didn't go away though. Superficially, joyful Christmas celebrations came and went. But Christmas was to be Ivan's last day alive. He was found dead in his cot Boxing Day morning.

That is when the real nightmare started, one she couldn't consciously face for a long time. So she suppressed all memories. Without consulting her husband, she even threw away the photos of that Christmas. She had never found the courage to look at them, and they haunted her. Needless to say, throwing them away didn't help. Years later, at her request, her parents gave her some of the family shots they had taken on that day, including one in which Ivan looks like a little Buddha in *blessing pose*.

In those days, Gabrielle had never heard of cot death, nor had any member of her family. They now know that the most likely cause was the borrowed bedding in which he was sleeping. Old mattresses tend to harbour a fungus that attacks fire-retardants in such a way as to produce poisonous gases. These fumes can be fatal to babies, especially if they sleep on their tummy and are kept too warm in a centrally-heated house. All those conditions were present in Ivan's case.

"Can you tell me in which ways your baby's death was a blessing?"

Hardly a second had elapsed since the question had been asked, and Gabrielle answered it without hesitation, although with a slightly croaky voice. Yes, there was still some emotion there, even after all these years.

"Ivan's death," she said, "prompted me to look at life differently—to ask different questions. Questions such as 'What is death?', 'Why are we here?', 'Why would a baby who was wanted, adored and well cared for die, when others who aren't loved or even wanted keep on living?', 'How did I know that he would die?', 'Did he choose to leave?', 'If so, why?'"

She paused, wondering whether to elaborate further. She could see clearly how this traumatic event had, in one single blow, propelled her on her life's path—to shed light on some of Life's great mysteries. Until then, she had been more concerned with what her neighbours thought of her mini-skirts and whether high boots would also be fashionable Down Under!

"And in which way was his death a blessing for the baby?"

It was the same man again. Another question she wasn't prepared for, yet to which the answer came easily.

"I believe, at the soul level, before we came to the physical plane we all made an agreement to help each other in our spiritual evolution. Ivan chose to go back to Source to allow us—his parents, sister and extended family—to grow very quickly.

Some of us need decades to fulfill our mission, to reach our potential and/or to make a difference for others. For him, his work was done in 7 months. In his journey, this transition was neither a sacrifice nor a tragedy because life isn't good *or* bad. Nor is death. They are just different planes of existence that co-exist on a continuum."

Gabrielle was happy to notice that she could now talk of Ivan without wanting to run away. Gratitude balanced sadness. She was centred in her heart and acknowledged the perfection inherent in all of creation, including her personal tragedies.

At the time of Ivan's death though, she didn't have such clearly articulated spiritual beliefs. She had many questions and no answers. And her biggest question was, "How did I know he would die?"

This thought changed her life forever. Because of it, she spent the next three decades exploring her inner world in order to understand existential mysteries: *What is reality? What creates or sustains our connection beyond time and space? What did Einstein mean when he said that the difference between past, present and future is just a stubborn illusion?*

With a smile, she cleared her throat and resumed her speech. The young woman in the front row was still crying. As for Gabrielle, she was at peace. She knew how she knew. She had just spent two years writing it down, giving birth to the very book about which she was now talking to this particular group of people.

It was, however, the first time she had become aware that Ivan's death had been the pivotal event that began her life-long quest for Truth.

Having changed her life—and those she touched with her hard-won wisdom— Gabrielle uttered silently in her heart, "Thank you, my darling boy."

CHAPTER 28

We Belong to Our Relationship

by Lon & Sandy Golnick

We sat in a bare clapboard meeting room with a post right in the middle of it, looking around us at about thirty people. There were six families in total. It was a balmy Tuesday evening on Mission Bay in San Diego.

The previous Saturday and Sunday, we had been in front of these same people in this same room (musty carpet and all) leading our newly-designed workshop. Our purpose was to uncover the *default design of families*, i.e. the one that produces so much disappointment, frustration and resignation. Our intention was to then co-create a *whole new design* that would produce a greater sense of peace, ease and fulfillment for the entire family, including all its members.

We had just raised the question: "When their parents get divorced, why do the children so often feel shame, like they themselves have failed? Especially since, for the most part, they are simply informed about their parents' decision *after the fact?*"

The first to raise his hand was Francisco, a nine-year old Mexican-American boy who had been mostly silent during the weekend. When we called on him, he said something that had never crossed our minds—and it rocked our world:

"Well, we *did* fail," he proclaimed. "Our parents belong to our family, and we didn't keep our family together."

Our parents belong to our family? What an amazing statement. We hadn't heard anything like this before, and it struck us as a revolutionary way to look at the family unit.

But it wasn't just us who found this statement impactful. No one else we knew of professionally or personally had ever thought of it this way. No parents had ever said, "The family I belong to…"

But why not?

Most of the time we hear parents use the terms *my daughter, my son, my children* or (less often) *our family*, implying that the children and the family belong to the parents. We will also hear children say *my mom* and *my dad*, but this is usually in the sense that the children have a mom and dad they belong to, not in the sense that their parents belong to them.

On that "fateful" Tuesday evening, young Francisco initiated us into a powerful realm of thinking that invited us to illuminate and explore a new perspective of everyone's role in the family. This was most certainly going to transform our approach to our work.

Two days later, as we sat in the warm afternoon sunshine on our flower-decked terrace, we found ourselves reflecting once again on what Francisco had said. While we were enjoying our beautiful surroundings and each other's loving company, it was then that his insight moved us personally, taking the revolution straight to our hearts.

Our <u>relationship</u> doesn't belong to us. We belong to it.

With that thought, and the energizing conversation that followed, we entered a new world that glorious afternoon; a world in which the basic unit of our existence shifted from the individual to the relationship—from "I" to "WE." And that "WE-based" world opened up to us in full techni-color as a whole new way of *being* to explore and enjoy together.

We decided the old Patti Page song, "You Belong to Me," was misleading and represented an out-dated way of thinking. In our newly-emerging paradigm, it would be more accurate to sing, "You and I Belong to Us."

We began to share our "thought" with family and friends. Each time we did, a light of recognition sparked in their faces.

Two of our closest friends, Barry and Suzanne, shared the impact this had on them. They told us how embracing the idea of belonging to their relationship with each other satisfied one of the basic human needs we all share—a longing to belong. They went on to explain how this new awareness then expanded to include their circle of friends, their community, and ultimately, a connection with their place *in* the World.

Soon after, with encouragement from other close friends—so close as to be considered our family—we expanded our exploration of this approach to design and offer relationship workshops as well as family workshops. This is the world we have been steeped in for the last six years.

In that time, we have observed how the conventional use of language seduces us into believing we actually *own* our relationships and families, even our World— e.g. *my* wife, *my* children, *my* house, *my* country and *my* land. We fail to notice that at our death, we return to the land: "Ashes to ashes, and dust to dust." The land doesn't belong to us, we belong to it. What many ancient peoples seem to be very aware of, many of us have forgotten.

While it may be true there is no relationship until we create it, what we came to realize was that often people fail to notice that "we" created it, not "I" created it. Once we create it, it ceases to be ours. (And maybe never was.) The relationship becomes an entity of its own, and it "owns" us.

Imagine trying to make a hand by putting a front of a hand together with a back of a hand. It can't be done. A hand is a whole, an entity that arises with a front and a back, each being distinct from the other. Neither the front nor the back owns the hand. Instead, it could be said that the hand "owns" the front and the back. Both sides belong to the hand *and each is a unique expression of the hand*, moving in perfect harmony.

Bringing this idea back to us, we recognized how we both belong to our relationship, and each of us is a unique expression of it. We belong to our family, and each of us is a unique expression of our family. Neither our relationship, nor our family, belongs to us separately.

Our family has grown to include our daughters' husbands and children, and each of us belongs to this extended family. Our "new" family now owns the twelve of us, and we are all unique expressions of it.

By the way, we have found that we belong to more than one family—and that's OK! As a matter of fact, we think it would be wonderful if we all realized that we belong to many families. And that we belong to communities. We belong to societies. We belong to our World.

During the recent economic uncertainty, there have been several times we've been faced with difficult decisions: do we abandon our work and do something else to ensure our financial future? Or, do we continue sharing our explorations and discoveries, trusting the World we belong to will take care of us? We have courageously chosen the latter.

George Bernard Shaw expresses this concept of "belonging" brilliantly in the following passage.[7] In it, we have substituted "I" with "we" (and, by the way, find it interesting that people capitalize "I" and do not capitalize "we"):

> **This is the true joy in life, the being used for a purpose recognized by yourselves as a mighty one; the being a force of nature instead of a feverish, selfish little clod of ailments and grievances complaining that the world will not devote itself to making you happy.**
>
> **We are of the opinion that our life belongs to the whole community, and as long as we live, it is our privilege to do for it whatever we can.**
>
> **We want to be thoroughly used up when we die, for the harder we work the more we live. We rejoice in life for its own sake. Life is no "brief candle" to us. It is a sort of splendid torch which we have got hold of for the moment. And we want to make it burn as brightly as possible before handing in on to future generations.**

Today, as we sit once again in the warm San Diego sunshine on our ever-flowering terrace, enjoying the relationship we have co-created and to which we both belong, we are loving our life. There is nowhere else for us to be, nothing else more important

---

7   Adapted excerpt from George Bernard Shaw's play *Man and Superman: A Comedy and Philosophy* (1903)

for us to do. For it is here and with one another that we truly and ultimately *belong*. And it feels glorious.

We like to remind ourselves and others, "The World is <u>not</u> our oyster. We are its pearls."

CHAPTER 29

Does My Perception Change Everything?

What Soap Bubbles Taught Me at Midnight

by Angelika Christie

It was a hot summer's night, and all guests had happily departed. I felt deeply satisfied because it turned out to be yet another truly successful evening.

The beautifully hand-painted dishes towered on my kitchen counter, leaning slightly out of perfect alignment. Four different sizes of plates stacked with silver spoons, forks, knives and left-over morsels silently lurking between the layers made the entire compilation seem dangerously high. Delicate, hair-thin wine and champagne glasses, carefully set down mostly in one place looked like a frighteningly large lot begging to be washed, rinsed and polished.

There were twelves of every sized plate and glass I had in my china cabinet. All of them were used now—soiled and waiting to be cleaned, dried and put back into their resting place, ready for next time.

So why did I not fill my dishwasher with what would have been several loads? I could not because this was my finest china, and these were my most delicate crystal glasses. The hand-painted design would fade, the fine Riedel glasses would break, and the silver cutlery would turn yellowish and dull. This was not an option! The only other solution was to leave it all and deal with it the next morning—which I hated to do. What I needed to face in that moment was just getting on with it. But where to start?

After a large meal and a few glasses of wine, I was especially tired and not at all happy about being left to clean up this mess all by myself. Oh yes, not only had our guests gone home to retire, but my sweet husband was also on his way to rest his weary head, giving me a last wave of "goodnight" through the open kitchen door. His eyes expressed sorrow and encouragement simultaneously as he offered a forced smile before disappearing out of sight. "Leave it until tomorrow," he said from down the hallway. As if fairies would surprise me in the morning with a sparkling clean kitchen! I love to start fresh in the morning, so I resigned myself to tackling the enormous chore right then.

I took a deep breath and started separating, organizing and scraping the dishes. This is when it started: echoes of self-deprecating, victimizing thoughts—all centered around feeling abandoned (yet again) after having labored all afternoon shopping, cooking, setting up our house beautifully, sensing every wish and fulfilling it before anyone could utter a word, etc. Serving my guests still thrilled me to a point, but the time in which all the food was consumed seemed fractional to the time it took to prepare. "This is not fair," I muttered. The entire monologue looped in my head over and over until I felt so sorry for myself, physical pain started to creep down from my head into every other part of my body. I felt miserable and had to force myself to continue.

Then, to make matters worse, the monologue turned into a dialogue—with nobody! Well, I imagined the "nobody" being my husband, to whom I complained heavily until I heard myself hissing unpleasant words through my clenched teeth. All the while, he was oblivious of course, sleeping sweetly in our comfortable bed, far away from our kitchen. The chaotic buzz in my head intensified into the red zone—a "four alarm" warning. My hands started to shake, and I knew I could not continue lest I became numb to the present danger of either breaking dishes or seriously overloading my nervous system.

So I stopped and walked out on the balcony where a warm breeze welcomed my quivering body. With its comforting embrace, my shoulders immediately relaxed. I slowly started to feel better. Then I looked up into the starry sky where a half moon raced through the clouds' sketched openings. Staring in fascination, I started to laugh at the trick my eyes played on me! Of course, it wasn't the moon but the clouds that raced across the night sky...

The optical illusion caused me to pause and turn inward. Then a thought magically appeared to me from behind the clouds in my *mind—Is perception everything?* It was so profoundly simple, and yet so incredibly powerful. What I was feeling that night was obviously a reflection of what I was seeing. But what if what I was seeing was merely an interpretation of the events around me? And, what if I changed the way I looked at things? Could my feelings change too? *In fact, does my perception change everything?*

My dream-like state first changed gradually, then powerfully into an almost uncontrollable shaking in my body. There was the urgency of a radical change taking place which I can only compare to the physical birthing of my five children—when my body was overtaken by a mighty, unseen power. Tears of release and gratitude streamed down my face as I felt a divine energy of great love and wisdom take a heavy burden from me. A deep inner knowing emerged. I could hear it clearly, even though it seemed to come from deep in the center of my heart:

It does not matter what happens around you or who is with you; it is only you and your conscious choice deciding how you see, experience and respond to a situation.

This sudden sense of *knowing* was so absolute, I felt as if a divine force burned it into my body with a non-consuming fire. *Does this mean my mind and emotions create my experience to which my body reacts instantly?* I wondered about this for a moment and made up my mind to return to my dirty kitchen and soiled dishes with new eyes.

Now, rather than seeing the left-over laden dishes, I gazed at the plates with their partially covered beauty that wanted to be fully revealed. Taking a deep breath and smiling, I was ready for a new experience. I slowed everything down—especially my physical movements.

Rinsing the china and cutlery under clear water became an observation, with no feelings of stress *or* pleasure. I felt strangely awake and alert now. In no time, all the dishes were stacked up neatly again and ready to be thoroughly washed and polished. I watched myself filling the basin with fresh, warm water and squeezed a small amount of dishwashing detergent into the running stream. Soapy bubbles appeared, displaying countless tiny rainbows. I felt the softness of the solution which stimulated my sense of touch. Immersing the first plate into the soft, soapy water became a sensuous experience.

While my fingers were gliding over the painted surface, I felt the smoothness of the glaze which was only occasionally interrupted by the elevation of a golden rim.

The beauty of the design dazzled my eyes when the shiny, wet plate emerged from the water. The delicate design of color and shapes started to communicate with my sense of beauty, bringing sound and movement into my meditative state of surrender. I lost track of time, and to my surprise, all the dishes were done more swiftly than I ever expected.

All exhaustion had disappeared. My body felt calm and surprisingly restored, as if I'd just awakened from a wonderful sleep.

And I *stayed* awake with a feeling of new life as the next day began, confirmed by a most beautiful sunrise. Once again, I stepped outside onto the balcony overlooking the turquoise ocean, smiled, and faced the sun, feeling a tremendous wave of gratitude and new empowerment. I had been honed to align with my true *essence*. I was alive with a renewed energy and passion and eager to apply this new awareness each day for the rest of my life.

From this night on, it became more and more natural for me to shift into a different mind-set each time I needed to accomplish a task that evoked feelings of resistance. From contemplating menial tasks to navigating frustrating situations and difficult moments in my relationships, whenever I feel resistance, I create a new pathway in my brain like I did that beautiful evening on the balcony, high up between the ocean and the starry sky in the moonlight. Invariably, I see a new possibility arise, and, magically, this allows me a fresh sense of enjoyment for what I have to do.

During the past 25 years, a deepening of my understanding has guided me to apply this truth and live it. This does not mean I live in constant bliss, but my spiritual awakening has continued to bring tremendous gifts of wisdom, harmony and love into my life. It became my mission to wake up and empower others—especially women—who are ready to take ownership of their lives. My greatest joy emerges from seeing positive shifts taking place in my family, my friends and clients.

Your true nature wants to be found and honored, and the time is *now*. All of us are waking up to a greater awareness about our own consciousness. As the veil of false beliefs disappears, it reveals the beauty, truth and authentic power of the Divine Self, which is embodied in every person.

Does perception change everything? That is a beautiful question I will leave with you to explore in your life.

Perhaps the soap bubbles have something for you, too.

CHAPTER 30

What Am I Waiting For?

by Kristen Moeller

Plopping down in front of the computer, I checked my email for the fifth time in fifteen minutes. And still—nothing. A sinking feeling came over me. *What was I doing? Why did I feel so unsettled?* Then, I wondered...

What am I waiting for?

In one profound, life-altering moment, my world transformed. As quickly as that, this thought began challenging me to become someone I was previously afraid to be. Eventually, it would propel me to do things I didn't know I could do. It would help me to stretch myself beyond self-imposed limits. It would guide me to experience my life in ways I hadn't before.

Was it a near death experience?

Not quite. But close.

It was the realization that I didn't want to die with any of my passions unexpressed or any of my cherished dreams unrealized. I caught myself waiting—for Jack Canfield in this case—and it was definitely time for me to pull the plug on that worn-out habit. On that day, I began the greatest journey of self-discovery in my entire life.

I would love to tell you that since that moment, I've *never* waited again. I can't say that. What I *can* honestly say is my life was significantly altered in ways that still reveal themselves to me daily.

For many years, I craved a sense of purpose. I wanted to arrive at some place where I could relax—to finally breathe a deep sigh of contentment and know I'd made it. I hoped if I read the right book, found the right teacher or attended the right seminar, I would hear what I needed to hear and everything would fall into place. Life would make sense. *I* would make sense.

Long before I opened my first self-help book, I struggled with feeling I wasn't "good enough." To deal with my angst, I hunted for the illusive ideal of perfection with an insatiable desire to claim it. Whether it was a perfect body, perfect life, perfect understanding, perfect *whatever,* it didn't matter. One way or another I simply *had* to achieve it. Or die trying.

For much of my life, I sought, searched and *obsessed.*

As a teenager, my intense feelings of lack led to seven long years of addiction and bulimia—a daily struggle with darkness and demons. For a very long time, I wondered if I would ever make it out of my self-imposed trap alive. But in 1989, I found recovery and assumed that freedom and fulfillment were mine to keep.

So on that fateful day in 2008, when I caught myself waiting for Jack, I wondered: *How did I end up <u>here</u>, again? How was it, after all my years of growth, personal work, education and professional experience, I feel so perilously close to the emptiness I sought to evade many years ago?* Sure, the brutal struggle of my addiction was absent, but this *feeling* was terribly similar to those of the past in a critical way: it appeared I'd once again lost sight of myself.

Had I fallen into the same trap? Here I was waiting for Jack—or someone or something like him—to fulfill me or let me know I was okay. The problem was he couldn't. Not then, not ever. So, there I was…alone…once again…waiting.

I'd first met Jack Canfield at a speaking event in Denver. At one point in his presentation, he stood in the middle of the stage and waved a $100 bill in the air. He challenged the audience by asking, "Who wants this?"

Without thinking, I jumped out of my chair, ran up on stage and grabbed it from his hand. This seemed to be the reaction he was looking for because he proclaimed a hearty "Yes!" to the audience. "We can't wait around for what we *say* we want in life. We need to go for it!"

Feeling inspired, I approached him after the presentation and asked for his personal email address. I wanted to continue moving boldly forward in my life and career, and I felt he was the man who could help me.

Amazingly, Jack handed me his business card. Over the next several months, I sent him lengthy emails about my dreams, goals, and what I was hoping to create. You see, during my addiction, I never entertained big dreams for myself. But after years of recovery, I finally allowed myself to envision even the most exciting of prospects—a career as a world-renowned public speaker; a coach who impacted the lives of thousands of people; the dream of being a successful author. I hoped to contribute to the World in a meaningful way—to use the darkness of my past to bring light to others' struggles and suffering—so they wouldn't feel the loneliness I once had.

After each lengthy email detailing my mission, Jack always kindly wrote back, typically with one-liners such as, "Keep thinking and playing bigger—it's much more fun that way. Love, Jack." Then, as time went by, the routines of life took over, and my once fiery vision receded into the distance. I slowly lost sight of my bigger dreams and even stopped emailing Jack.

Sometime later, as my passion came back into focus, a craving grew within me to reconnect with Jack. He seemed to represent a portal for me into the World I still hoped to create for myself. With renewed determination, I sent him an email…and didn't hear back. I sent another…and again, no response. Desperate, I thought: *What if I've blown my <u>one</u> chance to live my dreams? What if Jack never emails me again?*

This puts us at that fateful day in 2008 when, in the middle of a family gathering, I was sneaking into my room to check my email.

What made this moment different was the *revolutionary thought* that arose with my actions. I suddenly became the observer. I watched myself repeating a familiar, anxious pattern, and this stopped me dead in my tracks. All of a sudden, I thought: *What am I waiting for?* And then, the epiphany: *Why am I waiting…for Jack?*

There it was—the thought that changed my life forever. Although it arrived unsolicited, it has remained my faithful companion ever since. The thought even became a book title—*Waiting for Jack*—summarizing why we find ourselves waiting in life and why we look outside ourselves for answers. Oliver Wendell Holmes so powerfully captured the potential tragedy of this human tendency when he wrote:

Many people die with their music still inside them.

When I think back to the day of Jack's presentation, I can see the 800+ others in the audience, with fewer than a dozen running for the stage. When I interviewed Jack on my radio show recently, I asked him about that exercise. "What do *you* see?" He answered, "A handful of people get up and run toward me and that $100 bill. Most don't even raise their hands."

What stops us? Why aren't we willing to just *go for it?*

Practically speaking, we know we should strive for our dreams and "go for the gusto!" Yet many of us never do—just like the majority of the people in Jack's audiences. We wait…we hope. We think about it…or we don't think about it. We lose sight of our dreams…or pretend we don't have any. We blame others. We complain. We get depressed. We regret.

Helen Keller once said, "Life is either a daring adventure or it is nothing." When I caught myself waiting, I chose in that moment to dedicate myself to the "daring adventure," confronting head-on the part of me so prone to screaming out, "I can't do it!" With that one decision, that one dedication, my life has taken directions I'd never believed possible.

Don't get me wrong—I still have my moments when I think it might be easier to curl up in a ball, lie on the floor and quit. It's quite seductive to think that once we begin living our passion *on purpose,* we will never wonder or doubt again. It's easy to look at successful people or our idols and think they have it all together. So many of us think we have to wait to feel all "together" before we can even attempt to be like them. So we wait.

From what I've seen, no one has it *all* together. No one is completely without fears and doubts. Some may deal with their "stuff" more quickly, making it appear they don't have stuff to work out in the first place. Yet we *all* do! After two-plus decades on this side of addiction, with many fabulous accomplishments under my belt, I am here to tell you that there is no arrival. If we wait for *arrival,* we will wait…forever.

And while I now know there is no perfection *out there* to be claimed, gratefully I've come to realize there *is* a perfection at the heart of me; and living my dreams as fully as I can—right now—is *living my life to perfection.* Why would I ever wait for that?

CHAPTER 31

Who's Teaching Who?

by Hilary Bowring

Looking back at my younger years, the word "celebration" comes to mind. I was accomplished, good at my job, and popular in social circles. I was "magnificent," my father-in-law sometimes said.

Early on in my marriage, my husband and I were quite the couple, too: interesting, good looking, "party-goers," intellectual debaters. So much fun to be around in the '80s.

Then things began to go wrong.

Heavy partying turned into alcoholism for my husband, and our social invitations waxed, waned, then snarled to a standstill.

But we were bright, young and imaginative! If we set our minds to it, we knew we could fix this thing. Or so we thought. Full of optimism, we embarked upon a treatment program, knowing full-well the first step to conquering anything is to *recognize you have a problem*. If you put the effort in, things work out, right?

Not always.

As it turned out, things didn't go exactly as planned. In fact, it began to dawn on me this was a beast that would not easily be tamed. There were days I felt that treatment for my husband's serious disease may <u>never</u> work, and I'd be burdened with a beautiful man who was not fixable. My heart began to feel very heavy and hope started to fade. It felt like we were making no progress and there was nowhere for us to go.

Or was there?

Experts advised us to seek help in the United States. The Canadian healthcare system was limited at the time for this type of treatment, and many Canadians were going to places like Chicago, Boston and Dallas for care. So he went, returned, and went again. Each time he ventured south, hope would return, if only for a short while. Each time we thought, *Maybe this approach will be the one—the cure!* But nothing seemed to provide the answer we needed. The monthly spin-dry accompanied by the newest, thought-provoking angle worked for a week or two, but nothing had any real staying power.

I was becoming a "treatment centre widow." While my husband reached for the next panacea, in his absence, I would occupy myself with friends and mindless tasks. Often I found myself redecorating and renovating the house—once even laying a hardwood floor! From the outside looking in, I was doing a good job holding my life together, as his was falling apart.

But was I *really*?

Alcoholics Anonymous became an obvious and all-too-familiar meeting place for us. People there were welcoming and supportive—even laughing (not like the serious approach at the treatment centres: "Get serious, you have a problem!"). I discovered new practices like meditation, and my motivation was rekindled.

My husband felt the same, and with an AA sponsor, he acquired new-found determination, accompanied by a support group steeped in understanding, personal experience, goals and ideas. The 12-Step Program included a lot of self-examination, and this appeared to help.

Yet, after a while, my husband experienced a slip. (*It's OK, it was just a slip.*) But then another slip...and after a while another...and... I found it deeply distressing and hard to witness—he was a good man, after all, and working The Program the best he could. This wasn't supposed to be happening! As his loyal wife, I was sticking by his side, no matter what.

Not everyone saw the wisdom in my approach.

A close friend finally took me aside and expressed her concern for my welfare. She suggested I go to a deep trance channeler, confessing later she'd hoped I would receive advice from the etheric realms to get a divorce. When I heard my father-in-law saying, "Do *two* people need to go down?" I knew I had to take some radical action.

So, reluctantly, I went. But instead of the sage advice my friend was hoping for, out of my session with the channeler came a simple question:

Who's teaching who?

In an instant, this one question forever changed me. I was no longer the smart one from a spiritual perspective; what became clear to me in that moment was that my *husband* was the spiritual provocateur, the teacher—despite all his challenges and failures.

Although my logical mind could not wrap around this radical concept, in my soul I knew it was true. Out of this question came a deep, heart-felt appreciation for my husband and our marriage. Divorce was *definitely* out of the question now. (Much to my friend's chagrin!)

Everything I looked at from this moment on was through the lens of this new understanding. I continued at Al-Anon, but with a new perspective. I began to see more and more that every time he faltered, it was really a mistake that created an opportunity for me, contributing to *my* spiritual growth. Although the "old me" felt terrible that there might be a gift for me each time my husband suffered, I intuitively knew these gifts were somehow meant for *both of us*.

Sometimes the situation would reveal an insight about my own patterns, and other times I would connect with a deeper level of detachment. But there was always something to learn. To this day, I don't know how to thank another human being for giving benefit to others through his own suffering—but I do it anyway, practicing gratitude as often as I can.

In the case of addiction, many people cannot get beyond being judgmental. For others, it may appear to be a huge or even *impossible* stretch to consider that an alcoholic might be a spiritual teacher. Yet this was *my* truth. Our egos often cloak our soul's desires, making it difficult for us to be aware of anything other than what is happening in this physical body. From the moment I changed my understanding of my relationship with my husband, I *expanded*—and felt deep respect for him, for myself, and for Life itself. At the time, I could not immediately apply the idea of learning from difficult people or circumstances to other parts of my life. It took many years and his actual death for me to be able to see a bigger picture.

Spiritual teachings are Life's blessings, and our teachers can appear in the most unlikely of places. The *suffering* of some has the potential to serve to *enlighten* others. Our collective intention is to evolve in this lifetime, and as souls we spur each other on in surprising ways. Sometimes the most powerful spiritual lessons can be found in relationships where our roles become reversed—the vulnerable becomes the powerful, the parent becomes the child, the student becomes the teacher.

And our unexpected teachers can be young or old, advantaged or disadvantaged. We just have to tune in and look beyond what they physically represent in their societal role and actually *see* what they represent spiritually.

Who's teaching who?

Is your next spiritual teacher a child, a grandparent or an infuriating friend? Look closely at those around you. Do your family members or close friends know best how to "push your buttons?" Does this usually create an angry reaction? If you were to shift to a more spiritual perspective, might you consider they are simply doing what they are *supposed* to do to help you grow and evolve? Even though family situations can create unpleasant drama in our lives, these situations are often charged with the potential for personal transformation—an opportunity to break free from our old patterns and embrace a new consciousness, including the freedom to choose *love* over *anger*. What an incredible gift!

There are unlikely spiritual teachers everywhere.

When I was still grieving my husband's passing, I often refused to leave the house much or to socialize. That's when my dog came into my life. Introduced to this "angel" by my friends, she taught me many significant lessons. Unless I was grounded and in my body, she would absolutely run riot! She also forced me to go out for walks and be with other people—gradually leading me to step back into my life again.

We are all interconnected as souls, each one of us motivated by an innate drive to evolve. Everyone and every situation appear to us in our daily lives to teach us *something*. Embrace even the most frustrating experiences and ask yourself, "*Who's teaching who?*"

You may be pleasantly surprised when what first appears to be a *curse* later becomes a *gift*. Practice no judgment, no blame. Instead, celebrate the good with the bad, the shadows *and* the light. Embrace Life. Love *all* of it and learn—deeply, honestly and earnestly—thanking your teachers each and every day. Whether or not you can still see them.

I do.

CHAPTER 32

Life Is the Most Precious Gift You Can Ever Receive

by Lionel Philippe

I was born premature, weighing less than two pounds. My mother told me that when the nurse first presented me, she burst out, "It's not mine—he's a monster!"

From that auspicious start, my childhood with my mother was always difficult. I don't recall many moments of tenderness or closeness with her. I also saw her lying and having affairs with other men. In fact, the entire relationship between my parents did nothing to model what I imagined a loving relationship could be.

When I was 14 years old, I witnessed my mom kissing a man who was not my dad. Looking back, I see this was truly the beginning of the end for us. This so devastated me that I felt like the ground under me had collapsed; it was like I had lost all support. I completely lost confidence in my mother, and with that, lost confidence in women in general. All I could feel was confusion, rage and sadness. I started building up resentment toward her, completely losing all trust and respect. I even described her as a prostitute to my friends.

After a heated argument between us, at only 17 years old I left my family home.

As I moved through life, I found myself (unconsciously) choosing women who were very different from her physically. At 22, I married an African woman who I met in Dakar (Senegal) while I was in the French Air Force. Our relationship lasted 13 years. Later, I met an Asian woman while traveling in India. I moved from Paris to Los Angeles a year later to be with her, and this is where our daughter Seghara (now 15) was born.

My relationships with women remained very unsatisfying. This is what led me to embark on a path of self-discovery: I studied psychology. I tried all kinds of therapies, including individual and men's group work, tantra, primal scream and meditation. I went to India to meet with spiritual gurus. Yet after all this concentrated effort, my relationships with women *still* remained unfulfilling. To me, male-female relations were a toxic elixir of sexual passion, power and struggle. I could never feel the respect and deep, *true* love I so longed for.

Even with therapeutic commitment, my relationship with my daughter was difficult, too. I was over-protective and very impatient with her needs. At that time, I wasn't yet aware of how much I loved her—so I definitely *couldn't* and *wasn't* expressing that to her. Unfortunately, like my mother, I was not being a model parent.

Despite my significant discomfort with women, I felt myself compelled to learn more about them. I decided to focus on Feminism and came to learn of the abuse women have endured at the hands of men throughout history. I also started to see and equate this to the *fear* men have always had around the powerful energy of the feminine. I read about the symbolism of the Great Mother, the archetype of the feminine in different cultures, and studied mythology and stories about female deities. Although I found it challenging to connect at an intellectual level, I had a very strong intuitive sense that what I was reading was true. Yet there was so much more about women I didn't know and was still not able to see.

Then, at age 45, I participated in a powerful shamanic ceremony that became one of the most transformative journeys I've ever experienced. It opened my eyes and heart to all that I was missing in this area of my life.

During the ceremony, as the Shamans were singing and beating their drums, I began to experience life regression. At the height of my experience, I saw images of my own birth—the blood and the white floor of the hospital room. It was very strange and powerful, confusing my mind and inner being. As I felt I was losing my sanity, I remember consciously thinking to myself, *How could songs and drums trigger such deep memories in my psyche?*

This was quickly followed in my vision by the decision to live or die. Images of people all around me flashed in my mind's eye, yet no one was paying any attention to me. I had a strong sense of feeling very alone—*ignored*. I wondered, *Could this be how I felt in the incubator?* Madness came over me. At this very moment, a woman sitting nearby brushed my arm, suddenly triggering something very deep inside me: immediately, I understood that the gift of *Life* is given by each and every mother! It was such a profound realization—but exhausted, I could not yet fully embrace it.

During a long silence granted to us by the Shamans, I could finally rest. I savoured the stillness. Then a thought slipped effortlessly into my consciousness: *Life is the most precious gift you can ever receive.* At first, I did not get the deeper meaning of this—it was simply a Truth unfolding, like a butterfly from the cocoon. My <u>mom</u> was the one who gave me the gift of Life! *She* was the one who allowed me to be here!

This revelation transformed me. It wasn't just my mind that understood, but my entire *being*. The trillions of cells in my body all aligned to this realization instantaneously. I saw each woman, each mother, as the medium through which Life manifests itself. Deep gratitude, love and respect toward my mom washed over me. I felt connected to her as never before! I knew from that moment I would now relate with all women differently. Years of fear, protection, anger and mental resistance dissolved.

My eyes opened slowly, and all I saw was a woman in the group approaching me. My arms simply opened naturally at the sight of her beauty, inviting her into an embrace. And I hugged her like I'd never hugged a woman in my entire life. I opened my *whole being* to her.

My inner war with women had come to an end. I was finally at peace. My vision had become clear, and I could see women as they really are: Divine Goddesses that give us the gift of Life. I felt the urge to care for women, to be more gentle and respectful. I saw so clearly how priceless this Life is and that nothing, absolutely nothing, is more valuable.

After that experience, a permanent truce was called between my mom and me. I sent a letter to her in which I listed all the qualities I appreciated about her. I deeply thanked her for the beautiful gift she'd given me. I told her how sorry I was for my part in our suffering—how I had previously misunderstood her and hadn't recognized her own sorrow and pain. That I now understood some of the distress she'd felt in her own life. And for the first time in my life, I shared some of my inner life with her.

As our relationship blossomed, we spoke over the phone. I found I was able to listen to her, to accept her tears and above all, receive her expressions of love for me. I began to share both my profound spiritual experiences and daily banalities, alike. She loved it and often told me how relaxed she felt when I was speaking with her.

From my newfound inner peace, I also saw how much I love my daughter Seghara. I know whatever had or will happen between us, I love her without a single doubt. Even in my moments of anger, frustration or uncertainty, my love for her is the foundation of our relationship, and it's indestructible!

My inner struggle with women has now been replaced with feelings of humility and reverence. I'm becoming more and more aware of the giving, nurturing nature of women, as well as becoming more connected with my own feminine, intuitive self. I have shifted from viewing the feminine as dark and negative to light and life-giving. As my consciousness expands, a deep integration continues between what I experience as the physicality of women and the deep archetype and symbolism of the divine feminine—including Mother Earth and her power.

Recently I went to Haiti with a humanitarian association named Phoenix Vision that helps women heal their traumas and reclaim their self-reliance (in this case, after the 2010 earthquake). When we arrived there, we were teamed up with 10 female Haitians who were trained in trauma-relief. With these courageous women, I witnessed even more evidence of the female strength and connection to Spirit/God. Having lost everything during the earthquake, I never heard these women openly complain about what happened. Like wounded Goddesses giving birth to a new world—a new Haiti—they transformed their suffering as much as they could to empower and serve others. They nourished me with their spirit, inner strength, joy and songs. They helped me awaken even more to the feminine potential inside me, and my heart cracked open.

Given how difficult it was, never would I have imagined my early relationship with my mom could result in me dedicating myself to serving women in becoming more alive and empowered—all sparked by that one single thought: *Life is the most precious gift you can ever receive.*

Thanks, Mom.

CHAPTER 33

We Are One and the Same

by Gabriel Nossovitch

I was born in the Year of the Dragon, the only one in the Chinese zodiac based on a *legendary* creature.

There is little denied these souls. Our birthstone is diamond; our color, gold; our motto, "I reign." I paid no particular mind to the Chinese zodiac, but what had been bestowed upon me by accident of birth did not escape my notice. Everything about my life seemed plucked from a rugged, leather book with silken, gilded pages.

Take my ancestors: Having lost the life of the Aristocracy, my paternal grandparents made their separate and tortuous ways out of Czarist Russia during The Revolution, ultimately building a family and a business on their own merits, first in France, then in Argentina. They established a legacy of vigor and brilliance—forming the palette from which their descendants paint their stories even today.

Likewise, my maternal grandparents (of Italian descent) stretched a canvas which produced a beautiful, passionate woman. She would prove hesitant to spread her own wings, yet unwittingly resigned to riding (and ruffling) the feathers of a patriarch—as fate would have it, *my* patriarch.

I was acutely aware of the legacy that spanned the landscapes of power and resistance, of dominance and demurral, of city mice in spurs and country mice in furs, all with a warm patina of Old World grace. These served as both my blessings and my curse—for although I was granted economic and social privileges, I could not escape the existential questions facing us all. Even while thriving in five languages, living and learning on four continents, and taking economic and social privilege for granted...AND even though blooming in confidence, endowed with a soupçon of passable looks, and a spicy pinch of charisma...I was still genuinely tormented by the questions that surrounded the making of my *own* life and the discovery of my *own* distinctive voice in the Universe. Would the proverbial Dragon have a leg up on getting the answers? Not necessarily.

Unremitting questions began to raise their fiery heads when I was just a child. Chief among them: *Who am I?* That question would lead to everything else I have come to treasure or reject, to all I have conquered or surrendered. Without it—my journey would have been aimless. With it—my path has been illuminated, even in the darkest moments.

My response to that all-important question began with a single critical moment in which the notion "I am" presented itself to me. With my inquisitive and intellectual nature triggered by this simple, yet most profound statement, I used all the knowledge available to me at the time in a vain attempt to bring clear understanding to the very nature of my own mortality. Standing at the crossroads of my life at a very early age, the Truth appeared to spring forth from only one of two options:

1) "I am" is my recognition of my existence as a finite being of flesh and blood. Therefore, if who "I am" will one day end, then whatever I do or become is ultimately irrelevant and has no transcendental purpose. This "I" could only be meaningless.

2) "I am" is an awareness of my infinite nature—a reflection of the energy of creation. And, since "I" will continue to exist beyond this life form, endlessly, then by definition "I" would have no purpose, since purpose is defined by its very finality, its end point.

Given the inescapable and devastating conclusions that were being drawn from this inquiry, I did my best to set aside this dilemma. For I did not want to embrace the inevitable truth that *I did not matter*—yet if I was to move beyond this distraction, how was I to make the most of a rather bum deal?

I needed to come up with a more acceptable solution.

Eventually, another idea surfaced. I posited I must be a *spiritual* being that transcends this one particular human experience. Life on Earth must be nothing but a smaller part of a larger curriculum in which we teach and learn, gathering clues to our evolving consciousness. In the beginning, we forget who we "are" (the price of admission), and consequently recognize who we are *not*. Then, if we are fortunate enough, we come to experience the truth of being human—and in so doing begin to "re-member" ourselves.

Once I fully bought into the concept that I was a being who was taking this human "course," I committed to using my life as a laboratory. At the age of 14, in my first experiment with cultural unfamiliarity, I spent six months in a student exchange program in the United States. I caused quite a stir by regularly breaking the social mold in this arena, but it revealed to me the mere beginnings of a life dedicated to freedom. I came to believe that I could conquer the World if I just did what was really in my heart and trusted my own instincts.

At 20, after completing one year of college, I was off to Japan. I enrolled at Sophia University tending my appetite for the academic, and worked as a French and Spanish instructor at a nearby language academy. Sharing in the Japanese desire to venture beyond their island borders, I joined a group of students on a back-packing tour of China. The year was 1985 and the Chinese were still relatively unfamiliar with foreigners. We were constantly surrounded by people wanting to talk politics or simply stroke our hair or even remark on the whiteness of our teeth! The life-lessons were becoming more and more interesting.

Then, just when I figured I was getting quite good at the game called "making the most of a bum deal," a new thought came to me and took everything to a whole new level. I began to see myself and those around me as characters appearing in a play that was my life—a play I was creating! *I was not only one of the characters in the play, I was the playwright—the author who was revealed in every single character on stage.* What a life-changing thought! It brought with it even *more* freedom, joy, and a desire to go all out—and to enjoy the show, no matter what the plot.

That life could be a script in which I had <u>chosen</u> to play a part led me to the next life-affirming realization: There is no advantage in wasting time questioning the fairness of the challenges or obstacles presented by the scenery, the dialogue, the curtain, the other players, etc. Instead, I must choose to see challenges as opportunities to master my own script, and in doing so, recognize and accept all the inherent responsibilities—as the playwright, the director, the stage designer, the lighting director, the actor. If the "others" on stage are not doing things "to me" but are key characters showing up on the stage, on cue, to provide me with the dialogue I need to grow and expand—then everything that happens is a meaningful contribution to my story, whether positive or negative.

This shift brought with it an awareness of how much light, love and beauty actually surround me. What appeared to be protecting me from pain (defense mechanisms) kept me from fully waking up from the dream and experiencing the next level of joy. *If I kept you and the unique challenges you may offer me in the dark wings of the stage—if I didn't let the light fall on you at center stage, so I might recognize you as having shown up to teach me—and vice versa—then how shall any of us wake up from Act One?* With this thought firmly in place, the journey has never been a dull one.

Am I not part of your play, just as you are part of mine? Same playwright, different show? Different playwright, same show? Perhaps all <u>one</u> play, in which the creative tension demands that none of us know where we are really, not even the alleged Dragons!

You may wonder after reading this if I now say with confidence that I *do* matter. Absolutely not! And yet, as I melt into the relative realms where this show takes place and I continue to surrender to my humanity, I experience how much others matter to me. *I* have brought everything and everyone into my play so that I may awaken from this trance, master this game and bring the curtain down. Every person who shows up is perfectly cast!

So, do I matter? Well, inasmuch as here and now, <u>you</u> my fellow thespian, author, dreamer, student and teacher, <u>you</u> matter to me, then I believe I do, too. And in my life's play, both of us are but mirrors for each other. Mirrors in which we might ultimately see our own reflection and realize once and for all: *we are one and the same.*

That is the thought that changed my life forever. And it continues to do so every day.

CHAPTER 34

I Don't Need to Do Something Today Just Because I Did It Yesterday

by Ocean Bloom

I f you are striving to create the beautiful body you've always wanted or doing your best to maintain something you've worked very hard to achieve, trainers and coaches will tell you to successfully reach your goals you must have *structure* and *consistency*. You must have a clear plan and a routine to follow. You must always know when you will eat your next meal, complete your next work-out, sleep, etc. While all this may be true in the strictest sense—and it's the approach I embraced for most of my life—in the long run, how sustainable is it?

For fourteen years, I made my body my full-time job. I fixated on my physical body *so* much, in fact, it consumed me. As a competitive fitness athlete, I was *hyper*-focused on sticking to my workout routine—even making a living at it! But over time, when I stopped to check-in with my sense of happiness and excitement for life, it simply wasn't there. The truth is, I wasn't really excited about anything, yet I knew I had *every reason* to be full of joy and tremendous gratitude. *Why, then, couldn't I feel it?*

"No Pain, No Gain!" was the motto I lived by. To stay on track, I made choices to ignore other things in life that could bring me fulfillment, like time spent with family and friends or enjoying leisure activities and fun-filled hobbies. I had the blinders on and could only see one aspect of myself—the PHYSICAL BODY in the mirror! Slowly I began to realize how little of my awareness and attention was on my emotional, energetic and spiritual bodies. Although I was celebrating success as a result of my consistent efforts in one specific area, as far as my overall quality of life was concerned, I was not feeling particularly success-*full*.

In North America, we are taught to be thinkers and doers. We've been rewarded, encouraged and given praise for having high intellect, athleticism and beauty. We push ourselves to excel, and sometimes we do *too much* in an effort to achieve success and be accepted. I know I did. But what if the constant "Go, go, go!" is all we know?

As the pace of modern life keeps accelerating, we disconnect more and more from our *essence*, locking our nervous systems in a constant stress-loop. As I'd done, we continuously run around like hamsters on a wheel, looking outside ourselves for happiness and fulfillment. The same tools we use to create our ideals (intellect, athleticism and perfectionism) are also the ones that can serve to catalyze a kind of *madness*.

What are we doing to habituate this neurosis?

After years of trying really hard to achieve more and more, I came to realize how my addiction to a routine was actually creating internal and external suffering in my life. If quality of life was what I was seeking, it was imperative for me to take the time to let my nervous system unwind, to allow the fluctuations of my mind to settle, and to restore a sense of internal equilibrium.

With many personal goals in a career dedicated to competitive fitness already under my belt, I decided to step off the hamster wheel. I actually took some *time off*, and looked forward to being able to revel in a significant sense of relief. I felt empowered, and congratulated myself for making that all-important first step of adopting a new attitude.

Before long, however, I found myself actually yearning for the very structured routine I'd programmed myself to follow during my years of competition:

Eat, Sleep, Train!

I had created such strong beliefs about how my days were supposed to go (based on the years of discipline I'd forced upon myself), I found it incredibly difficult to change this pattern. Although my intention was to move in a new direction—living more balanced and free—the belief systems I'd created were so ingrained in my mind that my desire to feel joy was replaced almost immediately with a feeling of disappointment in myself for not measuring up to some unseen, unrealistic set of expectations associated with being an elite performer. Instead of finding the inner peace I was looking for, I found myself being judgmental, feeling guilty, and blaming myself for not being more motivated and focused.

In the midst of this struggle with myself, I discovered one of the fundamental truths about being human: Even if you have great desire to do so, it's challenging to initiate change when you're trapped under a blanket of under-investigated, unconscious beliefs. Many of us live in this paradox of *functional dysfunction*—although we feel we are performing at a high level, we remain aware that something important is missing, and we are left seeking more.

With this realization firmly in mind, I made a conscious decision: I would start looking at my beliefs, one at a time, questioning their origins. Was it from something that happened a long time ago? Was it given to me by someone else? Or, was it unconsciously taken on from the collective consciousness (or unconsciousness) of the society in which I live? Then I asked a *more* important question:

Which beliefs no longer serve me, and which ones best align with my new attitude and vision?

Adhering to this process of investigation, I recognized that the only way I would be able to move forward and achieve my new goals (including joy, peace and life satisfaction) was to let go of the limiting thoughts and patterns, and embrace the ones that served me best. I needed to integrate positive routines into my present life and leave the rest behind.

On this path to a new experience, I discovered that *self-awareness* would need to be my constant companion—an essential tool in creating the change I so desired. Through this self-awareness, I would use a *new* kind of mirror to look deep inside myself. A regular practice of meditation and yoga became the portal to this conscious mind-body awareness. Once I found I could start separating myself from my routines, it then dawned on me: *I did not need to do something today just because I did it yesterday!* Instead, I could empower myself to choose something else—something new, something expansive, something life-affirming.

By standing back and observing myself and my old beliefs, I've come to embrace the totality of my human-ness. The more I feel myself evolving consciously, the more I experience the holistic nature of this life, realizing the importance of my body, mind, breath *and* spirit. If we are to become balanced human beings, we must respect and integrate all aspects of ourselves, step by step.

I feel so much more alive now! I appreciate everything life brings to me in this present moment. And, the beautiful thing is that it all began with simply a change in attitude. As a result, I now believe that freedom for all of us lies in the possibility of considering our habits from a new perspective, and in doing so, recognizing our often thoughtless repetition. I can summarize this transformation with the idea I constantly remind myself and others, "We are more than our habitual thoughts tell us we are!"

But acknowledging this alone is not enough. When our understanding changes but our routines don't shift accordingly, we only create more suffering and discomfort. At some point, a decision must be made to move both feet in the direction of where we truly want to go. If we have one foot in the present, but the other in the future or past, we will never move anywhere and continue to feel dis-satisfied with our current reality. We must hold space for ourselves and all our emotions, good or bad. We must be a witness of our own thoughts and reactions if we want our limiting beliefs to evolve and transform.

Choose to make decisions, set goals, and structure new routines based on the reality of your life right now—not based on what used to be or who you thought you were. Use the positive tools you've learned along the way and apply them to your next beautiful, cherished reality. When you begin to live your life in better balance, and with more conscious present-time awareness, I guarantee you will also begin to experience the joy and freedom that have been there for you all along.

We are so much more than we were yesterday! Today is a new day, filled with *infinite* possibilities.

CHAPTER 35

It's Not Mine

by Stephanie Bennett Vogt

Wait a minute, what just happened?

The thought that changed my life forever wasn't so much a thought as an awareness that took years to bubble up into my consciousness and then appeared one day as that wondrous question, swiftly followed by, *Is it possible some unpleasant sensations we feel are not even ours?* The implications of a "yes" answer felt radical to me, yet the question was still begging to be explored.

I was sitting on a plane waiting for take-off, feeling very much under the weather. (*Again?*) I still remember thinking: *Didn't I come down with the flu the last time I visited my uncle? And wasn't I sick the time before that?*

Three visits to the same house, three sudden on-sets of the same mystery ailment. This couldn't be a coincidence, could it?

Then a second thought appeared—the thought: *Is it possible the symptoms I'm feeling aren't even mine? But if they're not mine, whose are they? And, why would I take them on and choose discomfort over feeling good instead?*

In my achy, feverish state, I began to connect the dots. I remembered other places that had had similar ill effects on me: The seaside house of a friend in Maine, the office where I worked for sixteen years, and the centuries-old colonial homes in Mexico City where I lived as a child. I remembered the sudden waves of nausea, the pangs of anxiety, and all those mysterious stomach aches that appeared to have nothing to do with what I'd eaten that day.

I also noted it hadn't mattered whether some of these homes were jaw-dropping stunners or their occupants were some of the sweetest people in the World. If there was something energetically funky going on in the space, it seemed I soaked it up like a sponge and took it home with me.

Why me? I wondered. *Can other people feel their spaces, too? Why do I feel really good in some spaces and not so good in others? Why does my uncle's beautiful home in particular make me feel so uncomfortable? Is there a connection to the fact that his first house burned to the ground?*

My inner floodgates opened to a swirl of related questions as I sat waiting on the tarmac of the Dallas Fort Worth Airport; questions I hoped would find their way to rational answers and give me some relief.

The significance of having these insights in an airplane about to take off was lost on me then. I had no idea my "a-ha" moment would launch me on a ten-year hero's journey—a sometimes turbulent flight of self-inquiry, physical challenges, clutter clearing, paradigm shifts, explorations in women's spirituality, and advanced-level study with the world's leading space clearing experts.

In my decade-long journey of discovery, I concluded that our living spaces are not just empty boxes that we fill up with our collections of stuff, life experiences and unique personalities; they are dynamic and alive places that respond directly to our own level of clarity, attentiveness and joy (or lack thereof).

I even found I could consciously tune into and follow the *energetic trails* that people unwittingly leave behind in their spaces by utilizing an ancient technique also used for locating underground water (called *dowsing*). With much practice, I became proficient at "reading" spaces by sensing the energetic residue of what went on there—even if the events had taken place centuries before!

Over time, I began to see how *negative thoughts stick* to our things and our spaces. I learned to identify the specific energy signatures of the more stressful patterns like illness, sudden or violent death, painful divorce, severe depression and financial drain. Using dowsing, I could tell whether the principal cause of a disturbance was coming from the current occupants or previous ones, from above the ground or deep below the earth, from environmental factors or electromagnetic ones. Where there was harmony, love and joy in a space, I could feel the distinct frequencies of those, too. There is no mistaking the clean-burning coherence of energies that feel good!

Each and every one of us is capable of detecting these distinct energies, but when we haven't been taught to tune in, decode and separate our natural reactions from their original cause, it is easy to get lost in the swirl and take the disturbing effects home with us. A headache becomes *my* headache; sadness becomes *my* sadness; worry becomes *my* worry. Without conscious detachment, we personalize all kinds of patterns and perpetuate the endless cycle of imbalance that affects our homes, our lives and our World.

We do not have to *take on* the stress in our environment. Yet, how do we learn to unplug and not identify with it as ours? My answer—which took years to process and accept—is quite simple: Be aware of what you're feeling and be willing to find the truth in it. You will just *know* what is yours and what is not, what is real and what is not. Awareness changes *everything*.

If you watched me walk from room to room with my little dowsing wire, tuning into disturbed "hot spots" and clearing them as I go, you might not see anything and wonder what exactly is happening. As the more intuitive cousin of *feng shui*, space clearing can be profoundly mysterious and unfathomable, sometimes unpleasant or just plain weird. It is a specialized practice of energetic clearing that harmonizes and balances the flow of energy in spaces at very deep levels.

Space clearing, as I practice it, is comparable to acupuncture—the ancient Chinese practice of inserting needles in various points of the human body to increase the flow of energy (chi) in order to restore balance. The one major difference is that in space clearing, the needle I use happens to be <u>me</u>! What I insert into the stressed and contracted areas of our living spaces is a pure, witnessing presence.

Some of the more visible and popular forms of space clearing—like smudging, belling, clapping, toning, praying, placing offerings and sprinkling holy water or salt—derive from ancient spiritual traditions based on the same ideal, which is having harmony with all life. After years of practicing many of these modalities and realizing it was not the "doing" that was changing the energy in a space but the practitioner's personal clarity and state of "be-ing," I revised my approach. I replaced all the various "do-dads" with the one essential tool that was much more portable, and in my experience, infinitely more effective in changing the way our spaces look and feel: the compassionate heart.

You don't need to know how to use a dowsing rod to experience the profound effects of a clearing yourself. Just identify an object or an idea that holds an emotional charge for you. It might be an object of clutter that is hard to release or something familiar that no longer feels "quite right." It could be a painful memory or a difficult relationship. Perhaps it's a bad habit you would like to break. Whether it's a thing or thought, person or place, your job is to simply focus on this item and allow sensations to arise without doing anything to fix, change or manage them.

As you quiet the mind and tune into your feelings, you might experience waves of emotion, shallow breathing, dry mouth, heaviness in your chest, tightness in your temples or any number of physical sensations. Or, you might feel nothing at all. You may pick up some energetic "off-gassing" that may lead to yawning more than usual, feeling tears well up in your eyes or burping. You might catch a whiff of smoke or experience a strange taste in your mouth. You might see an image or download an entire story.

If you can lean into and ride out any discomfort or resistance you feel with innocent curiosity—*remembering that none of these sensations have to be yours*—you might notice the object you are clearing seems a little brighter or the photo of the person with whom you want to heal a relationship looks softer. If you look around the room, you may even notice that everything looks more sparkly, more enlivened, more spacious.

Or perhaps *you* feel different. Maybe your breathing is clearer and less congested or you feel a little lighter—like a ten-pound weight (one you didn't even know you were carrying) has been lifted. To the degree that you don't personalize any of the emotional weather that arises, you are likely to notice the unpleasant sensations pass just as quickly as they came.

Next time you find yourself feeling just fine one minute and utterly exhausted the next, here's your chance to practice awareness. If you experience a pang or a wave of something unsettling or you feel inexplicably nudged off balance somehow, consider that maybe, just maybe, it isn't *you* having a bad day or coming down with something. It could be any assortment of disturbing influences or stuck energies that have been around longer than you have.

It doesn't take much to cultivate detachment. Try it—with a little daily practice of allowing uncomfortable feelings to arise without judging them as good or bad, you might just discover a divine and yummy spaciousness in your home (and life) that gently reveals itself...and can change everything.

CHAPTER 36

What Would Do the Most Good?

by Ted Kuntz

The thought came to me at a very difficult time in my life. My daughter Lani was just moving into her adolescent power. On this particular evening, Lani decided to exercise this power by ignoring her mutually-agreed upon curfew of 10:00pm.

At the time, my life was full of stress and tension as a consequence of having a young son with severe medical challenges. Josh had been neurologically damaged by a routine vaccine shot at five months of age and had developed an uncontrolled seizure disorder. As a result, his mother and I had to deal with his sometimes violent seizures, many times per day. The decision of my fourteen-year-old to disregard her curfew that evening was more than enough to push me over the edge.

I sat in the darkened living room of our home waiting for her return. As the minutes turned into hours, I became increasingly anxious, angry and resentful.

What is she thinking? I ranted in my mind. *How could she do this to her mother and me? Doesn't she know we have enough on our plates with her brother being sick? Doesn't she care?*

I vacillated between confusion and anger, volleying from concern to fear:

What's happened to her? Is she safe? Is she alive?

I conjured up all kinds of stories and images to feed my negativity. With each dark thought, I could feel the rage growing inside me. My mind rambled on with an infinite number of thoughts, questions and condemnations. I imagined all the things I would say and do when my daughter arrived home. Most of the thoughts and actions were painful expressions of my anger, resentment, disappointment and hurt. On and on I raged, a victim of my own emotional hi-jacking.

Suddenly, without any conscious intention on my part, a thought entered my mind. I confess that it was not me who was responsible for this thought. It was too foreign and unfamiliar. It was too unlike me. The thought stood in stark contrast to the uncontrolled venting I was undertaking at the time. With absolute clarity, I heard the following question in my mind:

Ted, of all the things you could do when your daughter comes home, what would do the most good?

I must admit I was caught completely off-guard by the question. In fact, I had never even *considered* this kind of question before. Until that moment, I had lived my life as if I had no choice in the kind of action I might take in highly charged circumstances such as this. I acted as if my behaviour was determined by my emotions. Further, I acted as if my behaviour was fully *justified* by my emotional state. If I was angry, I had a right to express my anger! If I was hurt or disappointed, I had a right to express my hurt and disappointment. Somehow, it was as if my emotions justified whatever actions followed.

As I sat there in that darkened room, I began to consider the question that had been asked of me by some unknown agent. I reviewed the range of actions I might take when my daughter eventually arrived home. And as I considered each action, I held it up to the criteria I had been invited to consider: *Would this action do the _most_ good?*

As I ran through the options in my head, considering the likely consequences of each, it became apparent to me that most of the actions I had spent the evening ruminating on were unacceptable. It became obvious to me that if I were to act on any one of those actions, the already-growing chasm between my daughter and me would widen even further. The pain and despair I was already feeling would only be worsened by my thoughtless responses.

I began to consider other options: I thought of actions based in forgiveness and love. I pondered the possibility of expressing gratitude that my daughter was home safe, rather than resentment over her lack of consideration. I weighed the possibility of acceptance, rather than resistance.

What I also realized was that my current challenge was faced by all parents in times such as this. But what response would I choose now? I began to feel my heart opening to the love I felt for my daughter, rather than responding to the constricting feelings of fear. My heart softened. As I connected with these sensations in my body, I knew my heart was affirming that these more sensible actions would do the most good.

It was literally minutes after I declared my intention to express gratitude, acceptance and love that my daughter came through the door. It was just before 4:00am. The Universe must have been coaching Lani all evening and had finally whispered to her, so only she could hear, "It's time to go home. Your dad is finally ready."

When Lani came into the house, I wrapped my arms around her small adolescent body, hugging her tightly. With as much warmth and sincerity as I could muster, I said, "Lani, I'm glad you're safe, and I'm glad you're home. I love you." I then added, so as not to ignore the transgression that had occurred, "Let's talk about an appropriate consequence in the morning after both of us have had some sleep. Goodnight."

I still remember the look on my daughter's face that evening as I expressed my love and gratitude for her arriving home alive. Lani looked shocked and confused! Responding with her beautiful adolescent humour, she said, "OK, so what did you do with my dad?" While I laughed out loud at Lani's response, at the same time I felt remorse. I knew what Lani must have been saying in her playful way was this was not the dad she was used to. She was familiar with someone who expressed anger, disappointment and fear in moments such as these.

This one experience with my daughter taught me something that will forever be emblazoned in my mind. What transpired that evening, in a rather unexpected way, was an awakening inside me that reinforced my capacity to choose—in each and every moment. Until then, I allowed whatever emotion was the most intense to determine my response. I acted as if I had no choice. I lived my life as a *reactive* being, using my uncontrolled emotions as my guide. Some might say I lived my life as a victim.

Once I received the gift of this thought, I made a silent vow to live my life in a completely different way—to live with choice; to live as a *creative* being; to take responsibility for my actions and my thoughts. In effect, I became "response-able." This evening was the first step in my journey of taking one hundred percent responsibility for my thoughts, emotions and behaviours. It was my first step toward personal mastery.

A lot has transpired since then. Although I have experienced many ups and downs along the way, I realize that now, whenever I am confronted with the challenges that life can present, I choose to pause and consider the thought: *What action of mine would do the most good?* Whenever I take the time to do this, I appreciate the more intentional and thoughtful source of my actions. When I choose to act consciously, I behave in ways that are more caring, loving and positive. As a result, I experience life as an act of constant creation. I experience a more profound sense of ownership of my life, rather than the thought that life is being imposed on me. I get a sense of feeling more human *and* divine than I've ever felt before. And for this, I am deeply grateful.

Can you imagine how our World would be transformed if we *all* lived this way? What if each one of us took the time to pause, especially in times of difficulty, and asked the question: *What action of mine would do the most good?* I feel certain this thought could not only change each one of our lives, but has the potential to change our entire World…forever!

What good will *you* choose?

CHAPTER 37

...i'd rather be seen for who i *am* and be alone... than be accepted for someone i'm *not* and be lonely.

by Brock Tully

In 1970, i[8] was at university in Vancouver. i was in a fraternity, playing varsity football, skipping class as much as possible, drinking excessively and experimenting with different drugs.

Although i was entertaining everyone with my fun and goofy behaviour, i would (unfortunately) sober up and realize i was depressed, lonely and suicidal. The amazing thing was *no one had a clue*. They thought i was very happy and fun-loving, and they had no idea i was just a tremendous actor!

But then i reached my breaking point. i didn't know where the "party me" ended and the "real me" began. It was so exhausting to hold up the façade, always *pretending* i was happy—but i didn't know what else to do. When i was the life of the party, i got fed by all the outward attention. By the next morning, however, i felt like i was starving inside again. A thought began to circle around my head—*maybe the easiest thing might be to just put an end to it all?*

---

8   For over 35 years i have always written "I" as a small "i" — i did that without thought at first, then realized that i personally never liked the big "I" — it represented to me the ego "I", whereas the small, soft, gentle "i" feels like it comes from my heart...in all my *Reflections* books it is the small "i".

But then another thought came to me: *What if i used my athletic ability to serve others instead of just serving my ego?*

So instead of taking my life, i climbed on my 10-speed bicycle, slung a huge canvas pack on my back, loaded on a big sleeping bag and heavy saddle bags, and began to ride. i rode all the way across the northern US to Washington, DC! i didn't know it then, but by doing this, i initiated the "kindness movement" i would eventually dedicate the rest of my life to. Before i could consciously realize what was emerging, it had already unconsciously begun *within* me—it just didn't feel that "kind" to me at first.

During that long journey, i had lots of time alone to think. My thoughts often turned to my wonderful family and how my two older brothers and i were brought up. My parents were very focused on helping their boys become successful—at least by society's terms. A high-paying, respectable job was top of the wish list because it could buy security. Security for them was a big house, a fancy car, and a wife who would take care of us.

Their first two boys lived up to these expectations very well: Brent, the eldest, became a world-renowned astronomer; Blair, next in line, was a deputy minister for the Ontario government. And then there was Brock—a "granola bar jock"—who just loved to play sports, never read books, and was totally unmotivated by money and "stuff." To me, success was enjoying the simple things in life, like bringing people together in laughter and fun.

As i pushed my legs, day after day, i started to realize what i was missing all along and why i was having such addiction issues: Our family never talked about feelings, never hugged, and we never took the time to look into each other's eyes and say, "I love you!" As a young, sensitive boy growing up, i felt a hole inside me that i desperately kept trying to fill. i felt unloved and unworthy. Even though i was popular at school, i thought it was only because of my athletic abilities, not because of who i was inside. The truth under all this was that i was very insecure and self-conscious! I often thought, *What would people think of me if they knew?*

Disconnected from feelings of worthiness, but not ready to die just yet, i'd set out thinking the trip was about me being the first person to ride across North America (this would surely make me feel better about myself!). By the time i finished the trek, however, it was no longer about doing an 18,000 km bicycle trip. For me, it had become all about the 18-inch journey from my head back to my heart! Slowly but surely, kilometre after kilometre, i was becoming more reconnected with the *real* me...

And i was connecting with others, no matter where i went. The cycling trip continued from Washington, DC all the way down the East Coast to Florida. i even trekked through the scary South (Mississippi, Texas, Louisiana) during the Vietnam War, the racial riots and the Hippie movement. This was followed by a lengthy figure-eight: Mexico to Central America and back up to the United States. Unfortunately, my journey ended as suddenly as it began with an emergency operation on my rear end (a real "bummer!"). In the end (go ahead, laugh) it didn't matter—i was already a changed man because the true journey back to my heart was complete.

Ironically, the skills i'd used when pretending to be happy and becoming popular at school were the same ones i used to find my *true* self. As i enlisted my athleticism to ride thousands of kilometres, my thoughts and my mind were being used to develop a completely new attitude! No longer would i ever consider *taking my life*—all that mattered now was how i could *give with my life*!

Reconnecting with my heart was the key.

i realized whenever i was in my head and full of fear, i thought things like marks, trophies, money and relationships were going to "make" me happy. As i rode, i let go of those ideas. i realized instead that i *am* happy when i stay in touch with my heart—joy comes from loving the things i do, no matter what they are!

Following this incredible *life-saving* journey, i wrote the thought that captures the essence of what i learned over those many months on the road:

> **...i'd rather be seen**
> **for who i am**
> **and be alone...**
> **than be accepted**
> **for someone i'm not**
> **and be lonely.**

i realized *why* i had been SO incredibly lonely as a young man. Even though i was surrounded by many beautiful people, i was following their expectations of who i was for *them*—or who they wanted and needed me to be—instead of following the deep, beautiful voice i had inside.

i know this is the same voice inside <u>all</u> of us. It is this voice in our hearts that brings us together—as *one*.

When i chose to take a stand to be myself—even if that meant being alone—it actually brought me *closer* to others, more deeply and beautifully than ever! Now, i use my voice to inspire others to know that happiness comes from following their heart—and that when they act from that place, kindness comes naturally. It really can change the world!

i am grateful for my parents, too, and what they taught me, both consciously and unconsciously. Although their values and choices were so different than mine, that difference helped me appreciate myself for who i truly am. With the lessons i learned through our relationship, i realize i can either feel like a victim or i can become a more understanding and compassionate human being.

As i set out on my bicycle trip, i felt rejected because my parents threatened to disown me. But many, many years later, i found out my dad would go to the golf club with his buddies, pull out a map, and show them all where i was each week—for six long months! It turns out my parents were just rejecting what seemed like crazy, grandiose ideas—not ME. They were actually very proud of me!

Because of my journey, i reflected upon how all parents love their kids the best they can—even though for mine it was expressed mainly through money and gifts. It wasn't until my brother passed on that i saw more clearly how they would give their lives for any of us—in an instant—if it meant one of their kids could live instead. How can anyone's love be greater than that? i've only witnessed this in a few people in my lifetime, and they truly inspire me: Gandhi, Martin Luther King and Winnie-the-Pooh. Pooh, in particular, represents forgiveness, innocence and being in the moment. These are the *keys* to kindness!

For me, true happiness appears when we move out of ourselves and into service, when we consistently think about being kind to others, and do what is in the best and highest good for all. When we take a stand to be alone in our fullest, truest expression, we can ultimately learn we are never alone…because we are ALL ONE.

i will be forever grateful that i had the courage to listen to my heart, and even more importantly, to take action and follow it!

CHAPTER 38

What I See, I Can Be

by Dr. Derek Porter

I remember it like it was yesterday—as clichéd as that sounds. It was a beautiful, sunny, *calm* morning. I say calm because to a rower that is a *very* important detail. Weather is always key when you are sitting in (perhaps more accurately, sitting *on*) a 35-foot boat that's little more than 12 inches wide! Such is the life of a rower.

Truth be told, I was not *much* of a rower at the time. I'd started out on this new athletic journey when I joined the novice team in my first year of undergraduate studies at the University of Victoria. Now into my second year of rowing, the early advantages of being 6'5" and having natural athletic ability were par for the course, so I duly focused on learning the subtle nuances of the rowing stroke to develop a competitive edge.

To the outside eye, rowing looks simple enough. Most of us can picture a rowing shell skimming effortlessly across a lake or river in the wee hours of the morning, the fog rising gently off the glassy surface, loons calling in the distance and the long, sleek oars entering and exiting the water in perfect rhythm…

Or is that just my romantic notion of rowing?

The truth is, like most sports, rowing is a lot harder than it looks. I often reflect on my fifteen-year career and marvel at how much time, energy and focus I invested in one seemingly simple movement. As I sought to perfect the rower's stroke, I realized *the more I knew, the more I needed to know.* It was a passionate and humbling journey, where I came to learn more and more about less and less.

On that particular morning, I was sitting in a "pair" (two oarsmen with one oar each) at the entrance to the channel connecting the two main areas of the lake we trained on. We were slowly turning the boat around preparing for the next workout piece while our coach talked to us about some technical point we were working on. The morning sun was rising behind us. At that exact moment, another pair being propelled by two Canadian National Team athletes hummed by us in perfect synchrony—blades coming out of the water simultaneously with utter precision, their body movements driven by some invisible connection, as if one person was moving in two places—exactly how rowing should look.

As they passed, something caught my eye and completely captivated my attention, freezing this moment in time: The bowman's oar emerged from the water at the finish of the stroke right beside me, and I sat there mesmerized as the blade was liberated, pushing sternward a puddle of quietly gurgling, swirling, whitewater. The puddle seemed to float across the surface like a water bug, creating a few concentric rings on the water before dissipating into the flatness of the surrounding lake. With that one stroke, the boat glided by effortlessly, and after a few more, was out of sight. A beautiful example of the transcendent grace of rowing.

I was hooked. From that moment forward, this timeless image served as the technical focus for the development of my own rowing stroke: *Extract my blade from the water that cleanly—that perfectly—and I too can row on the National Team!* When I envisioned that image with me inside it, I somehow knew it was possible.

And so began my singular dedication to becoming a world class rower. Wherever I was, whether participating in events at clubs, universities or regattas, it was that sole image emblazoned in my mind that consistently served as the motivation to keep pressing forward to my goal.

My decision to pursue a career in rowing was not unlike many decisions: when they are *right*, they don't seem like decisions at all. I made a commitment to do whatever it took to make it onto the Canadian National Team, to compete at the World Championships, and eventually, the Olympics. I had my fair share of ups and downs (also par for the course), but since I'd committed to myself with a clear goal (even though it seemed lofty), obstacles were never deal-breakers, just mere hiccups along the path. It became natural for me to push through, my goal always kept in plain sight, driven by desire and a laser-like focus.

Anchored by my image of the perfect rowing stroke, within two years of that fateful morning I *did* qualify for the National Team, and over the next two years, I won 10 National Championships, 4 World Championship medals and 2 Olympic medals—one silver and one gold. This was my path, set in motion by that one magical image.

Similarly, I believe we *all* have a path. This does not mean our way forward is set in stone—rather this path serves to guide us and focus us toward our *potential*. I believe we all have greatness within us, but not all of us find the way to expand and express it in the World. Like all things worthwhile, however, you have to find that something special within you that wants to come out; then nurture it to fruition.

It was that snapshot in my mind of that perfect moment on the lake that ignited the thought—*that same perfection is possible in my life*—and led me to set the lofty goal of being a National Team rower. Thoughts alone, however, could not create the results I envisioned for myself. It was my *actions*—repeated over and over, day in and day out, over the many years of the course I'd set forth that *galvanized my vision* into my physical reality. What a difference one thought can make!

The power of a thought can be the magnet to which specific, powerful action can attach itself. For me, that puddle skimming across the surface of the water stood for so many things: focused desire, tireless efforts, technical mastery and a commitment to creating grace of movement. The image of the blade coming out of the water propelled me to *want to get there* no matter what it took. And, I knew it would <u>only</u> come with a lot of hard work!

It has been said, if you define your goals, you are 80% more likely to achieve them. Yet, less than 1% of people ever do! Most of us never set goals for our lives, effectively sailing along on a rudderless boat. Try answering the following questions: Do *you* have goals? What do you want to achieve in this lifetime? Is there a legacy you want to leave behind? When your life is over, what would you want others to say about you?

If you really want to achieve something, announce it to all those who will listen! At the very least, announce it to yourself—write your goals down in black and white. It may not be easy to establish this degree of clarity, but it isn't difficult either. Most of us don't get around to it because we think we're too busy. Are you *really* too busy to plan your life? Are you truly too busy to be the architect of your own powerful existence?

I don't believe everybody can do *everything*, but I do believe that everyone can do *something* very well. The trick is finding that something you *love* to do and seeing how far you can take it. At the outer reaches of your ability is where real growth begins—where the true magic of life happens. These are the moments you look back on your life and say, "Yes, I laid it on the line!", "I pushed the envelope!" or "I really couldn't have done more!"

This is living your life without regrets.

When we are truly on purpose, there seems to be an ease to the way things unfold. Mihaly Csizksztentmihalyi called it "flow" in his book *Finding Flow–The Psychology of Engagement With Everyday Life* (Basic Books, 1998). If your life seems like a struggle, you are almost certainly not on your path of effortless flow. Perhaps there's something just waiting for you to see—closer than you think...

To this day, I see that image of the rowers whisking by, showcasing the elegance of that perfect stroke. I can't help but think about the lasting effect of a single ripple— like the one left by the blade of those National Team rowers. Every day, we are all casting pebbles into the water with our thoughts, feelings and actions—creating concentric ripples that can go on forever. Each one begins gently but can ultimately grow to move mountains of water. As one of the founders of my chiropractic profession once said:

> *You never know how far-reaching something you think, say or do today, will affect the lives of millions tomorrow.*
> — **B.J. Palmer**

That one image created a powerful ripple in my mind—shifting my thoughts and actions, and ultimately changing the path of my life forever. Never underestimate the power of a single thought to dramatically alter your future: with persistence, dedication and a passion for your vision, anything is possible!

CHAPTER 39

I Am Not Bad.

by Reverend Bruce Sanguin

Before I entered therapy, if you'd asked me if I was bad, I would have thought it a strange question. I had a couple of degrees and a good job; I was an accomplished athlete and a spiritual leader; I enjoyed healthy self-esteem; I was "normal" by any contemporary psychological standards. The reason I went to see a psychotherapist was not that I felt like a bad person—I was grieving. My recent decision to end my marriage also carried with it the consequence of being separated from my two-year-old daughter by 1500 miles.

I chose a body-oriented school of therapy to find relief. In these sessions, I found that my body expressed grief by curling into a fetal position. I was being guided by a skillful and loving therapist, but I'd hide my face from her whenever I regressed to a very early time in my life when I experienced profound shame. This was unexpected.

To feel shame is to feel like a *sham*. Needs, wants and impulses get internalized as invalid and out of place. At a pre-verbal level, it felt like the very fact I'd shown up in the universe at all was *wrong*. I did not fit in—it was all a big mistake. More to the point, *I* was a mistake.

This experience repeated itself over quite a few sessions. But then, in one particular session, a *protest* began to arise from deep within me. I turned my full face toward my therapist and looked into her eyes. The words that voiced that inner protest were simple and life-altering:

"I am not bad."

They seemed to emanate from a place I can only associate with my *soul*. This far exceeded looking into a mirror and parroting positive affirmations to try to convince myself of something I didn't actually believe. This was my *soul's* proclamation, my way of letting the Universe know I'd come for a reason. I was worthy, delightful, and my needs and wants were *not* bad. My soul's voice had been recruited as an active ally in my journey back to health, wholeness and the enjoyment of intimacy. A quality of *presence* arose in me, and I began showing up for life in a new way.

I wonder how many of us construct our world out of an unconscious assumption that we are (in one way or another) bad? For unless these assumptions become conscious and then corrected, we will unknowingly remain imprisoned by the "small self's" futile attempts to prove to the world that we are worthy. *Futile* because when we labour under the belief of our "badness," the proof of our *worthiness* can never hold. We will find ourselves mysteriously sabotaging our own success. We will find fault with our intimate partners and create elaborate stories to justify our perceptions. We will experience an overwhelming urge to *exit* relationships at the very moment they are becoming most intimate. Ultimately, we will thwart the promise of our one precious life—all to avoid the shame of being unmasked as "bad."

Unconscious shame explains, in part, some people's attraction to fundamentalist Christianity. This approach is premised on the doctrine of "original sin"—that we are each born into the world deeply flawed. While not *actually* true, it can *feel* true because it resonates with our unconscious shame. Following this "logic," once we accept our badness, we are then offered the solution: the unconditional love of God—which is actually *conditional* upon our believing that Jesus died for our "sins."

This rather gruesome condition (of having to accept that God executed his son for *me*) is also strangely compelling: Jesus takes on my essential "badness," and I am *liberated*. This liberation can actually be felt for a time, but under stress, we eventually default to the original, unconscious assumption that's much more powerful than this temporary solution: *It is me who is flawed.*

What's the remedy?

I'm afraid there are no shortcuts when it comes to repairing and evolving the self. Harvard psychologist Robert Kegan's classic text, *The Evolving Self: Problem and Process in Human Development* (Harvard University Press, 1983), tracks the maturation of our "self-sense" through every stage of human development. At each stage, a "holding environment" (first mother, then both parents, then family, then school, the workplace, etc.) either facilitates or blocks our evolution. The three functions of these environments are: 1) *holding*—signaling "this is a safe environment to identify with," 2) *letting go*—signaling "my need to differentiate is good," and 3) *challenging*—signaling "it's time to move on." Each of these holding environments is a potential source of shame.

For example, when I was in high school, I arrived one morning and was marched down to the lunchroom where I was asked to complete a series of tests. I wasn't particularly interested in the tests and didn't know what they were for. Rather than focusing on answering the questions properly, I just figured the sooner I finished, the sooner I could get to the basketball court. It turned out they were IQ tests! A few weeks later, when the guidance counselor called me in to discuss the results, he outright told me I should consider manual labour as a career. I left with the belief *I'm not smart enough* indelibly etched in my mind.

In this experience, the particular holding environment called "school" failed me. Even after two degrees, academic scholarships and four books, I still catch myself defaulting to this negative belief at times. When these kinds of beliefs remain unconscious, we will find ways to prove they are correct with our unconscious behaviours—over and over again. Each time this happens in *me*, I depend on my soul to rise *above* and sound a protest in support of my intellectual capacity.

These unconscious beliefs not only create personal tragedy, but result in a loss of *universal creativity*. For the self is not merely personal—it's the *personalized form* of 13.7 billion years of universal evolution! We are the manifestation of the *heart of the Cosmos* rising up out of the material universe with its impulse for increased complexity, unity and consciousness. This is expressing itself in each one of us! We tend to think of the self as a discrete and separate entity. But it's not a thing, and it's not separate. It's the evolutionary *process* showing up *as* each of us. This means that the self is meant to continue evolving just as the Universe continues to evolve. The self enjoys the same "blessed unrest"[9] as the entire Universe in its desire to realize deeper and expanded potentials.

Therefore, we *have* a personal self, yet our *being* is more than that personal self: we are personal *plus*. The "plus" is the transpersonal Self—I call this the "Cosmic"

9   Martha Graham (choreographer/dancer): "No artist is pleased. [There is] no satisfaction whatever at any time. There is only a queer divine dissatisfaction, a blessed unrest that keeps us marching and makes us more alive than the others." *The Life and Work of Martha Graham* by Agnes de Mille (Random House, 1991).

or "Universal Self." To awaken to this dimension of ourselves is to discover we are each an immense centre of creativity. We realize that we are concentrated amalgams of every physical form and intelligence that's ever come into being since the "Big Bang." In fact, we're what the Big Bang looks like after 14 billion years of shape-shifting!

In the Cosmic Self, *natural* selection becomes *actual* selection. We gain the capacity to consciously select a preferred future, both individually and collectively—with our thoughts, intentions and actions. This expanded Self wants to take full responsibility for the realization of that future as an expression of itself. Doing so is a source of deep joy, an ecstatic privilege—not a burden, as some might see it. We are *vocationally aroused*[10] to bring forth a new humanity in service of our one Earth community.

Until we make this fundamental shift in identity from personal self to Cosmic Self, we will not have the clarity of consciousness or the spiritual energy required of our species to contribute to collective evolution at this juncture in Earth's history. Instead, our creativity will be chronically in service to the projects of the small self and the limiting, unconscious beliefs that keep us in a contracted state. Unconscious beliefs like "I am bad", "I am stupid", "I am helpless" and "I am alone" are not only untrue, they present stumbling blocks for the realization of our Universal Self.

The practice for releasing yourself from these beliefs is simple, but not easy. It requires that you bring awareness to your *reactive* behaviours, thoughts and feelings. When an innocent comment from a friend feels to you like a personal assault, you can be pretty sure that a core negative belief has been triggered. By bringing this into your consciousness, you can first take responsibility for your reaction, and then recruit the authentic protest of the soul—thereby liberating your Universal Self to be of service to this precious Earth community.

As we embrace our authentic identity as the presence of the whole Universe consciously evolving, we will eventually learn to take it all less personally. We will gain the capacity to witness our early evolutionary instincts for sex, security, sustenance and status as good and necessary—but will not identify with them. Rather, we will come to identify with the transcendent *spiritual* instinct to be of service to a higher purpose—the evolution of the Universe's capacity for love, compassion and justice.

And this is *good*.

---

10   Barbara Marx Hubbard: "Vocational arousal is the Universal Self's equivalent of sexual arousal in our biologically-based self. With seven billion people on the planet, it is vocational arousal and not sexual arousal that is the key to the emergence of a new order of humanity." www.barbaramarxhubbard.com.

SECTION IV

AS ME

*God is a metaphor for that which transcends
all levels of intellectual thought. It's as simple
as that.*

— Joseph Campbell

CHAPTER 40

A New Name, A New Way of Being

by Reverend Sophia Ducey
(formerly Mary Kay Lutz/Hornick/Ducey)

When asked, "Why did you change your name?" the answer I give is, "Actually, it changed <u>me</u>."

Many of my friends and family wondered if I'd *lost it* when I announced I was thinking of changing my name. But they were just getting the tail-end of a profound journey for me.

Perhaps a little personal history might provide some valuable context for this life-changing decision:

I grew up in southern California in a family that chose its church by the vibrancy of the youth program (good criteria if you ask me!). This resulted in me attending a Presbyterian church where, as a teen, I tried to follow in Jesus' footsteps, learning the attitudes and behaviors of being a "good" Christian.

When I could not get a satisfactory answer about why the supposedly "geographically undesirable" people of Africa and Asia would go to Hell based on where they were born and because they had not been exposed to the life and teachings of Jesus, I chose to become part of the "un-churched" for the next 14 years.

After this time of feeling "spiritual but not religious," I discovered the *New Thought Movement*. Specifically, I connected with Religious Science and learned about "the Law"—the subjective, impersonal, creative aspect of God. This new understanding allowed me to participate in co-creating my life with the divine presence of the Universe.

What followed was an amazing journey of becoming an ordained minister in that tradition, studying and learning to embody the Universal Truths of various faiths and philosophies, and endeavoring to integrate my understanding of "new science" into the realm of spirituality. The teachings were indeed powerful for me, and a new foundation was laid within for further explorations of ever-evolving approaches to life and God.

Yet, in the summer of 2008, I began questioning every aspect of my life, including my concepts of God, my call to ministry, and my marriage. During this time, I read a quote about God by Eva Bell Werber:

> **You have now had it shown to you that I AM CAUSE, and I AM ABSOLUTE.**
> **These terms seem cold and hard at times,**
> **but when you have fully mastered them, made them part of your life,**
> **you will know that I AM warm, vibrant and lovely within you…**
> **Go now and carry the sweetness and warmth of MY PRESENCE with you.**

I yearned to have the experience of this comforting Presence with me and within me. I began to meditate on this quote and explore it with my spiritual counselor and breath-worker. In a beautiful transcendent moment, this "warm, vibrant Presence" came to me in the form of Divine Wisdom—Sophia.

My first experience with the Divine Sophia was in Ukraine four years earlier. During that trip, I was overcome by the grace and glory that emanated from her in a beautiful mosaic in the Cathedral in Kiev. When her image re-entered my consciousness in 2008, the energy was palpable. Sophia became my constant companion during that season of deep pain and hard choices. I experienced her around me, with me and within me. Even in the darkest of moments, when I felt her Presence, I was comforted.

As we journeyed together, I felt called to *be* Sophia. It felt as if she were "claiming" me as one of her expressions in the world. As I contemplated adopting her name for myself, the "Mary Kay" that still existed within me needed an explanation, a reason and a greater understanding about this change. So I researched everything I could about people who changed their names, as well as the myths, stories, teachings and texts about Sophia. I had a few name analyses done and meditated on Sophia. I explored all kinds of combinations of my old and new names. And then something magical happened: I simply…*surrendered*. After all the musings and machinations, Sophia gently guided me to just *let go*.

It's not that I'd spent my life feeling discontented with my birth name. I just didn't feel like I was Mary Kay anymore. Hearing that name spoken by me and others or signing it on documents felt incongruent.

Changing my name was an opportunity for rebirth—a chance to discover my True Self. As I contemplated the meaning of the name, I found myself starting to embody its qualities and vibration—and this began to slowly change my life. Divine feminine wisdom, creativity, compassion and generosity started flowing through me with more and more ease—and I was so grateful to both embrace and be embraced by this new identity.

Shortly after I'd adopted my new name, I began the process of consciously and fully expressing it in my life. This included a powerful experience as a client in an Integral Coaching program. In one of the practical exercises, my coach worked with me to identify a metaphor describing my *"Current Way of Being"* as well as my desired *"New Way of Being."* Just as I could imagine how my *current* metaphor would respond to a particular situation vs. my *new* metaphor, I realized I could also ask myself, "How would Mary Kay respond to this situation?" vs. "How would Sophia respond?" I was fascinated to discover there were *clearly* things Sophia would do that Mary Kay definitely did *not* feel comfortable doing.

As I began to see my *current way of being* more clearly, I came to appreciate both its strengths (which I wanted to integrate as I evolved *my new way of being*) and its limits (which I wanted to release). The same was true for Mary Kay and Sophia— some things in the way Mary Kay showed up in the world no longer served me and were ready to be released, while others were parts of me I cherished and wanted to bring into my new way of being Sophia.

The life changes that have resulted from embracing myself as Sophia have had to be integrated not only cognitively, but also on an emotional, somatic, spiritual, moral and interpersonal level. This has been a continuous journey of consciously awakening, practicing, falling asleep—only to awaken anew and begin again. In this process, many things have been revealed to me—not the least of which are many of my own inner gifts.

How often do *you* stop and wonder, "What are *my* gifts that were known before I was born and that are emerging in and *as* my life?" Or, "What was I consecrated to *be and do* in this precious life I've been given?" Most of us live our lives day-in and day-out without such questions looming in the forefront of our consciousness, yet I believe they are latent within each one of us, just awaiting our attention. We may experience them in the form of a deep longing—that "divine discontent" that asks for something different or something *more*. As we spend time in quiet contemplation—going to the mountain tops of our consciousness to see what Spirit is revealing to us—we open ourselves up to a "higher idea" of our lives and the gifts that are waiting to be expressed.

This is what allowing myself to be changed by Sophia has done for me. As I use my new name, as I hear it spoken from me and to me, I am reminded to live as my True Self—full of Divine Wisdom. And while you may not have a mystical experience that inspires you to change your name or to embody a new way of being, I believe we are *all* called to experience and express our True Selves at some point in our life.

Whatever your gifts, you must be willing to open up and listen to Spirit's whisper and then give your sacred *Yes!* to that longing in your heart that says, "Be true to Me!"

I recently bought *Tinkerbell's True Talent* (LeapFrog™) for my little friend named Miracle Sophia. The summary on the back jacket caught my eye:

> **"Read along in this magical tale, as Tinker Bell discovers
> that *being true to herself* will take her furthest of all."**

Changing my name opened up a powerful well-spring of my own heart's potential that I otherwise may never have discovered, and brought me to an even truer sense of myself. I have also found a way to re-integrate my religious roots through some new branches: evolutionary Christian mysticism, the Wisdom teachings and Anthroposophy. For all this, I am eternally grateful, for it has given me a whole new vision for my life—and along with it, the experience of a warm, comforting God, with me and within me.

I leave you with this prayer, one that came to me after writing this chapter:

May we each be True
To that which was consecrated AS our lives
Before we were born.
May we open to the reasons we are here:
Our Gifts. The Highest Idea for our Life.
Spirit's yearning for expression.
May we live in Trust,
That as we share our gifts,
As we answer the call of Spirit,
There is a power that is always present in our Yes.
A Power that is with us,
In us,
And as us.
Always.
And in all ways.

CHAPTER 41

The Universe Plans Better Than You

by Nina Talley-Kalokoh

Dear Ella,

I know we've had many conversations about how Life can surprise you with circumstances that are challenging and even down-right scary sometimes. You and I share a similar habit—attempting to control what is happening to us by over-planning events and circumstances. Some might think it's a silly pattern, but *we* know it has brought us a sense of safety when facing the unknown. We do this so we won't be overwhelmed with fear of what we do not know or understand.

When you asked me about my experience in Africa and how it came to be that without planning a single event I ended up meeting dignitaries, successful female leaders and even my future husband, I was tongue-tied. Instead of describing these events as chance circumstances that occurred by fate, I should have described to you the deep internal shift in my thinking that occurred months before. I'd like to share that story with you now, in hopes it will open up a space for you to consider the possibility that our thinking has an impact on our lives. I believe the more conscious we are of this, the more amazing our lives can become.

My story begins in the winter of 2004. I had just moved back to my parents' house after graduating college because I couldn't find a job (a frustrating blow to a 22 year old's sense of freedom). After a few months of working two hourly-paid jobs, I realized what I really wanted was to travel abroad. A friend suggested I apply to the Peace Corps. I wasn't enthused about this idea because I was morally opposed to organizations that usurped the term "peace" when their actual philosophy and activities were structurally and traditionally violent. (At the time, my studies of Conflict Transformation informed me of a very different approach to peace than the politically influenced activities of Peace Corps volunteers.)

Despite this attitude, I ended up applying to Peace Corps to appease my parents (who viewed it quite rationally as the safest way to work abroad). I also researched and applied to other organizations doing similar work but who were taking an approach and philosophy more in alignment with my values—like The Mennonite Central Committee (MCC). No, I'm not Mennonite, I'm not even Christian, but what I found in the way the MCC operated (and in my conversations and friendships with many Mennonites since I was younger) was that they were less interested in sharing the story of their religious doctrine as they were in the principals of it: compassion, justice, collaboration, empathy and love. Their concept of peace—an active power of spiritual and social well-being and connection to God—was something that aligned more closely with my heart.

After applying, I began my daily routine of affirmative prayer and intention about being accepted into the program. I visualized myself making a difference: working with religious leaders in Africa, conducting trainings on conflict resolution, sharing my spiritual perspective, and learning the stories I never heard in the U.S. (about Africa's diverse history, as well as the traditions and languages that didn't come from Europe). In my mind's eye, I saw the land; in my heart, I felt its beauty and ancient wisdom. I was confident I would get there.

As it turned out, things didn't go as I imagined. Surprise, surprise! Although I was accepted to Peace Corps and MCC, my strong preference to work with Muslim and Christian religious leaders in eastern Nigeria alongside the MCC was denied. The explanation I received after weeks of probing was that my youth and gender were less than ideal qualifications for this extremely delicate, inter-religious project.

After reading the letter, I stormed outside and ran—and kept running until the cramps and tears forced me to stop. I wondered out loud to God how this could have happened when I was so sure about what was meant for me! The only response I heard was the cool March breeze weaving through newly-budded tree branches and annoying blue jays singing their spring songs. I fell on the brown-green grass and stared up at the sky, dotted with clouds. Any other time, I would have thought it a perfect day. But I was angry and only saw what was missing: my confidence in prayer.

Literally a week later, I was sitting in a staff meeting at work when my boss announced that a guest scholar would be joining us in the office for the next few weeks. The scholar was planning a Homecoming Trip for an African American woman from South Carolina to the place where her great-great-great-great-great-great grandmother (yes, that's seven generations) was sold as a 10-year old off the coast of Sierra Leone. My ears perked up at hearing the country, as my college roommate was from Sierra Leone, and we'd spent many late nights talking about the politics, music and food of that amazing place. My boss asked me to stick around after the meeting. She knew about my desire to travel to Africa and about my recent disappointing news with the MCC.

"I've already planned for you to meet him," she said, before I could even ask. "He needs some assistance formatting some images and writing up some project descriptions, and I've volunteered you to help out with that."

Still dazed, all I could come up with was a simple "Thank you." I was immediately looking forward to doing *any* work that had something to do with Africa. It was leaps and bounds more interesting than mundane office filing and coordination. I felt a flutter of hope that this could turn into something more.

While my logical mind was hesitant to get excited about the possibility, my spirit whispered that this was my dream. And, in the days that followed, I prayed that whatever happened would be good. A thought occurred to me that I didn't really need to have it planned ahead of time—that the Universe/Spirit/Source/God knew what would be best for me. I found a sense of peace in those prayers. I experienced a deep feeling of relief that I didn't have to plan. It might actually be fun to be surprised! I've been planning my life since I was eight. This was the first time I considered the possibility that I didn't have to have all the answers.

As this realization became clearer and clearer, my hope about traveling got stronger. In the weeks that followed, the scholar-in-residence invited me to come to Sierra Leone on the Homecoming Trip he was planning. My boss secured university funds to pay for my flight, and in return I wrote about my experience for the university magazine—as an African American in Africa for the first time. A friend from college convinced her sister and brother-in-law to host me in their home for the entire trip, securing my housing needs. Once I arrived in Sierra Leone and decided to stay longer, the scholar introduced me to a renowned female leader who offered me a paid internship that covered all my additional expenses. While planning a major conference for Muslim and Christian leaders (did you notice that I had hoped for this earlier?), I met a young French interpreter who I later fell in love with on the dance floor of the city's beloved night club—and married a year later in Oakland, California.

I don't feel that I can take credit for any of the events that took place leading up to my time in Sierra Leone. Not in the usual way that one takes credit for producing or organizing something. I didn't worry about finding funds for my $2,000+ airfare. I didn't research the country's political history to try and work for the first woman who ran for President. I didn't search out hotspots so that I would go dancing at one of the few clubs that locals and ex-patriots dance together. I simply followed my intuition that Spirit would provide—and It did.

There are probably a number of thoughts we should change about our lives to invite in more confidence and joy. For me, however, shifting out of my deep-seated belief that planning was the *only* way to make things happen just right has freed me beyond anything I could have imagined! It has opened me up to the idea of focusing on qualities I want to experience in my life: peace, health, joy and love. Praying for more abundance in all areas feels a lot different than asking God to pay my rent. And when I focus on abundance, I receive a lot more than just a single check.

Ella, the challenges you are facing can also be perceived as opportunities to lessen the need to control your life circumstances. This shift alone has truly changed my life forever, and it has magnificent potential to transform your life, too! I look forward to celebrating with you, the amazing manifestations you have yet to create!

Always with love,

Nina

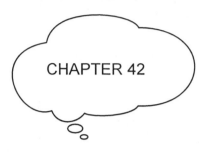

It Doesn't Matter What You Do: Just Make Sure It's Something You're *Passionate* About

by Sean Aiken

My toes creep over the edge of the metal bridge to which I'm attached by only a thick elastic bungee cord.

How did I get into this situation? I think to myself.

Oh yeah, passion, I nervously admit, trying to build up the courage to step off the perfectly safe bridge. *To find a career I love. Gotta try new things. Gotta take the leap.*

The bridge spans a river canyon. I glimpse towards the mountains on either side covered in old-growth forest and rugged basalt column cliffs. For a moment, I forget my current reality, lost in appreciation for the beauty that surrounds me.

The countdown of the cheering crowd (that wants nothing more than to see me jump) jolts me back to the task at hand. I peer past my toes. The river, 160 feet below, eagerly awaits my descent.

I gaze behind me at the energetic crowd, smile, and give a "thumbs-up." Then I turn back to the raging river below, take a deep breath, and check my harness one last time.

I've put this off much too long, I think to myself. *Ready or not, it's time to take the leap.*

Two years earlier, I'd struggled with a different leap.

Having recently graduated with a Business Administration degree from Capilano University, I found myself tormented by the ultimate question:

"What should I do with my life?"

I scoured various job-posting boards and flipped through newspaper classifieds. All the different industries and ambiguous job titles sounded cool enough, but I had no clue what the jobs would actually be like.

I thought back to the advice my dad gave me in my senior year at university: "Sean, it doesn't matter what you do, just make sure it's something you're passionate about. I've been alive for nearly sixty years and have yet to find something I'm passionate about besides your mother."

Sage advice we often hear, but what we don't get is *how* we can find our passion.

We hear people complaining about their jobs, working for the weekends, and becoming numb to the possibilities of life (and the moment) along the way. In today's economy, most are happy to simply *have* a job. But whether we are in dire *or* prosperous economic times, how do we find a career we can love?

I've learned that oftentimes a leap is required.

Not many jobs require we jump off a 160-foot bridge attached by an elastic cord, but in order to find a career that we are truly passionate about, some significant concessions are definitely required. We must be willing to step outside our comfort zones, take risks, and try new things. We must be willing to jump—not just think about it.

But where do we start? Where should *I* start?

I gave it some thought, and then came up with an ingenious plan: instead of pressuring myself into committing to one job, why couldn't I try many different jobs over a one year timeframe? It just might work! I called it the *One-Week Job Project.* My goal: To work 52 jobs in 52 weeks to find something I was passionate about—to help prevent me from getting stuck in an occupational rut *now* that I would find difficult to get out of *later.*

It was the first day of my first job that I found myself about to leap off that bridge as a bungee jump operator at *Whistler Bungee* in Whistler, British Columbia.

During the 52 weeks that followed, I trekked more than 46,000 miles, slept on 55 couches, raised over $20,000 for charity, and tried every job I could: baker, teacher, real estate agent, advertising executive, Hollywood producer, NHL mascot, radio DJ and more. Wherever I could line up work, I'd go there, find a couch to crash on, and immerse myself in whatever profession was at hand. Then I'd move on.

It wasn't long before the media was covering my story extensively! *The New York Times, The Rachael Ray Show, Good Morning America, CNN, 20/20, Time, CBC, MTV* and countless other outlets around the World peered into *my* world. When *Yahoo.com* sent over 30,000 visitors to my website *OneWeekJob.com* in under an hour, it crashed the server! It seemed there was some resonance out there with respect to this topic...

Indeed, I soon realized I wasn't the only one kept up at night struggling to decide what I wanted to do with my life. Thousands of people were following my journey in various ways, looking for inspiration in their own lives. They wrote about the journey in their blogs and made comments on my website. College students were relieved to find others uncertain of their careers. Baby boomers wrote about how they'd found the courage to change their jobs or return to school to discover their passion once again—even if the passion itself had changed!

I admit my idea was a little wacky, especially when compared with the traditional route: go to school, get a job, buy stuff, start a family, buy more stuff, retire— die. But seriously, isn't it far <u>less</u> wacky than getting out of bed in the morning, absolutely dreading going to work because you hate your job?!

I was consciously committed to avoiding that fate. I wanted to find something I'd LOVE—something I'd gladly spend forty hours of my life doing each week that would also allow me to pay the bills. Whether this was simply the unrealistic hope of an inexperienced, idealistic twenty-something, I couldn't be sure. But I suspected my hope could easily become regret if I didn't find out for myself.

Launching the *One-Week Job Project* was my leap into the working world—the "real world," so to speak. Each week, I put myself in unfamiliar situations, continually operating outside any sense of familiarity. I was constantly being presented with new challenges and sometimes nerve-racking uncertainty. In the past, where I may have avoided situations that required I step outside what seemed comfortable, now I found myself *seeking them out*.

As a result, I discovered what I need in a career to be *truly* happy.

Throughout this crazy year-long journey, I've seen myself grow and develop in ways I never previously thought were possible. By exposing myself to ever-changing environments, I forced myself to continually learn, evolve, and step up to the challenges of an uncertain future. The ultimate discomfort of my "comfort zone" had nothing to do with losing sight of the familiar after all; the *real* risk was losing sight of myself and my passion for learning new things. The situations all these jobs placed me in were amazing— diverse opportunities to overcome my fears and learn more about what the world and I have to offer one another.

In my search for the ultimate career *destination*, I discovered that my passion is *the journey*. And now, my journey involves teaching others how to do the same.

But I never would have learned this truth about myself unless I was willing to first take the risk to step off the path of the predictable and embrace experiencing the exhilaration of the free-fall. I had to summon the courage to take the leap.

It takes guts to put ourselves out there when an uncertain future lies ahead. Most of us are all-too-familiar with those moments of anxiety and self-doubt, as we stand on the precipice of choice—acutely aware of our fear of failure—looking around for somewhere soft to land. Career decisions, serious commitments in relationships, moving out of the house to be on our own, taking that dream trip around the world—these are all situations that can easily challenge the internal boundaries of our comfort zones.

Venturing out on a limb represents a leap of faith that many avoid in favor of more conventionally "secure" decisions that, while they leave us feeling safe, also leave us feeling unfulfilled somehow. My quest reminds me it's often in these moments of uncertainty that we learn the most about ourselves and uncover our true potential. And if it doesn't work out as planned, life invariably gives us a second (or third) chance.

I've met thousands of people during my "experiment," and those whom wholeheartedly pursued their passion all shared one common trait: they may not have ended up exactly where they thought they would, but none of them regret their decision to take the risk.

I also noticed most of those passion-hunters hold a similar, humble confidence: they *know* and *fully accept* they are the co-creators of their destiny, they captain their own ship, and rest-assured, they will never be haunted by the question, "What if?"

If you find yourself at the edge of yet another important life-changing decision, dig deep and ask yourself this one question: "Which choice will best reflect my *passion*?" If you answer honestly, connect with your personal values and take the leap, you will never look back on your life and regret *any* choice you make.

Isn't that worth the risk?

There's only one way to find out.

CHAPTER 43

Ask and You Will Receive

by Petey Silveira

After being trained by past-life regression expert Dr. Brian Weiss in 1991, I was ready to put my lessons to good use. The first situation that presented itself to me was a female client with *current*-life sexual abuse issues. What happened that day has since become one of my life's most memorable experiences— something that truly changed my life forever!

The beginning of the session was very straightforward. I started by quieting her mind to facilitate the journey back in time. After a relatively short period, her mind was open and ready for the healing to begin. Up to that point, everything went completely according to plan. However, once the "regression" steps were initiated...

Instead of going into a <u>past</u> life, she actually started going <u>between</u> lifetimes!

In her altered state, she proceeded to describe an unbelievably peaceful "space" where the masters and guardian angels reside, and where family members transition to before they decide to re-enter as a new human life form. In this space, souls replenish and bathe in the white light of healing and knowledge from the journey they've just taken and receive soul lessons to grow from and use in the "next-life" opportunity.

As if this weren't surprising enough for my first past-life regression therapy session, she began to communicate *personal messages* from spirit guides and masters, instructing <u>me</u> to write a book about the experience! They were very specific, adding that I had been "appointed" as the right person to transmit these important life messages to others throughout the world.

I was surprised and flattered, but mostly shocked! It took me more than 19 years and at least 12 more personalized messages from these masters to finally take action. However, when I did, the result was a book I wrote called *Stepping Into My Happiest Lifetime*. This was a labor of love. I feel truly blessed to be able to pass on this deeper level of understanding to the world.

While this was very fulfilling professionally, on a personal level it felt very limited: I'd only received these helpful nuggets while interacting with clients. As a truly "spiritual" person, I wondered, *Why aren't the messages coming directly to me, through me?* After asking myself this question, thankfully I didn't have to wait long for the answer.

Meditation was the key to uncovering the Truth.

From a very early age and as the daughter of an open-minded, incredible mother, I was fortunate to receive some amazing and unique training. She took me to seminars and meditation rooms at the Association for Research and Enlightenment in Virginia Beach where Edgar Cayce was known as the "Sleeping Prophet." I participated in meditation groups, learned to see auras, and could comfortably sit in silence by the age of 10.

Even though I was very familiar with the power of meditation to transcend stressful human experiences—and was trained to help others do the same—I simply hadn't thought to use meditation to find the answers to my most profound and personal questions. I went deeper and deeper into my meditations to look for the answer. The message I finally got one day—loud and clear—was five simple words that touched the very depth of my soul:

Ask and you will receive.

I *knew* this was the answer I'd been waiting for! I never had to wait *on the edge of my chair* for clients to give me messages. I just needed to be *open* to receiving them on my own; to *ask* for what I wanted.

So I did—and *once I allowed myself to receive*, the gates were thrown wide open!

I will never forget the first time I went into my meditation with the intention of asking to receive my *own* messages from Source. It was January 2, 2008, and I remember being rather nervous and unsure! I sat with my laptop, lit a candle, closed my eyes, said my affirmations, recited prayers, asked for protection and announced I was READY to receive. I tentatively put my hands on the keyboard and paused. I had no agenda. I had nothing in mind.

These were the very first words I wrote:

I have been waiting for you to be ready for me. There is a realm of information here to be shared with mankind.

Goose bumps went up and down my spine, and I wondered, *Is this just coming from my unconscious or truly from my spirit guides?* Doubt tried to creep in, but I kept reminding myself to trust what I was hearing and just go with it. The results were astounding!

When I went into my meditations with complete faith and trust, often times I would have two entire pages written out in five minutes with the most profound metaphors coming across the page. These metaphors would have normally taken me several hours to create (if ever), but they flowed effortlessly through these sessions.

Each day's message started out with: *The messages for you this day are...*

They always addressed some aspect of my *own* life, yet somehow I knew they were also meant to be heard by *others*. They spoke about unconditional love, forgiveness, tolerance, peace, and all the other attributes of souls on a highly evolved plane of functioning. I felt truly blessed to be receiving this Divine knowledge and understanding *first-hand*!

Sometimes I would sit down in a highly agitated state, produced by the typical stresses associated with my role(s) of wife, mother, sister, friend, daughter, therapist, author and so on. But by the time I received all my messages for the day, I would be completely transformed, with an entirely different, more peaceful disposition. I would sometimes receive instructions with specific action steps that were required of me, but most often I would simply be encouraged to let go, love unconditionally, and accept what has been placed before me in this lifetime as experiences necessary for my soul's evolution. As time went on, it made more and more sense to me.

I wrote every single day. In one session, I received messages that helped my daughter sort through personal challenges with guidance and insight. In another session, I helped some other family members deal with their grief over the death of a loved one: beautiful messages came through to help bring them solace, including the Great Truth that there is no death. According to the Spirit Masters, the soul never dies. It only transitions into another space where there is no pain and suffering. I have page after page of messages transcribed from the Source, and the unifying theme is: *We can create our own healing*. How comforting and empowering is that?

I believe we are <u>all</u> messengers. I was told it was *my* time to take on this role because my established level of training, education, qualifications and body of work would allow others to listen to the message from a reputable and highly respected source— *me*. I was also ready to let go of any suggestions that I might be a little "kooky" or somewhat unbalanced because of my new "skills." I know I am as sane as they come: I am analytically-trained as a therapist from the University of Virginia, with the credentials and degrees to back it up. I know all paths have led me *here*; to deliver *this* message, in *this* way, to *you*—right *now*.

If after reading this you feel inspired to sit down and receive your own messages, I encourage you to do so. The beautiful thing about more and more of us seeking (and receiving) Truth from Spirit is that we will elevate the consciousness of our entire world. Peace is ours for the asking.

The first step in hearing messages—from Spirit, God, Guardian Angels, Divine inner voice or whatever you choose to call it—is to acknowledge that you are READY. It is easy to get encumbered with such thoughts as:

Could I really be talking to spirits?
Have I gone mad?
Am I just hearing voices in my head?
Am I just making this up?
What will people think when they find out about this?
What will they think of me?

I had every one of those questions flowing through my mind until I finally decided it didn't matter anymore! As Anais Nin so succinctly put it:

> **And the day came when the risk to remain tight in a bud**
> **was more painful than the risk it took to blossom.**

I took the risk to let my thoughts go and invited Spirit in!

If *you* feel ready, then I am ready to go on a journey of spirit *with* you. It is your Divine right to also be able to communicate with your guides. It would be such an incredible privilege to help you—all you need to do is ask.

May you be as *shocked* as I was, and feel as *blessed* as I do, when your answers appear!

CHAPTER 44

Who Does This Belong To?

by Brenda St. Louis

The summer of my first year in high school began with a cycling accident that left me with a seriously injured lower back.

For almost 15 years afterwards, I struggled with frequent bouts of debilitating pain. Running and jumping were completely out of the question, and intense physical discomfort punctuated most of my activities. I saw countless doctors, chiropractors and a plethora of energy healers, but nothing could consistently alleviate my pain.

Frustrated, I focused with dogged determination on finding a "cure" for *myself*. I studied acupuncture, dissected cadavers, and investigated some of the more popular energy healing techniques of our time, including Shamanism. At one point, I even acquired a healthy "addiction" to *Vipassana* (10-day, silent meditation retreats), where I focused on transcending the pain with my mind. Although my efforts were rewarded at times, nothing permanently took away the pain and suffering. And, whenever I needed it, my trusty friend Percocet (an opiate-derivative painkiller) was always ready and willing to come to my rescue.

Eventually, I decided to turn my quest into a career and took the formal training required to become a massage therapist. Once I graduated, I soon discovered I was better at helping others than I was at helping myself! I would often receive credit from my clients for "taking away their back pain" when no one else could. As the news spread regarding my dramatic success rate, chiropractors and doctors began to refer their patients to me—and my practice grew fast.

Ironically, it was this success in helping others that led me to the thought that would change *my* life—and transform the way I related to pain in my own body—forever.

It was a Monday morning at 10am. My client arrived with a huge smile on her face. She exuberantly wrapped her arms around me and lifted me off the ground. "I don't know what you did last week, but my back pain was totally gone after I left! You're amazing." The ease in her face and the lightness in her step warmed my heart.

I politely thanked her for the compliment then prepared for our session together. After several minutes of working on her, I started to become aware that *the pain in my back was increasing*. Although I was accustomed to having pain in my back, for some reason this time it felt different. My mind, triggered by this new sensation, began to make a powerful connection. Before long, it brought to my conscious awareness an idea: *Perhaps I was literally taking the back pain out of her body and into mine!*

Immediately, the thought transformed into a question: *Is this my back pain or hers?*

As my mind pondered the question, my tailbone started to burn. This was followed by a loud popping noise in my lower back which literally took my breath away! Suddenly, it seemed like every cell in my body began to celebrate in unison at this long-awaited release and the accompanying realization:

I've been taking on the pain of my clients—and storing it in my lower back!

The elation I felt at this understanding was so intense that tears filled my eyes. I smiled and tried not to laugh out loud as tingling heat filled my whole pelvis, and lightness engulfed my heart and being.

Once the session was finished, my client noted with surprise that her back still felt a little sore. It made me wonder whether my newly gained awareness inadvertently blocked pain from leaving *her* body as I disallowed it from entering *mine*. Although I felt a twinge of sadness for her, there was no way I was going to take on her pain right now! My body was singing, and I couldn't remember the last time I could breathe this easily. With this revelation of how my body, mind and work were connected, other points of awareness began to arise:

Firstly, it was galvanized in a whole new way that *my body has an innate ability to heal others*. In fact, all of us do this to varying degrees—with a hug or a loving touch. I now realize we cannot turn off this capacity, but with awareness and curiosity, we can certainly enhance it and take the time to understand the effect it may have on our own body, so we can release it when necessary.

Secondly, it brought me to the realization that *almost everything I experience in my body is not mine—it's just energy*. However, when I perceive it as belonging to me, it becomes solid, dense, and sometimes even painful. When I began to offer up the question, *Is this mine?*, it was the first time I allowed myself to be separate from the pain. I opened myself to another possibility, and since the pain apparently did not belong to me, it lightened and virtually disappeared.

Embracing this concept, I have since reflected on why my own back pain took so long to go away:

As a teenager, I was involved in a tumultuous relationship with a friend. She was always threatening to kill herself, and I was always there to talk her out of it. In the weeks before the cycling accident, however, I'd become exhausted by her behaviour and truly annoyed with her antics. Nevertheless, we had arranged a trip to the cottage together and were on the way there when I fell from my bike. It was a painful struggle to make it the rest of the way, and once we arrived and I laid down to rest, I was unable to move off the bed.

With no apparent concern for my welfare, she initiated a rant about how cold and unfeeling I was being to *her*—and proceeded to threaten harming herself (again). Out of frustration and anger, I blurted out, "Just do it then and get it over with!" At this, she ran away for two days, leaving me stranded. In my state of agony, I couldn't chase after her (as I'd previously done).

What I realize now is for years I must have locked all the guilt and shame from my intense, reactionary comment about her on-going antics squarely in my back. It's ironic how brilliantly I was able to put these feelings "behind" me so that I never had to *look* at them. I'd just spend the next 15 years *feeling* the pain!

My new practice of inquiry (and energetic release) was later honed even further by a phenomenal teacher of mine. He invited me to ask the question, "Who does this belong to?" for *every* thought, feeling and sensation I had. If an uncomfortable feeling got a little lighter after the question, he instructed me to say, "Return to sender." It didn't matter whose thought or feeling it was. I just needed to be aware it wasn't mine, and therefore not take it on. He challenged me to do this for three days continuously. Knowing how successful the technique was for my back pain, I was very curious to see how this would unfold. So I did it!

Almost every time I asked the question, any existing emotional or physical discomfort got lighter, confirming my mentor's theories. What a concept! My whole world opened up for me. With regular practice, my mind became clear and my body felt a peace and joy like never before. I began to experience life as a fluid meditation.

Before this, I believed I had to figure everything out logically. I felt I had to examine all my thoughts and feelings as important portals to the healing and expansion of my life's experience. I now realize this is not necessarily true. I simply need to be present with the feeling, question its origin, and know that I am far greater than my physical sensations.

"Who does this belong to?" is a simple question, and it may challenge your current beliefs about pain and healing. Once the leap of faith has been made, however, you will find it a very powerful and highly transformative experiential tool. Throughout the years, teaching this tool to others has created some of the most dynamic shifts in my clients' lives.

If you would like to try using it yourself, begin by first asking the question for anything you are thinking, feeling or experiencing. If, as a result, an uncomfortable experience gets a little lighter, tell yourself to "return it to sender." Remember, you don't need to know exactly where it is coming from, just know it is *not yours.* You can simply release it because it doesn't belong to you!

Imagine if every one of us on the planet stopped making anger, hate, shame or fear real by taking it into our bodies and owning it. Imagine how much more beauty we could create instead of pain by releasing it into the universe where it can be dissipated! With this thought and this question, you too have the opportunity to be free! How does it get any better than that?

CHAPTER 45

Your Perception of Your Life IS Your Life

by Dr. Russell G. Kennedy

When I was young, I remember my father being very mentally ill. My perception was not only that I was powerless to help him, but also if *he* could get sick, any*one* of us could get sick. As a result, I would conjure up elaborate, scary stories about other members of my family contracting rare or even deadly diseases. I developed a profound fear of illness, and my behavior began to follow suit. I became vigilant about avoiding anything that could "get me" and this led me to see the world as unsafe—full of things that could hurt me.

I'm sure this is the main reason I became a doctor—it's my valiant attempt to gain some control over the fragile nature of our mortality.

In the course of my career, I've learned myriad causes for human pain and suffering. However, what hurts us most is not in our World: the most common reason for our ill-health is a function of our minds. It's the *perception* that the environment in which we find ourselves is a scary place that fills us with dread or fear.

Everything we see, feel and do in life depends upon our perception. It is our mind's interpretation of our experiences. The strange thing is, we are likely to see what we *think* we see, even if it is not an accurate representation of the truth. Just like the

85-pound anorexic who falsely perceives she is fat, your own perceptions (and the stories you create around them) don't have to make sense, they only have to make sense to YOU. And thus, your "reality" is born.

When we react with fear to something, an instinctual "fight or flight" response is automatically initiated: our hearts beat faster, our digestive and immune systems grind to a halt, and our muscles become taut and ready to act. This allows us the best opportunity to fight whatever's scaring us or to run away as fast as we can. Although this is a perfect survival response to immediate, *actual* danger, if it becomes a chronic reaction to non-life-threatening perceptions, it will harm us more than help us.

This happens because the body simply reacts to the information it's given. It doesn't distinguish between actual and perceived danger. All it needs is permission to be afraid for the survival response to be initiated, and our perception is what gives it permission.

This survival response was far more necessary in times when environmental threats were mostly physical. In modern society, however, the vast majority of our perceived threats are mental, but the body's response is still the same: it creates more feelings of fear. Primitive man feared his predators and modern man fears his creditors! Human beings are the only creatures that use fear to protect themselves from fear. Unfortunately, we don't see ourselves doing it, and anxiety can slowly take over our lives.

In my twenty years as a medical doctor, I've counseled and treated thousands of people with stress and stress-related illnesses. Time and time again, I find the onset of illness preceded by a fearful reaction to something that's either happening or only *potentially* happening in their lives. Since most of our fear-based perceptions are created in our impressionable years, they're rarely examined or questioned and, therefore, easily hide in plain sight. Sure, anything could happen, but rarely do these worst-case scenarios come to fruition.

This "fear-creating-stress" phenomenon happened to *me* when I was in pre-med. For the first time in my life, I actually *failed* a course—Calculus 100. Talk about devastating! I was very hard on myself, and my negative self-talk included things like, "I'm obviously not smart enough to get into medical school!" and, "There's no way a medical school is going to take me with a big fat F on my transcript!" What I failed to consider was that all my other grades were excellent! I focused instead on the one negative event—which only reinforced my stress reaction.

Failing that one course didn't stop me from being accepted into one of the highest-rated medical schools in the country, so the story thankfully had a happy ending. However, by believing that one mishap truly threatened my future career in medicine, I created a tremendous amount of unnecessary suffering for myself. It was all just a story.

When we are young, we are taught what to believe—and what to fear—and this belief system is used to create our unique life stories. Those stories are translated into our automatic self-talk, and these mantras can be repeated so often inside our heads they cease to register as our own fabrications; they become who we think we *are* and what is *real* for us. I summarize this phenomenon with my patients when I tell them:

The more you perceive it, the more you'll be(lieve) it. We don't see the World as it is, we see the World as WE are.

The good news is, just as perception can be used to create a negative reality, with a simple mind-shift, we can also change our reality for the *better*—leading to a healthier, happier future.

Having a biopsy doesn't mean you have cancer, being in couples' counseling doesn't mean you'll get a divorce, and making a mistake at work doesn't mean you'll be fired. But if our personal stories are full of fear—and our perception does not change—our repetitive, unquestioned negative stream of thoughts can lead to physical or mental dis-ease.

To this day, I admit I'm still a *bit* of a hypochondriac. Whenever I become stressed, my thoughts tend to revert back to their old, automatic patterns of negative self-talk, and I start looking for illness in me. This creates a chain reaction of thoughts convincing me that something really *is* wrong, which produces even more stress and anxiety and perpetuates a vicious cycle that is uncomfortable—albeit familiar.

Fortunately, I now recognize this pattern. To change my perception, I start by practicing *awareness*—separating reality from the way I perceive it, based on my conditioned past. I've found this awareness can be cultivated by three ancient practices: meditation, breathing techniques and yoga.

With regular practice, I can embrace my true essence as very different from my thoughts. By shifting my awareness to a more peaceful, centered place, I can appreciate better *what* I perceive and *why*. I don't automatically look at myself as a victim of the world, needing to keep myself "safe" by being judgmental and pessimistic. Instead, I ask myself, "Do I know for certain these thoughts are a true reflection of reality?" Almost always the answer is, "No."

Once the negative energy of my pessimistic perception is dissipated by awareness—and I release the need to attempt control over my life—I'm able to focus on how I *want* to live instead. It's always a challenge, but I'm comforted in the knowledge that I'm able to direct my thoughts, instead of my thoughts directing me. This has allowed me the ability to SEE my stress and not BE my stress.

One of my favorite T-shirts says, "Don't Believe Everything You Think." Awareness practices can help you see your fears objectively, but you can also simply make a choice to become present with your thoughts. Becoming more aware that *we are more than we've been trained to think we are* is a brilliant starting point. In my own life, incorporating meditation and yoga has accelerated my process of self-awareness and created an energetic environment that has allowed me to expand beyond my self-limiting perceptions and inaccurate beliefs.

When I'm afraid now, I don't get seduced by my automatic responses and the ensuing perceptions of my reality. I use the experience as a signpost instead—an opportunity to question why I'm afraid—and I almost always find a false belief that propagates the anxiety. Diffusing false beliefs using conscious awareness is a much better use of mental energy than being trapped in fear's vicious cycle. I no longer let fear use me—I use it. I release the need to control what is ultimately uncontrollable, surrender to the present moment, and let go.

Or at least I try to. Releasing my old ways of thinking is an ongoing process, but it's certainly worth every effort. And I've made incredible progress!

On a very personal note, I have a congenital heart defect that has recently surfaced (so there IS something wrong with me!). My cardiologist has been watching it for many years, but at the time of writing this, I've been told I will soon need open-heart surgery to correct it. This makes me even more grateful for the consciousness I now have in my life. Even if it is a potentially scary procedure, I know all my practice will serve me well.

This MD has just prescribed you a refill on your <u>perception</u>: take one good dose of awareness with a full glass of optimism, and enjoy the feelings of well-being and happiness. You deserve it!

CHAPTER 46

Faith, Persistence and Surrender Are My Trusted Guideposts

by Rita Soman, M.A.

Like most people, I've gone through many major challenges throughout my life. After exploring different healing methods and making many failed attempts to solve my problems, three principles became the lights guiding me out of the darkness. With faith, surrender and persistence, I was able to find the love, happiness and inner peace I'm sure will accompany me for the rest of my life.

How It All Began

As a child, I looked up to my parents to guide me through the rough spots. My parents raised me the best way they could with what they knew—yet, unfortunately, they missed the mark for me in many significant ways. Instead of preparing me to reach my potential, I now recognize how my childhood experiences severely undermined my personal growth and well-being on multiple levels—physically, emotionally and spiritually. I was left feeling like I was not allowed to be happy, healthy, successful or prosperous.

My parents were forced into an (unwanted) arranged marriage while they were both teenagers. Having to stop their education and assume responsibility for the whole family must've been quite a blow to both of them. Although I'm sure they suffered many personal frustrations because of it, they each chose to suffer in silence. Somehow, this silence would come to engulf our entire family.

As culturally prescribed, within a couple years they started to have children. I was fourth in line after my three brothers (followed by another brother and sister afterward). After my birth, Mother began her full-time career as a teacher, leaving us with uncles, aunts and grandparents to raise us. For me, the inconsistency in my upbringing was almost unbearable. The "rules" I had to obey varied from overly strict to wildly lenient, depending on who was in charge at any given moment. Money was always short, too. As a result, there was no shortage of tension in our home. We were not allowed to ask for things we wanted or needed, or even to talk about our feelings.

As a girl, I was subject to even stricter rules than my brothers. This is common in my culture. But still, it injured my personal sense of justice and led me to behave more like a boy in order to gain more freedom. Unfortunately, that didn't work out the way I intended; it only made me a rebellious person, powerless to do anything but fantasize about liberating myself from my controlling home environment.

When I was in my early twenties, I decided to take the chance at creating freedom on my own terms. When I overheard my father suggesting he'd found a suitable match for marrying me off, I was so scared of following in my parents' footsteps that I set out immediately to find my own man.

I met my first husband while pursuing my Masters in Psychology at the University of Delhi, India—marrying him against my parents' wishes at age 23. The very first day after our wedding ceremony, he let me see him drunk for the first time. I was shocked by this behavior and quickly went into denial, convincing myself it was an isolated event. When his habits and behaviors continued to get worse and worse in the six years that followed—including emotionally and physically abusing me—I realized he was an alcoholic and he wasn't going to change. I could ignore it no longer. Looking back now, I know my shame and fear kept me tied to that relationship. Many of the personal issues I have since had to face were born of this marriage. Several of my childhood challenges were reinforced as well, including a feeling of helplessness and an inability to control my own life.

Thankfully, this is when the first guidepost appeared and began to restore my long-lost sense of hope for myself.

Since I'd tried but failed to get him out of my (grief-stricken) life, I turned to the only other source I imagined might work—I sought the Divine for help.

I surrendered, seeking guidance and asking for assistance to remove this man from my world. It's a much longer story than this chapter allows, but in a few short weeks (and after countless prayers), he disappeared from my life and never came back.

I felt a sense of relief mixed with guilt and fear. My previous sense of helplessness was quickly replaced with feelings of loneliness and depression—and physical illness soon followed. Scared of living alone, I attracted yet another dysfunctional relationship to fill the void, and that one turned out to be just as emotionally damaging. My only solution: once again, I surrendered to the Divine. I prayed for God to take care of me better than I could take care of myself, and asked specifically for a loving and caring man. It was at this point I discovered the importance of my second guidepost: Faith. It was my faith in the Divine to supply a new and better outcome for me that helped me quickly attract my current husband (to whom I have been married for 24 years).

Although I was very happy during the first few months of marriage with this wonderful man, to our surprise, my mental state began to deteriorate. I realized it couldn't just be my capacity for relationships that was lacking, but something within me that wasn't allowing me to be happy. As a Drug and Alcohol Counselor, I knew how to help others break free from their pain and suffering—why did I find it so difficult to be healthy and happy myself?

My search for the answer brought me to various methods of healing such as Talk Therapy, Hypnotherapy, *Reiki*, Shamanic Healing, Soul Retrieval, Rapid Eye Therapy, *Ho'oponopono* and more. They all granted me varying degrees of relief, but I still found myself going in circles.

A Ray of Hope

My practices of faith and surrender led me to a book, *The Biology of Belief* (self-published, 2005) by Bruce H Lipton, PhD. In it, he talks about the mind/body connection and introduces an intriguing new process called PSYCH-K® originated by Robert M. Williams, M.A. I decided to give it a try, enrolling in a two-day workshop to learn this method. This was completely different than any healing approach I'd ever come across. Strangely, I recognized its potential for my clients before I considered applying the process to myself. But once I started noticing BIG shifts in their lives, I could no longer deny there must be some promise in it for me, too. Each and every time I worked on myself using PSYCH-K®, I felt a positive shift!

It was only when I committed to using it regularly that I began realizing breakthroughs in my own life. The third guidepost—persistence—had been officially called in.

The Realization

The amazing truth I discovered while working with PSYCH-K® was that all my problems seemed to stem from my beliefs—those I acquired from my parents! Not only had I inherited their physical likeness, but also some of their behaviors when facing similar challenges in my life! My negative reactions mirrored theirs, as did my beliefs about myself and the World. I finally realized I'd been living their story my whole life.

I didn't know whether to laugh or cry—I had been programmed to behave just like the people I criticized and blamed for my own suffering. But it was not their fault. They, too, got their programming from *their* caretakers. A deep sense of compassion and unconditional love for them washed over me. With faith that I could get my innate programming back in place with the PSYCH-K® process, I completely surrendered and sought with persistence to reprogram my subconscious mind with beliefs that would actually serve me! With a lifetime of erroneous beliefs to deprogram, to my surprise it didn't take as long as other modalities. In fact, the results were quick, long lasting and worth every bit of my effort. What a relief!

How Do I Feel Today?

I can honestly say I feel totally resolved of my past issues. My thoughts are automatically positive. There is total harmony and peace in my life. The accomplishment of 24 years of marriage feels incredible; it's like a communion of two great souls free of any personal agendas. I look forward to each new day as an opportunity to feel happy, healthy, abundant and fulfilled. People sometimes ask me if my joyful attitude is real, and indeed it is! I am excited to watch my life unfold beautifully according to a Divine plan. I feel completely satisfied on both a personal and professional level.

I feel very excited to educate and support all those who are ready to reach their highest potential. My goal is to facilitate shifting the current paradigm of treating addiction and mental health-related issues; to instill hope in all those who have come to believe they are powerless.

My journey continues...

Utilizing this amazing process (PSYCH-K®), I continue to depend on faith, surrender and persistence as my guideposts—for myself and in supporting others—as we all progress along our life's journey. Can you imagine a life based on forgiveness of self and others...a life based on shedding fears and accepting love...a life of true inner peace?

It *is* possible, and I am proof!

CHAPTER 47

I Have A Choice

by Lorri Dalton

To choose or not to choose? That is *my* question.

As I look back now over my personal journey, it was not always an easy question to *see*, let alone *answer*.

Incredibly, the answer was first presented to me as a thought—a single, powerful, life-changing statement:

I have a choice.

Although it felt like a foreign idea to me at the time, it has since become one of my core beliefs—as essential as the air I breathe. It directly affects not only the quality of *my* life in each and every moment, but the lives of others that share this journey *with* me.

This is my story.

In my early years, I was a "person of circumstance." An incident would occur, and I would go along with it, accepting the consequences or possibilities it offered me. I'd wait and see what was "served up" rather than considering what I actually wanted for myself. All too often, the end results were not of my liking and definitely did not reflect my preferences!

What I didn't realize at that time was the immense personal power I was sacrificing—giving away little pieces of myself to whatever or whomever, simply hoping for the best. I acknowledge I did make some decisions along the way, yet many of these were more reactive to what was going on around me rather than conscious choices that would make me happy.

My tendency to be passive or reactive to my surroundings had the most dramatic effect on me in my later teen years. At a time when most girls are highly sensitive to their changing bodies and emotions, a family friend made derogatory comments about my weight. It had never occurred to me that I was overweight, and looking back now, I realize I never was. However, those comments and the impact they had on my subconscious mind—and ultimately on my sense of self-worth—were profound and long-lasting.

As life would have it, this transpired around the same time the *Scarsdale Diet* became popular. Several members of my family were trying this diet regime, and because I was just recently convinced I needed it, I went with the flow and joined them. Unfortunately, the consequences of my reaction turned out to be worse than the earlier comments themselves. Months later, I found myself in the serious, life-threatening throes of *anorexia nervosa*.

At the most horrendous stage, my weight bottomed out at a paltry 90 pounds. This had nothing to do with the diet *per se*, but was more a reflection of my personal mission to take action in the face of these hurtful comments. It didn't help that I had a boyfriend who insisted I truly *was* fat—even though I could barely cast a shadow! Sadly, this belief became my inner reality. I literally felt powerless and out of control. Food had become my number one enemy, and yet oddly, this was the one thing I had deceived myself into believing I *could* control.

It became a slow spiral downwards into unconscious resignation, and ultimately a feeling of overall defeat. It's no wonder I felt extremely empty, unhappy, powerless, depressed and frustrated—even victimized. Although I was surrounded by exceptionally loving and concerned parents and friends, I still felt incredibly alone. I did not like myself at all, and in turn, this negatively impacted my life and kept me from the happiness I so deserved—and certainly could have otherwise achieved.

So how did I change from slowly dying to living a life of *conscious choice*?

This transition required me to get very real and very personal with myself. The first step was to take ownership of my life. I could keep starving myself and continue to die or I could decide I really wanted to live. I needed to hold myself accountable for <u>every</u> decision. The shift for me began with the realization that by making conscious choices, I could restore my personal power. And, this shift continues for me every time I remind myself, *I have a choice.*

"Taking ownership" can be a tough road to walk. I acknowledged and accepted I would require assistance to work through the issues I had attached to food and weight, as many of these were emotional for me as well as fear-based. When I got this help, I was encouraged to question my feelings and thoughts regarding *all* situations, not just my choices around food. In doing so, I created a whole list of questions I could ask myself whenever I faced important decisions. When I asked myself these questions, no longer was I able to accept my typical reactions associated with being a "person of circumstance." Significant changes began to occur in my life, and I began to heal from within.

These are examples of "choice questions" that help me to stimulate internal dialogue and hone my discernment:

- Will this serve me well in my body, mind and spirit?
- Is this going to enhance my personal growth?
- Who do I want to be in this situation?
- Do I want to be a positive person and offer this positive energy to others?

Centering my questions about what type of person I wanted to be, I found myself searching for my "Higher Self." This continually led me to seek the most reflective outcomes and positive choices:

- What can I learn from this experience?
- Do I need to step "outside the box"?
- What can I do differently right now?
- How can I turn a negative into a positive from this circumstance?

When I confronted perplexing decisions, which did not contain any achievable positive outcomes, I knew that I required digging deeper within myself:

- Why am I feeling this way—what is it that I need to do in order to change how I feel?

- Is this about being right? Do I want to be right or do I want to be happy?
- Is this pertaining to an issue I have locked away within myself?
- Is this issue really my own?
- Is this going to matter in 5 years? In 10 years? In 20 years?

Now, when I find myself confronting anything negative—be it a situation, a person or even my own self-talk—I find it necessary to acknowledge, *I have a choice*. Even amidst negative thoughts and patterns, there are always conscious choices for me to make. By asking a series of questions, I always find myself raising my own level of consciousness. When I do, life for me steps up a notch: I start to embrace choices that will have higher positive impact not only for me, but also for others. I accept the fact that I may make mistakes, but I can always choose to learn from them instead of criticizing myself.

I cannot heal or change what I'm not willing to question. I can either choose to stay powerless with the same negative feelings and reactions or I can choose to interpret the situation or person differently. When I do, I take ownership of—and responsibility for—a new set of feelings and actions. Committing to choose consciously has enabled me to reveal new dimensions of my thoughts and personality.

Most importantly, *conscious choice* saved my life.

It has been 26 years since I left behind my life of reactivity. Today I live a healthy, balanced, joyful life filled with many accomplishments. As a result of my experience with *anorexia nervosa*, I have had numerous opportunities to help others. I've come to realize one of my greatest strengths and joy in life is to "pay it forward." Each time I do, I feel truly grateful and blessed.

In order to serve others as their coach, I realize I need to be the best person I can be in each and every moment! When I make a conscious effort to do this, it keeps me motivated and inspires more positive choices. What goes around truly does come around. This karmic wisdom has proven itself true to me in countless situations with positive outcomes. To motivate other people to be their absolute best serves to create a powerfully positive ripple effect in life. We cannot know how far reaching the effects of this positive energy can be for the world. As well, I believe it is fundamental to our own internal healing. This journey starts within each individual—whether it's me or you.

In every situation, in every endeavor and in all people we collaborate and communicate with, we *always* have <u>choice</u>. And, in the answers to the series of questions asked of oneself, we can find the deeper truths that make all the difference.

To choose or not to choose?

May it be *your* question, too.

CHAPTER 48

Stuck Energy Creates Dis-ease; Loving Energy Creates Healing.

by Janna Moll

As a very young child, I possessed a special *knowing*. While I didn't necessarily understand the ways of the world yet—particularly adults—I intrinsically *knew* Earth was a magical place, and that I was more than I (physically) appeared. I was keenly aware of my own spiritual intelligence and, even as a child, knew I was awakening to my human role as an observer. For instance, I was really good at observing others while they conversed and then "reading" what the feeling was behind the words. I not only heard the conversation—I *felt* it.

For example, if someone was telling another "I really love you," but what I felt energetically was "I'm afraid I'm losing you," the emotion of fear and sadness welled up inside me. Since it was apparent to me that others didn't feel things the same way, living day-to-day in this world was often frustrating. I found it increasingly painful and difficult to be around others, and so I learned to block most of this frustration by living in the dream, daydream or "spirit" world.

Always an introvert, I replenished my energies by being alone and exploring these other realms. I spent many, many hours in what could be called contemplation or meditation, and this nurtured a deeper sense of clarity in me. I began to formulate the understanding that as human *beings*, we're not really male or female—but both.

I related easily to this androgynous feeling within myself and saw others that way as well. I realized that we connect with others as a way to be complete, and this changed the way I perceived love and loving relationships.

In fact, I was very sensitive to *all* energies around me. I would take them in, processing the world on an emotional level—empathically. By the time I reached my teen years, my unique perspective on the world brought me to a breaking point. I was 16, and I had one of the most vivid dreams I could imagine. In that dream, I had a brief "audience" with God, and was given the opportunity to ask Him one question. I told myself it needed to be a good one. I had to ask something that would contribute to my life and stay with me always. I was very nervous! Not about making a mistake, but because I was humbled by God's presence. My knees were shaking. I knew this was a defining moment.

All I could think of to ask was, "What is the meaning of life?"

God replied with only one word. It was said with such depth, clarity and feeling that it answered every question I had or would ever have:

The answer that was given to me was "LOVE."

This liberated something inside me! It initiated new prophetic visions and dreams, including several where I was being trained by a guide to work with energy. I remember very clearly being taught to walk through walls, to fly, and to use intention to create objects, shape shift, communicate telepathically and other really incredible lessons. It was at this point I started truly experiencing myself as an energetic being. Unfortunately, each time I awoke, although I could remember everything, I couldn't re-enact the lessons I'd been taught in my sleep—no matter how hard I tried!

Remembering them alone was enough to change me, and I started to share with others what I was learning—about how we are energy and much, *much* more than we appear to be. Most people just scratched their heads and thought I was crazy. There were only a few who were open-minded enough to listen. But with my accelerated spiritual maturity, combined with the fact that I never felt like I fit in with my teenage peers, life became barely tolerable for me. A deep and painful need to belong led me to turn my back on my early energy lessons in an effort to try to fit in.

Years later, I was to pick up the energy path again at another "breaking point" in my life. I was living with my second husband, two small children and two cats in the yard. "There HAS to be more!" I said to myself. But I couldn't quite put my finger on what *it* was. Fortunately, a good friend convinced me to join her as she went to meditation sessions, energy workers and spiritual retreat weekends. I started to *remember*—and began studying energy again with renewed enthusiasm.

Over the next 20 years, my understanding about Life and my life's purpose were greatly expanded. I experienced many personal lessons along the way, including recognizing my need for personal boundaries, how to engage my personal power, and seeing more clearly my ever-present self-esteem issues. I even had my heart broken and faced some of my worst fears. But ultimately what I learned was that we are *entirely* energy. Everything about us is in flux, always moving and ever-changing. When we resist this change, it creates a kind of stuck-ness—a barrier to who we essentially are as energy beings. What we know as physical disease is created where our energy stops flowing. It is dis-ease, and when it concentrates over time, patterns of this expression will manifest physically, emotionally, mentally and spiritually as illness—or worse.

Energy is wisdom—it is Source. When we let it flow, when we are literally IN the flow—we are expressing who we are on the highest frequency of possibility. But when we resist or constrict this energy somehow—through unprocessed emotions, rigid thoughts and unnatural patterns of behavior—we become the breeding ground for dis-ease.

I bring this understanding to my practice as an energy worker. As a hands-on healer, I run or channel high-vibration energy into my client. The intention is to create more flow where there is little or none. Like an earthquake sending out a vibration that concentrates in solid objects and can shake them apart, the energy I channel does the same—only more gently. By creating more flow in energetically "stuck" areas, we can create a path to healing and wellness, often by releasing what has been holding us back.

When we get un-stuck and allow our energy to flow unimpeded through our entire bodies, we not only influence our health and wellness, but we also facilitate a better understanding of who we really are—more than just a collection of flesh and bones. We begin to connect to our essence.

As an introvert and an empath, my lessons have taken me to the edge of my isolation and brought me back out into the world to share with others that as energy beings, we are all One. I'm sure you have heard these words. When *I* first did, a raging fear was sparked inside me. I thought: *How could this be? It's been so difficult for me to relate to other people. How is it that we can all be the same?*

I recognize this idea as the great dichotomy we all experience in life. When we isolate ourselves in some way within what or whom we identify closely (like culture, family, sex, spirituality), we see the world through the "I". It is then that we have an experience of being separate. Yet, when we stretch ourselves, reaching out across the barriers of identity, we create more movement in our energy and more flexibility in our awareness. We become the "we" or the ONE.

I now embrace the answer I received so many years ago—that LOVE (as God said it) is the meaning of life. What is the universal energy from Source? Love. What carries inspirational information between our hearts and is "chicken soup to the soul?" Love. What is the mysterious force that defies the research, the predicted outcomes of medicine, the disease process or a trauma of any kind? Love. If this love is the energy that flows through the body, then love is the highest form of us—*loving energy is healing energy*. If we are to stand as facilitators of healing for one another, we must be able to carry this love, express this love, and bring others into this love.

Today, I share with my students and clients much of what I've learned from my own lessons. As I continue to work with this energy, my understanding grows. If what we *don't see visibly* when we look at another is their very best part—Love—and if that is also what makes us Divine, then it is this hidden part we need to practice seeing and expressing! When I view the person before me as LOVE—perfect in every way and an expression of the Divine—and invite them to embrace that energy, then they can enter their fullest, most expansive expression.

Our own healing is created in the presence of Love.

This is healing of the highest magnitude.

CHAPTER 49

When I Am Weak, Then I Am Strong

by Gregg Taylor

*Lonely is the person who projects great strength
while suffering alone in self-sufficiency.*

I'm a pretty "together" and successful guy. At least that's what people have said about me over the years. I have a solid career, I'm recognized in my sector, I own a thriving business and I have great connections with friends, colleagues and clients. I grew up in a good family: My parents (who have now passed on) loved each other—showing us what it meant to commit to love, for better or worse. I have three older siblings, each with kids and extended relations, so I've always had a lot of family around. Ours is a family where we put one another first and *truly* love each other.

Home was a safe and comfortable place growing up. We were "middle-class" with enough to go around, never going without. I had the support and resources to attend college and university, and building on this beautiful foundation of family, I have cultivated enough focus and drive within myself to succeed in running my own career-counseling business for the past seventeen years.

It's been a good life. It has also been a hard life.

Along with the all the amazing, tangible, *visible* things life has brought me, there has also been a shadow side—an alternate reality that, earlier on, threatened to take over as the dominant force in my life. I do consider myself "human" in the fullest sense of that word: I have expressed the amazing capacity to dream, to create, to love and to choose. Yet I am also "only human"—one who has struggled with insecurities, compulsions, fears and pain.

I remember the days when I first experimented with alcohol.

Although I had all the common experiences with liquor that most people do—laughing, stumbling, and *Oh!* those nasty hangovers—I also remember the first time a recognition sparked inside me that when I drank, the gnawing fears, anxieties and shame I had hidden within me would disappear! For this reason, alcohol became the star coping mechanism I used during life's challenges and most stressful moments. Yet because of these seemingly favourable mood-altering properties, my use of alcohol turned to *abuse* of alcohol—which ultimately resulted in much self-destructive behaviour (and many unfavourable consequences).

It did not help that I possessed a deep secret; a secret that had become the vessel for a potent cocktail of emotions from embarrassment and shame to utter confusion and deep fear. I remember these haunting feelings as far back as elementary school, but it was only after finishing university when I finally attached the thoughts and attractions I'd been experiencing to the word "homosexual."

Unfortunately, due to an absence of any context for my life-changing insight (including not knowing anyone who was discernibly gay—and then getting involved with a very fundamentalist Christian denomination), embracing my feelings, let alone "coming out" never seemed a possibility for me. Ultimately, it wasn't being gay that left me feeling disoriented and weak: it was being unable to resolve my internal anxieties or express my *true* self that led me to derail my good life through excessive drinking.

So why tell you all of this? Because after my profound, decades-long battle with addictions and personal identity issues, there came a point when I realized I could no longer contain my secrets; the cost to my mental and physical health of hiding behind the façade I'd created had become too much. It felt like I might implode at any moment from the stress! All that was left to do was surrender, and it was then I connected with one of life's deepest truths—one that continues to be a great source of inspiration for me today:

When I am weak, then I am strong.

This thought, one that has profoundly changed my life, comes from a passage in the Bible that says:

For Christ's sake, I delight in weaknesses, in insults,
in hardships, in persecutions, in difficulties.
For when I am weak, then I am strong.

The Amplified Bible translation expands upon this concept and expresses the last phrase as:

For when I am weak in human strength, then I am
truly strong—I am able, powerful, in Divine strength.

This is when I began to explore: I chose to admit my weakness, my inner confusion and my powerlessness over my compulsions. To my surprise, by feeling the fear but facing myself anyway, I found the strength to admit and release my addiction to alcohol; and I felt the weight of the entire world lift from my shoulders as I embraced my identity as a homosexual man. The courage to choose and act in ways that supported my life was only possible by exposing myself fully—my *true self*, in all its frailty.

Being a child of North American culture with a desire to convey success and strength at all costs, I'd been hiding my struggles and perceived weaknesses, partly out of shame and partly from fear that exposing vulnerability would not be accepted by others. In this day of television shows like *Survivor* and *The Apprentice*, society's focus is on being strong, strategic and winning. After all that hiding, it was only when I came to acknowledge and share my limitations and vulnerabilities with others—and asked for help—that I was able to let go of my addictive habits, face difficult circumstances head-on, and become more accessible to help those around me.

I was finally revealing my beautiful, authentic self to all.

Jacques Delors (former President of the European Economic Union) observed that, "Cinema explains American society. It's like a Western, with good guys and bad guys, where the weak don't have a place." I feel *everyone* has a place, just as they are. To me, admitting weakness to yourself and others is one of the more uncommon acts exhibited by us humans. Yet when we do, we enter the fullest experience of what self-acceptance, community and Divine connection really mean.

My career transition program owes its success to this principle. Early on in the program, all the instructors and I share our personal career challenges, missteps and failures with the participants. This has proven time and again to set a tone of humility and openness within the group that would otherwise not occur, and has resulted in a group cohesiveness that participants admit they've never experienced before. Demonstrating and accepting our individual weaknesses with others allows people in transition to admit and share that: 1) they don't know where they are; 2) they don't know how they got there; and 3) they can open themselves up to alternatives, even if they feel vulnerable, uncertain or afraid. This authentic vulnerability might otherwise be called a "weakness," but in actuality, it serves as the foundation upon which a solid, *new* life plan can be built.

I believe the loneliest people alive are those who project great personal strength while suffering alone in their human struggles and feelings of weakness. They live trapped in false self-sufficiency, cut off from the help they need. After years of living this way myself, I now know I would rather have the strength to admit weakness than endure the loneliness of pretending to be strong.

We humans are miraculous, resilient beings that are also vulnerable and fragile. Born into this world dependent on others, we rely on those around us to sustain, teach and protect us. As we grow, we develop an individual sense of Self, and with this awareness, take on these roles for ourselves. For some, this newfound independence represents freedom and excitement—the opportunity to spread one's wings and soar. For others, this same independence is associated with a sense of uncertainty, along with feelings of insecurity and fear. Yet even those who are most afraid will often project an aura of strength, all the while living an internal life of loneliness and isolation—solitary pain.

True strength, I have learned, comes with authentic self-expression, whether that means displaying your capacity and talents boldly for all to see or admitting your weaknesses and vulnerabilities with an openness to ask for help. When I've been true to myself in this way, I've always felt more comfortable in my own skin. I recognize my strong points and am very comfortable with those, too! But I don't waste energy propping up an image of independence and strength when it isn't there; people know the real me without pretense, and my clients never feel judged or pressured to be anything other than themselves.

With this perspective on living, I enjoy a life pursuing activities with a grounded integrity and authenticity, never judging myself as unworthy. By being more true to myself and others, I never have to hide anything or fear that my "true feelings" or vulnerabilities will be found out. Instead, I get to experience the joy of authentic human companionship, support and friendship!

In the midst of a success-driven world driven by self-reliance and striving where the formula for success is believed to be independent effort and personal fortitude, may you, too, find the ultimate strength: the willingness to be authentic, vulnerable, and dare I say it? Even weak.

CHAPTER 50

I Love You Just the Way You Are

by Susan Phelan

I t was a Sunday evening, the end of a wonderful weekend. Having enjoyed a yummy dinner and with the dishes done, I settled in for some rest and relaxation. Suddenly, I felt a strong urge to call my mother.

My mom and I have become very close in my adult years. I jokingly tell people she's not the mother who raised me because we were two very different people some 40 years ago. But we have since shared many stories, turned unexpected corners, and lived through significant changes and transitions together. We have now forged a special bond—one I truly treasure. I see her differently with adult eyes: young and vibrant at 81, simple, kind-hearted and insatiably curious about people.

Like so many octogenarians, my mother has gleaned years of wisdom from a rich, challenging, and somewhat troubling life. Being disconnected from her mother at age 7—never to see her again—was the first of many disappointments, losses and difficulties that followed her from adolescence into early adulthood. Yet she survived to become a going concern as a fantastic cook, a "Red Hat Club" member, a volunteer and aqua-size "buff"—as well as a dear friend to many.

Our conversations over the past decade have typically been honest, open and heartfelt. This particular evening, however, the sharing was to go deeper than I expected. It led us to a place I never would've imagined, nor predicted.

After saying hello, followed by a little light conversation, she asked me how things were going with a challenge I'd been experiencing in a very dear friendship. I mentioned I was feeling perplexed and troubled at how deeply my sense of struggle for power and control in this friendship was affecting me. To this, my mom reflected, "You know, she must be reminding you of the way I was with you as a young child."

The theory was not foreign to me, yet I found myself curious to explore what *she* meant by the comment.

She immediately began sharing with me how angry she felt as a younger woman. Specifically, she referred to how she had to cope as a mother of three young children all under the age of five, with a husband who was not very supportive or energetically available for her. She appreciated he was working tirelessly to provide for the family, but this left him stressed, exhausted, and often sick in bed with stomach ulcers and indigestion. I, too, was aware of these aspects of our shared history, but in this conversation, there was a different energy in my mom's voice—a kind of remorse or regret which I'd never heard before.

She then turned her focus to a specific incident which had occurred when I was four years old. It had to do with teaching me to make my bed—a *specific way* of making my bed—which included perfecting the folding of a sheet over the blanket to form a special cuff. She was taught this "proper method" in nursing school, and she thought this technique was an ordinary, everyday skill a child could easily learn. Apparently, it wasn't for me. She kept saying, "It's so easy, you can do it!"—to no avail. I got more and more frustrated and discouraged. It was a very unsettling affair for both of us, and in the end, I just couldn't get it *right*.

One weekend not long after this incident, I went to stay at my (paternal) grandmother's house. There, I learned an alternate form of bed-making, and I excitedly returned home absolutely thrilled to show my mom! I was beaming with pride. I remember my mom saying she was totally floored by what I demonstrated because she had absolutely no idea you could do it any other way than how she had been taught. I could tell by the tone in her voice she really meant it. As she spoke about it now, she confessed she didn't realize back then how much suffering I experienced trying to "make the damn bed" just the way she wanted me to.

Something in the way she spoke with such genuine feeling cracked open a place of forgotten pain in my heart. Suddenly, I stepped into the memory as if it were happening right then, and I found myself telling her how difficult it was for me to live up to her expectations. Making the bed *her way* was only one of many examples. Overcome by emotion, I went silent on my end of the phone, feeling that hurt and disappointment all over again. From the young child's perspective, all I could remember was I had do it "right" for her, exactly as she dictated. It left me trying to squeeze myself into a pretzel—striving, yet feeling helpless, powerless and stupid.

After the silence extended between us, she gently asked me to remind her about the steps of *Ho'oponopono*—an ancient Hawaiian tradition of healing and reconciliation. Pulling myself back to the present moment, I obliged her request. As I began outlining the four steps involved, I could hear her shuffling papers to write them down: *I'm sorry...Please forgive me...Thank you...I love you.* After what seemed like just enough time to accomplish the list, I heard three tiny, heartfelt words:

"I'm so sorry."

She said it slowly, purposefully, and it immediately evoked lots of feeling in both of us. It was the kind of "I'm sorry" every kid would want to hear from a parent—the kind that rips the scab off a deep wound so the healing can really begin.

With her next words, "Please forgive me," she burst into tears, aching over the raw realization of how controlling she had been and how difficult it must've been for me as a child. It was truly touching.

What happened next really surprised me: unexpectedly, I went *numb*. I simply shut down and then became very...*angry*. I wish I could have been different in that moment, but I couldn't hide the truth. I was just so mad! Courageously, I told her, "I honestly *can't* forgive you in this moment. I am so angry, so pissed off and so hurt remembering all the times you were so controlling with me..."

Then came her surprise response: "It's OK, you don't have to forgive me right now." I was stunned. Her authenticity blew me away, and I knew she really meant it. Next came the statement that would *change my life forever*:

She said, "I love you just the way you are."

I'll never really know why or how my heart *heard* her just then, but it did. Instantaneously, my anger transformed into compassion, and forgiveness began its magic. I felt so respected and loved by her willingness to surrender and simply accept my anger without seeking to change how I was feeling in that moment.

She concluded by saying, "Thank you, I love you."

As the call came to an end, she dedicated our conversation "to all mothers and daughters who may never be able to have this kind of talk." I remember thinking, as I hung up the phone, how absolutely transcendent that gesture was, and how blessed I felt in that moment to have had this conversation…instead of just *wishing* it had happened once she was gone.

We finished talking at 12:15am. I fell into bed and into a deep, relaxed sleep. Suddenly I was awakened by my home phone ringing, followed in short order by my cell going off. I immediately had a sick feeling—the one you have when you know something's terribly wrong. It was my mother's neighbor telling me my mom was in an ambulance on her way to the Emergency Room with a life-threatening heart arrhythmia. I felt my body flood with fear, apprehension and urgency, realizing I might lose her that night. My next thoughts turned to our conversation just a couple hours earlier, and I selfishly prayed for more time to enjoy more of that same closeness we'd shared.

Gratefully, my prayers were answered. She got to the ER just in time and was treated with medication that set everything straight. It was the closest of calls. But it was the synchronicity of this incident with our earlier conversation that stays with me. As I sat at her bedside all through that night, her words kept echoing in my head, "I love you just the way you are."

By expressing her unconditional love and acceptance, my mother gave me the key that has helped evolve all my relationships. I am much more open-hearted and compassionate with others, especially when they are being vulnerable with their anger, disappointment or feelings of betrayal; it has also revealed a whole new dimension of giving and receiving that, until our discussion, had been foreign to me. This precious gift impacts virtually every area of my life, yet what is most special to me is how my heart finally let in the *reality* of her love for me—that bond of transcendent caring and kindness that can never actually be broken. And in Truth, it never was.

I truly hope you benefit from my story, even if it's just to let yourself feel something that's deeply real for you. But most of all, may each one of you find the courage to tell the truth to yourselves and those you love while you still have the opportunity to do so.

CHAPTER 51

This Is *My* Vision

by Janette Martin

t was December 31ˢᵗ, 2006—New Year's Eve. Just minutes before the clock struck midnight, heralding in the start of another new year, an unexpected clarity struck me instead: *Can I actually do this for the rest of my life?*

I was truly between a rock and a hard place. If I stayed with my husband, there was a very good chance I would never fulfill my life's purpose—remaining instead, forever in his shadow, as well as in his darkness. If I left, well, I had no idea what that could mean for me. The thought of staying caused me to tremble and cry, but the thought of leaving left me feeling even more anxious and vulnerable: *How could I possibly live and support myself without his help?*

I'd just recently started my own wellness company, and in those early days, it was by no means a thriving business. As a matter of fact, I was barely making any money for my work. Despite my good intentions, it seemed I was my own worst enemy: either I gave away my services for free to those who needed it (but could not afford it) or I charged only a nominal fee, even to those who had sufficient (if not significant) means. Clearly, I had not yet established any real confidence in my own abilities, consistently under-valuing what I had to offer others professionally. It certainly didn't help that I was also under-valuing myself *personally* and feeling diminished because I wasn't receiving any moral support from my husband. Still, somewhere inside, I understood it was *my* life's vision (not his). Yet I somehow felt trapped in my own dream.

From a purely practical (business) perspective, I came to realize it was rather selfish to ask for his financial support, since the way I was running my company was more like a charity than a money-making proposition. Many lonely and frustrating months later, I finally understood it was neither my husband's nor anyone else's responsibility to facilitate my vision—to help others become *"Well in Body, Mind and Spirit."* This was *my* vision, not theirs. It was a sacred, personal quest, and thus, *my* sole responsibility—entrusted to me by the Divine Himself—to be carried out *against all odds*!

Six long months after that New Year's Eve, my husband's behaviour threatened my own physical and emotional well-being, as well as the growing possibility of bringing my vision to successful (and profitable) fruition. After much anguish, I left the marriage—fueled with a new confidence in myself that I *could* make it, if only I remained true to my divine vision.

Still, many dark days followed where I felt uncertain if I'd made the right decision. Even though I'd left, I still loved my husband, and adjusting to living on my own was hard for me. I found it challenging to remain focused on my vision for the business in the midst of this emotional pain. Then a ray of light: One year later, on the morning of my 50th birthday, I woke up with a renewed feeling of resolve that I *would* make it. I knew my life's purpose was at the heart of my vision, and if I didn't take the risk to swim in uncharted waters, it would be lost—and life for me would be empty. If I didn't follow my dream, I would forever be unfulfilled and never come to know my true, *authentic* self. It was clear to me that glorious birthday morning: the price was too high to *not* take that chance.

Our meaning in life is found in the process, not in the results. In order for me to fully see and activate my vision, I had to first connect with my heart and confront my core beliefs about who *I am* (and who I could become); I needed to accept myself and the value I could add to others' lives so I could embrace the totality of my true purpose. Once I felt I was on the "right" path, it became clear how important my thoughts were to this process. While it had become easier to choose positive thoughts more regularly, I knew I also needed to take responsibility for all of them. I had to keep moving forward no matter what, instead of crumbling in the face of Life's disappointments and everyday challenges.

This is my on-going process. I've had to learn to honour and develop my own uniqueness in the hope this way of being will positively affect others as I invite them to join me in my journey of self-actualization—to become well in body, mind and spirit.

I now realize my vision has been with me a long time and is ever-expanding, too. I started out as a registered nurse in 1975, but always had the desire to complete my graduate studies in psychology. I firmly believe that when we understand how human beings think and act, we are better able to accept and love each other (and ourselves) without judgment. One year after leaving my marriage, I took the final steps to actualizing this academic dream when I enrolled in an online course of study for my Masters in Counseling Psychology. The journey toward my goal had many setbacks, but by continuing to keep my sights on my passion (studying human behaviour), I graduated with my degree in September, 2011! The excitement continues: I've been accepted to the PhD program and will complete my advanced studies in human behaviour in 2014.

My other dream, to own a robust health and wellness company, has also come to fruition; my company has matured into the only one in my country that offers comprehensive disease management plus individual and workplace wellness programs, —all designed to help people learn healthier ways to live and to increase their personal well-being.

My vision has now truly come to life!

Our thoughts are powerful, albeit subjective tools we use to manifest our life's experiences. Because they can be both positive and negative about the World, our thoughts can (and do) influence our path both these ways—depending upon which ones we choose to follow. Thoughts can either assist us in achieving our life's goals or paralyze us to the point where we are afraid to move forward because of the perceived dangers that lie ahead. The critical thing is this: If we selectively choose our thoughts, and stay true to the ones we *want* to follow, our thoughts can motivate and inspire us, help to create our reality, and, most importantly, reflect and shape our *vision*.

Today, many of my thoughts centre on how to become a better person, a better sister, a better friend and a better therapist. I focus on thoughts that call on me to exercise my highest standards in life and business, and these thoughts continue to propel me toward achieving the best that Life can offer! An even greater vision!

If it's true that "We are what we think we are," (and I believe it is) I must continue to purge my negative thoughts on a daily basis because I don't want to become what I think if it's anything but life-enhancing and positive! My journey is now one of seeking out the best way to accomplish my expanding vision, one step at a time. I am dedicated to my future as a continuous expression of my true inner self, my (positive) core beliefs about who I am and where I'm going. I believe I can accomplish anything I envision if I remain focused and persevere through the challenges that may arise.

Embracing my life's purpose has had its daily challenges, but my strong energy reserve and faith in myself (and God) have given me the strength to overcome obstacles that have ultimately landed me in *grace*. I feel empowered! I now *enjoy* taking full, personal responsibility for bringing all aspects of *my* vision to life—for my business, for my own radiant well-being, and for serving others well. I now honour the uniqueness that was withering in the shadows of my unhappy marriage, and challenge others to live authentic lives, too.

Whether it's clear to you or not, I believe each of us has a special purpose, and the dreams we have for our lives are glimpses into a larger vision. Yet the vision you have or are beginning to glimpse is unique to *you*. Everything will change when you claim it and believe *you* are the one to bring it into reality. As I did, empower yourself to say, "This is *my* vision," and let your conviction and faith clear the path ahead to a whole new way of *living on purpose*, bringing that vision into the light.

My wish for you is that this process brings you *wellness in body, mind and spirit.*

CHAPTER 52

I Love You...Too

by Gillian Laura Roberts

T he man standing in front of me was easily 6'5". The room around us was dark—as were his eyes and the emotion I could feel stirring behind them. I stood perfectly still, the gravity of this moment pulling at every cell of my body. My hands were heavy as he held them out in the space between us. An undeniable stream of adrenaline began flowing to my heart. As I looked into his face, I had no idea what would happen next.

This was my first time in prison.

A part of me pulled back from my body, rising up to survey the space and assess the moment itself, amazed to find myself here, doing what I was doing: I stood in a dimly-lit room filled with 114 male inmates—one of only a few women. The *rest* of me, however, intuitively recognized the truth: I was here to learn about Love.

In this of all places...?

It was the last night of a 3-day course being provided in a medium-security men's prison. This exercise was the culmination of the entire 72-hour process: facing forgiveness. In prison, forgiveness is not the most intuitive concept—where is there space for it behind high walls and in tiny cells? In this exercise, it was the very heart of the matter.

Everyone in the room had paired up. The opportunity: Partner A plays a real person in Partner B's life; B either asks *for forgiveness* OR offers *to forgive* the proxy. The simple role of Partner A (me) is to listen, then offer "I forgive you" or "Thank you" in return, appropriate to the request.

As Sal[11] prepared himself to speak, he slowly shifted his weight from right to left, alternately looking deep into my eyes then shifting his gaze just enough to dodge direct eye contact. The energy in his hands was tentative—like he wasn't entirely comfortable touching my skin or being *that* close to me. I felt this strong man steeling himself, holding up the walls of a highly protected inner sanctum which, even now, he sensed was about to crumble and fall. Would he survive this?

I was steeling myself, too. It was not lost on me where I was (a state penitentiary), and that this enormous man was not only a convicted felon, but also the rumoured head-honcho of the entire prison. I didn't know why he was in (not something one asks), I only knew he had three life sentences. I sensed I was about to be told something that might be hard to hear.

Time to begin: speaking softly, he asked me to play his wife. I inhaled silently but deeply at this intimate request—at once, ready to rise to the challenge, yet aware a tender (now nervous) part of me was being tested like never before. I agreed, grounded my feet, and stood fast. I was committed to *being* her—to standing in front of this man (my husband) and having him see the face of this woman (his wife) fully present, fully prepared to hear him out. Tentatively, he continued,

"Please forgive me. I need you to forgive me for what I did that night. What I did to you."

With that, he pulled back the veil for me to peer into what was clearly the deepest, darkest place within him—a cavern concealing the most shattering of experiences. Devastating factors had converged that night—exploding in his body, breaking his heart, and melting his mind all at once. Too much to bear, he'd erupted in red fury, unleashing a raging animalism no man would *dare* believe lived inside him:

He'd come home to find his wife having sex with another man in their bed, his young son in the very next room. Transformed by rage, he threw the man from

---

11   Chosen to replace the real name of the man with whom I shared this experience, respecting his anonymity.

the window to his death, kidnapped his wife and baby, and ultimately raped her—ending life as he knew it, forever. Moments earlier, he'd just been Sal: a successful businessman, former professional athlete, and good guy to all who knew him...with unlimited possibilities and the World at his feet.

It was at these same feet he now stared, his head hanging heavy—our eye contact now broken, too.

The air around us was still. Time stopped. Then a breath...

It had been rising in me as his confession unfurled. From a well deep within me, energy slowly began swirling, surfacing with increasing strength. At first, it felt like an anxious response to standing in the shoes of his wife (a victim of rape and other terrors), having experienced an assault myself years earlier. But as I brought myself back to my role, I realized I was hearing more than his story: I heard—really *heard*—not only his remorse, but *pure devastation* at the heart of this man. Even with the incredible pain he had caused others, there was no denying his own shock and heart-break.

When I squeezed his hand, he raised his head. Looking him straight in the eye, (as his wife) I said, "I *forgive* you."

He exhaled like he'd been holding that one breath his entire life. Our hands dropped slightly as his shoulders slowly surrendered. Although this was the intended end point for the exercise, I couldn't let his hands go. Something just felt incomplete to me. I heard myself say, "May I ask *you* something?"

Surprised, he nodded his silent agreement.

Taking a deep breath, I said, "I want to ask you to forgive *me* now. I want you to forgive me for how I hurt you; for betraying your trust and our marriage. I'm so sorry for what I did to *you*—for all that's happened to you and our family."

At this, the giant man visibly crumbled. His eyes went from confused curiosity... to a kind of bewildered resistance...to surprised...*appreciation*. Given his actions, I suppose it had never occurred to him that his feelings mattered at all. But in terms of that relationship at least, two people were ultimately responsible and both had faltered, hurting each other irrevocably...till now.

With this unexpected opening, he courageously let himself forgive, too.

Shortly after, the weekend process completed with a round of gratitude. Joy and celebration filled the room! Amazingly, the inmates *joined hands*, encircling our volunteer group. As music played, we mirrored them, rotating our own circle so each man could offer us a nod, a smile or some gesture of appreciation. I saw the faces of men I'd worked with and observed that weekend, all reflecting a beautiful new lightness. As I rounded the circle, I saw Sal sitting like the king he was on an elevated platform behind the men's circle, a big smile on his face. When he saw me, he stood, pointed directly my way, and yelled over the music, "I <u>love</u> you!"

And I, in an instant, yelled back, "I love you, too!"

As I felt the words escape my mouth, I checked myself…where I was…and then realized…it was *true*. No matter what this man had done, no matter where he lived or what his life would be from that day forward, in this moment, he was honestly *loved*. And so was I. In the purity of this exchange, my heart and the entire Universe expanded beyond measure—never to be the same again:

I discovered there's a powerful love beyond fear, beyond rules and circumstances, beyond reason. I experienced how deeply honest sharing, taking personal responsibility, and embracing forgiveness leads to a sacred portal—the opening through which, when we pass together, allows us to discover this special kind of love. The one I believe we all truly long for: unconditional love.

The truth is we've all been in prisons of our own making. We've made mistakes— some big, some small. We've judged others and been judged. More than likely, we've been judge, jury and executioner to *ourselves*—imprisoning our own tender hearts without reprieve. In the instant "I love you, too!" flowed from my lips to Sal—without a nanosecond's hesitation—I was changed forever: I learned I could be a vessel for this Love, bigger than I'd ever imagined. I also discovered that like any gift, there's significant responsibility that comes with this newfound capacity—the exploration and refining of which has been my path ever since.

Because I've come to understand that even when love is unconditional, it doesn't mean relationships are. This powerful love is a gift to be cherished, not a free pass from self-responsibility. We all *still* falter. It's continuing to love someone beyond their painful choices—and the sometimes shattering impact on our lives—that can truly challenge the human heart. It definitely has mine. To genuinely see beyond someone's self-imposed limitations, reckless actions or personal pain to stand whole-heartedly for the power of Love—*no matter what*? Well, perhaps that's the *peril* of the remarkable gift I was given in prison.

The *pearl,* however, is I came to feel the simplicity of my calling in this life—the one I'd so long been seeking. It'd been here all along, right at the centre of my heart: to love, just *love.* If I fall and skin my knees or feel my heart shatter into a million pieces, to simply get up and love again—even through the pain—until it is gone and only beauty remains. I guess I had to go to prison to see that even on the "outside" I'd held my heart in too small a space for its powerful purpose. To truly *Love,* I needed to break down the walls and be that bigger vessel.

Thank you, Sal.

Perhaps the greatest challenge I've experienced in cultivating this capacity—as the Buddhists say, "for the benefit of all"—has been in developing the discernment and compassion to love *myself* unconditionally, too. Particularly in the face of fear, heartbreak or disappointment. Sometimes this has meant being committed enough to step out and love another faithfully *from a distance*; sometimes it's meant forgiving myself for the pain of believing I should give or do *more.* For loving and being loved unconditionally—beyond desire or even hope—is truly an extraordinary undertaking: the greatest responsibility is remembering to be gentle along the way and to offer myself the same gift I truly believe everyone else deserves.

Even when I falter.

My first and cherished spiritual mentor Reverend Candace Frank used to say, "I love everyone, and you're next..." What would our World be like if we each took that on? To love without limits—seemingly the most natural thing in the world—*does* take courage. But what if, like Sal and I did, we take this step together?

My wish for you *and* our beautiful World is that you will discover Love is *your* purpose. And that with every opportunity, you will also take care to say to yourself, *I love you, too...*

○○○

This chapter is dedicated to the timeless memory of the awesome Elvie Graham—a true Love Warrior of the unconditional kind. You were a cherished member of the "Aunty Brigade" - thank you for your many gifts of the heart to pass along to my treasured nieces and nephew. We see you in the red sky and full moon—and love you...forever.

For more information about the program referenced in this chapter ("Free The Heart"), please go to: thethoughtpublications.com/gillian-laura-roberts/.

Our Creator would never have made such lovely days, and have given us the deep hearts to enjoy them, above and beyond all thought, unless we were meant to be immortal.

Nathaniel Hawthorne

A THOUGHTFUL
QUESTION

When Our Thoughts
Transcend Us:

The SPIRIT of Changing Your Mind

by Gillian Laura Roberts
& Dr. Christian Guenette

At the end of the Middle Ages, as the first fingers of the Early Renaissance began to stretch out across the lands of Europe, there began an awakening within thinkers and artists of the day. This gave birth (a rebirth actually) to a beautiful energy of looking, *feeling,* and building upward-and-outward to express, celebrate, and emulate the beauty of God—and the great mystery of existence. Magnificent cathedrals were designed to exalt this great power and reverence, and it was said that those journeymen who began laying the foundations for these transcendent masterworks knew full-well that even as they did so, they would never live to see the day of completion. The technologies of the day simply could not allow for it, and some creations would take upwards of 100 years to finish.

Imagine that! Beginning something so meaningful, so magnificent and beautiful—to shine in the World as a beacon of the very best of human creativity—knowing you would never witness it coming to fruition? Imagine contributing such a critical effort to its eventual majesty, only to have your life end without ever fully understanding what your work meant to the World; to never enjoy the unveiling of its wonderful purpose in the service of others...

If *you* knew you would never see the fullness of a great mystery revealed, but also realized your contribution was critical to its revelation—would you still lean in and do your part? We believe this is not only a very powerful question, but truly relevant to the purpose and potential gift this book can be in *all our lives* on the planet today.

Mystery. Mortality. Purpose. These seem to be the very cornerstones of the foundational question so many of us have burning in our hearts and minds: "What is the meaning of Life?" Perhaps in these times of spiritual awakening and global consciousness, a more apt question may be, "How do I give my life *meaning*?"

In our personal and professional work alike, we (Gillian and Christian) feel it's very important to understand not just the *how* and *what* of mindfulness, but the *why* of it all: that is, "*Why* pay attention to and direct your thoughts?"

Why even ask why? Because in order to keep our circuits firing and juices flowing, to continue taking the necessary steps to joyfully stretch ourselves into a new way of being, we simply *must* clearly identify, engage, and embody a powerful reason. *Our personal Why!* This is the fire to the spark of any inspiration; in the pursuit of our dreams, it's the force for creating sustainability as we make any kind of lasting, *meaningful* change.

Changing your mind *is* meaningful.

You don't need to change your mind about everything, but it seems wise to consider changing those things that don't serve you well—those things that, if changed, will make you *happier*.

As we set out to create this book, we lovingly discussed our own internal impulses—our motivations and intentions—for illuminating the power of the mind. We felt committed that each reader be touched in a way that inspires not only some new understanding of themselves and the World, but might also initiate a new level of awareness—even *reverence*—for his or her very own completely unique and beautiful mind. Because for each thought that arises (even if we don't know where it comes from), each one of us has the power to assess and "handle" that thought—discerning how to respond. Even those thoughts that seem unconscious can be *made conscious* in this way, allowing us to see the ball clearly as it comes. By catching it and deciding in which direction to throw it—or whether to catch it at all—it's the ability to *respond* that we develop in this practice; a kind of response-*ability*.

Now that's power.

But why is harnessing this power important for *you*?

When we discover that "the power we have inside is greater than any power in the World" (as Michael Bernard Beckwith says), we are immediately free. Free to experience, express, and create *whatever we put our minds to*. Have you ever heard that before? Notice it does not say, "Whatever happens to arise in your mind as a thought that you react to in whatever way you *happen to*." It says, "You can create, have, do, be whatever *you put your mind to*." Dr. Dispenza points to this as a very active process. We passionately posit that this idea of self-empowerment is not only worth your while practically, but it is *critical* because it will change not just you—it will change the World.

Change Your Thinking, Change (Your) Life[12]

We experience our thoughts in different ways—they surface, emerge, and hit us from left field; they come and go, sit and await our attention or take up residency. Some are like anchors, some are like fireworks—weighing us down or absolutely making it impossible for us to attend to anything else around or within us! Regardless, it's what we choose to *do* with our thoughts that makes all the difference. When we have a powerful *why* as our touchstone, this becomes much easier.

What is *your* Why?

Many people say, "I just want to be happy!" We recognize this as a universal, human desire—and say yes, go for that! The key question for us is—why? *Why* do you want to be happy? Is it because your life would seem easier, you'd feel like you had everything you needed or you wouldn't really have to *do* anything anymore?

What if being happy could mean so much more than that?

Happiness is a vibration—literally, a unique frequency. When it's moving through you, your *being* vibrates in a particular way. You've probably already sensed this.

When you are happy, don't you feel lighter or perhaps find it easier to smile, laugh or look someone right in the eye and connect? When we are happy, it feels like our hearts are more open, our outlook is positive, and the World shines a little brighter—maybe even moving from shades of black and white to techni-colour.

---

12   This phrase was coined by Ernest Holmes (1887-1960), Author of *Creative Mind* (R.M. McBride & Co, 1919) and many other written works. He was also the founder of the spiritual tradition Religious Science and the Science of Mind philosophy.

Tasks that previously seemed unmanageable suddenly have clear, swift resolutions, and relationships seem to flow with ease. We feel *good*.

We believe the most important reason why we should all focus on being happy on the planet these days is that it ultimately breeds *service*. Yes: happy=service. This is the natural progression of happiness!

Since happiness starts with thoughts in *your* mind and sensations in *your* body, you may be self-focused on it at first. And that's great! However, it's what you come to desire *next* that is so incredibly powerful: you want to *spread* your happiness. This vibration of happiness does not wish to be contained! It radiates with the beauty of its nature and seeks to transform everything around it.

Happiness—or feeling good—does not have to look like puppies and flowers, skipping through the fields or waving your arms about in grand gestures. Of course it could look like that. But what we're really hoping to engage (also) is the quiet, clear, *grounded* happiness that moves us with strength and purpose and has an enduring quality. Because this is the kind of happiness that initiates the mindful directing of our thoughts and manifests in clear, intentional actions aligned with our most meaningful personal and collective values.

Like those magnificent cathedrals and works of art, Consciousness on our planet is something we are all contributing to each day in every moment—thought by thought, choice by choice. And like those journeymen and artisans, we may never fully understand or experience the full picture of the grand mechanism to which we are each contributing. This is the greatest mystery of them all. Yet there's a place in each of us that is either awakening to this larger reality or, at the very least, *suspects* it exists—something bigger than ourselves, something beautiful beyond measure. And that is, we believe, what has brought you to these pages.

We hope this awareness (or curiosity) will also evolve into the answer to your personal *why*: to discover your true purpose, one thought at a time. For even if you never really know the fullness of the grand mystery, we hope we've shown you how to transcend your everyday existence by turning your mind to thoughts of love, healing, creativity and giving—in ways that make your soul sing and bring you to your own great, personal happiness. When you do, may you come to *know* you're also contributing an essential part—the fullness of *you*—to the evolving story of the Universe.

What will *your* chapter be?

You're never given a dream without also being given the POWER to make it come true...

Richard Bach

Our Final Thoughts...

This book has been *our* dream.

The experience of bringing it to life has served as its own chapter in the book of not only our creative partnership—*The Thought Publications Inc.*—but also in our lives and those of our fellow contributors. The collaborations were many, the vision was singular: *Let's showcase revolutionary thought <u>in action</u> and share with the World our perspective on how it's possible to tap into the Universal Intelligence in new and magical ways—to create the future we <u>all</u> desire...*

Along the way, this ideal has certainly tested us! We've walked the talk, sometimes tripping and falling in the process, mind you—but most importantly, we've gotten up, brushed ourselves off and kept moving in the direction of our dreams. We say dreams *plural* because there are many: some of them are shared and others are our own. Regardless, the combined experience has been rich, inspiring and life-changing for us. Most definitely this is one journey that has changed our lives...forever.

We hope and trust the words you've found in these pages have done that for you, too. Perhaps one (or many) of the thoughts rang a bell, awakening your mind or heart to a new possibility for your life. Or maybe you've been reminded of some powerful thoughts of your own—ones that could easily have been shared in this book, too. Our hope is the power of your mind and your power to *choose* have become infinitely clearer. As Oprah says, "Once you know something to be true, you can no longer pretend you don't know."

What do you know now that you didn't before you opened this book? What will you do with this golden awareness now that it's been illuminated?

Move and the way will open (Zen saying)

We are committed to continuing this journey with you and bringing the next steps to light for all who want to keep learning, growing in power and happiness, and contributing to evolution of Consciousness on this planet! It is beautiful to read a book, to feel inspired, and to see a new way. Like many other experiences, however, these can often fade into distant memories all too soon—we've all experienced *that* from time to time, haven't we?

> *As a single footstep will not make a path on the earth,*
> *so a single thought will not make a pathway in the mind.*
> — **Henry David Thoreau**

While it's true one thought can indeed serve as an infinitely powerful starting point for personal transformation, it is also true we must revisit these new thoughts and feelings often if they are to become part of our newly desired reality! With this in mind, we wish to serve as fuel for your enlightenment engine—to help you remember your personal *Why* and fill you up when you need it!

In addition to this book, we have also created a website you can use as one of your fuelling stations—where we will keep creating for you and with you—to ensure the Truth you are now experiencing continues to live "As You" in the days, weeks and years to come! You will find more details in the *Coming Soon!* section that follows.

To begin, simply visit us at: www.thethoughtpublications.com where you are sure to get your fill of inspirational quotes, spiritual insights, healing resources and more! Plus, you will get to meet the people who helped bring this vision to your doorstep, including links to our contributors' websites and lots of other really cool opportunities—see you there!

The Thinkers

Angelika Christie is an international Coach, a transformational Speaker, bestselling Author of *Your Intelligent Cell,* and the Founder of The Freedom Whisperer. Her unique understanding of our soul-power and how we use our inherent cellular intelligence to free our hearts is revolutionizing the way we enjoy life. In her upcoming book: *Be Fearless Now,* she gives a clear roadmap on living a life of purpose, joyful abundance, harmony and peace. Angelika's motto is: "Change your mind and your body will follow." Her mission is to form a new human consciousness, releasing the destructive presence of fear in people's lives. Angelika says, "Fear, anxiety and doubt are the greatest destroyers of happiness, freedom and global peace." Visit her website: freedomwhisperer.com, or email her at: Angelika@ FreedomWhisperer.com.

Annemarie Gockel received her Ph.D. in Counseling Psychology from the University of British Columbia in 2007. She is both a psychologist and a Licensed Spiritual Practitioner with the International Centers for Spiritual Living. She specializes in researching how people draw on spirituality to cope with physical and mental health challenges. Currently, she teaches clinical practice, works with clients, and studies how people create healing in their lives at Smith College in Northampton, MA. If you have a story to share about how you draw on spirituality for healing, contact Annemarie at agockel@smith.edu.

Bernie Siegel has touched countless lives. In 1978, he attracted the attention of an international audience when he spoke about patient empowerment and the choice to live fully and die in peace. He created ECaP (Exceptional Cancer Patients), in which he and his wife and co-worker, Bobbie, remain active today. ECaP is helping patients interpret their drawings, dreams and images to express their feelings about mind-body healing. Bernie embraces a philosophy of living and dying that stands at the forefront of the medical ethics and spiritual issues our society grapples with today. In May 2011, Bernie was honored by the Watkins Review of London, England, as one of the "Top 20 Spiritually Influential Living People on the Planet." He continues to break new ground, seeking to humanize medical practice. berniesiegelmd.com

Brenda Michaels is an inspiring, insightful and passionate communicator. She spends most of her time as a syndicated talk-show host (*"Conscious Talk... radio that makes a difference"* and *"The Women's Hour"*), a public speaker, workshop leader, plus spiritual and emotional coach. Brenda also contributes her time as a member of the Advisory Board for the Emerald Heart Cancer Foundation. Brenda's participation and leadership in raising awareness is a true demonstration of her commitment to living upon this planet as a conscious being. To learn more about Brenda's contribution to the World, go to: conscioustalk.net.

Brenda St. Louis is an international speaker on the topics of consciousness and transformation. She currently lives in Vancouver, BC and works as a Licensed Access Facilitator, writer, coach, healer, CranioSacral Therapist and Registered Massage Therapist. She has been facilitating workshops on Access Consciousness internationally since 2004. From India, Korea, Japan, Australia, Italy and now Canada, Brenda has invited hundreds of people to use the tools and techniques of *question* and *possibility* to transform lives. She has a true entrepreneurial spirit and enjoys creating new and innovative projects that will enhance and expand possibilities for everyone on this planet. More information can be found at her websites: brendastlouis.com OR knowthatyouknow.com.

Brock Tully is an inspirational speaker and author of 8 books, including the best-selling *Reflections* series. Brock has taken 3 epic bicycle journeys around North America—covering close to 50,000km—to raise awareness in support of random acts of kindness. He is the founder of the World Kindness Concert (worldkindnessconcert.com) and the co-founder of Kindness Rocks (kindnessrocks. net). He has also founded One of a KIND Stories (oneofakindstories.com), and is the co-founder of the Kindness Foundation of Canada. For more information, please visit: kindnessfoundation.com OR brocktully.com.

Bruce Sanguin spent his teens and early twenties as a jock. After reading a book by Maharishi Mahesh Yogi on Transcendental Meditation (TM), he awoke to a vocation that transcended his dream of dunking the basketball and playing professional tennis. Bruce has been an ordained minister in the United Church of Canada for 25 years, now serving a congregation in Vancouver, B.C. He is a fellow of the American Association of Marriage and Family Therapy, not to mention he is also Ann's husband (24 years and counting), a father to Sarah, a grandfather to four, and author of five books—all available in both digital and hard copy from his website: brucesanguin.com.

Caroline P. Mueller resides in Richmond, BC where she enjoys playing tourist in her own community. She is currently working as a traveling "medicine woman" doing locum work as an OBGYN in rural BC & Alberta, honoring a belief that patients are best served by physicians & healers in their own communities—sustainable only if local physicians have time for self-care and continuing medical education. She spends her free time coaching people in cleansing and detoxifying their bodies, a process she believes is critical in the maintenance of good health and managing society's increasing burden of chronic disease. Her greatest joys are traveling with her life partner and spending time with her nephews. She can be reached at: cleansewithcaroline.isagenix.com.

Catherine Kozuch, raised in Adelaide, South Australia, entered Arizona State University in 2006 as a Communications major with an emphasis in Journalism Studies. In April 2008, during her sophomore year, she was paralyzed in a horrible accident and was forced to medically withdraw from school. Her positive attitude and self-motivation led her to a miraculous recovery, and Catherine taught herself to walk again! She graduated in 2010 with a Bachelor of Arts in Communication Studies and went on to work for Fox 10 News as an Associate Producer. Catherine plans to publish a book about her miraculous journey of faith—from being paralyzed to walking again. To learn more, go to: catkozuch.com.

Cathy Matarazzo, affectionately known as the "Heart Doctor" to her clients and comrades alike, is ALL heart! Her private practice of almost twenty years has served as a beacon of light for thousands of people seeking soulful navigation through the waters of life. As a writer, natural intuitive healer, peace minister and genuine love keeper, this "Sistah" shows up in a way that will always awaken and serve the purest of clarity and vision the heart is waiting to receive! This heart doc believes there is nothing too big for the heart to heal, it's only ever about the love, people! Reach out at info@freedomwake.com or visit cathymatarazzo.com for your own loving heart boost!

Christian Guenette was born to help others. He has served his community of Vancouver as a Chiropractic physician for the past 12 years at a clinic he owns called *Back2Health Chiropractic*. Christian educates his clients using the advanced training he's received in a number of different disciplines, including: Applied Kinesiology,

CranioSacral Therapy, Trigenics Functional Neurology®, EFT®, PSYCH-K® and Life Coaching—creating a unique and personal wellness plan for every patient. Online, as The CommonSense Coach™, he encourages people to embrace what he calls, "The ART of simply living." As the co-creator of the book *The THOUGHT That Changed My Life Forever*, he intends to spread the message of infinite possibilities to the rest of the world. To learn more about Dr. Guenette, go to: back2health.ca OR thecommonsensecoach.com.

Daniel Mauro enjoys seeing people come to life when they embrace their inner spark. As the founder and director of Speaking Visionaries Inc., Healing Ottawa Live Auction (HOLA), and Dream Weavers Mastermind, Daniel has discovered the power of merging science with heart-centered disciplines to facilitate transformation in others. He is a regular contributing author to two consciousness-raising magazines in Canada's National Capital Region, holds a Masters degree in Cognitive Science, and is considered Ottawa's leading expert on the science of Musical Medicine. Believing whole-heartedly in the art of self-mastery, Daniel incorporates sound and music as key components of his empowering personal development programs on "Heart Intelligence", "The Musical Brain" and "Fearless Speaking." To learn more about Daniel's dynamic workshops and live speaker events, visit: SpeakingVisionaries.com.

David Jan Jurasek inspires powerful connection. He loves working with sensitive people who yearn for authentic relationships and wish to make a conscious imprint on the World. He is a Child & Family Therapist and Mindfulness Martial Arts Instructor at INTEGRA, a certified mental health clinic serving families with Learning Disabilities. He is also the Founder of The Inspired Playback Theatre Company which helps creative folks to master the art of truly connecting through playing and performing "improv" theatre. To learn more, go to: inspiredplayback.com OR to find out more about David, go to: davidjurasek.com.

Dena Churchill is a Doctor of Chiropractic and dynamic keynote speaker remembered for her ability to deeply connect with audiences through clarity, wisdom and humour. With a humble confidence, she draws on a wealth of real-life experiences to help you "Envision and Achieve Your Best." As a doctor, speaker, author, coach and radio/TV show host, Dena integrates her extensive studies in Psychology, Biology, Chiropractic, Acupuncture and energy healing to provide you with fresh ideas in healing and transformation—unleashing the power of the "Authentic You." She is the author of the book entitled, *Divinity in Divorce: The Power In Gratitude and Love*. It explores how people going through divorce and other life crises can find healing, wholeness and wisdom. Explore more at: drdenachurchill.com, OR loveyourdivorcesite.com.

Derek Porter is a 3-time Olympic athlete who competed for the Canadian National Rowing Team. On the Olympic stage he took home one Gold and one Silver medal. He is a practicing Chiropractor and co-owner of West Fourth Chiropractic in Vancouver, BC. Through his involvement in high performance sport, he has gained an appreciation of the power of the nervous system in health and performance. His clientele include those looking for a way to improve health and function—from kids to high level athletes to octagenarians. His main focus is on wellness and optimal performance. Visit: drderekporter.com.

Dixie Gillaspie has been a consultant and analyst, fire-starter and mentor, alchemist and general trouble shooter for more years than she cares to admit. (But just ask—she'll tell you.) She says she is blessed to have come to a wonderful convergence where "What I am and what I do is the same thing—I am a coach." Dixie has been featured in books such as *Go-Givers Sell More*, by Bob Burg and John David Mann, *The Referral Engine*, by John Jantsch, and *–Able*, by Scott Ginsberg. She will release her first full-length book, *JUST BLOW IT Up: Eliminating Life-Limiting Barriers*, this November. She shares her home with a 14 year-old tom cat who thinks he's a kitten, and a 95 pound Boxer/Lab mix she calls "The Dragon Dog,"

Gabriel Nossovitch is the co-founder of several personal transformation companies throughout Latin America. He is currently the Chairman of the Board and the Director of Training for both Worldworks México and ChileWorks. These organizations offer personal growth and transformational seminars and sponsor large scale community service projects aimed at raising awareness in underprivileged populations in the Americas. Gabriel is a member of the Transformational Leadership Council where leaders of personal and organizational transformation support each other in their contributions to the world. He is also a founding member of the International Coaching, Consulting and Training Group (ICCTG)—an association that ensures appropriate knowledge and conduct of international coaches and transformational seminar leaders. He has triple citizenship (Argentinian, French and US) and is fluent in Spanish, English and French.

Gillian Laura Roberts sees something special in people and is passionate about illuminating everyone's unique genius. She's the Owner of Centre Space Spiritual Coaching, co-Director of The Thought Publications, Inc. and co-Creator of *The Thought That Changed My Life Forever*. As a Licensed Spiritual Practitioner, she enjoys coaching and teaching her clients/students using spiritual tools and principles to assist them in discerning which beliefs and actions serve their highest vision. A student of Science of Mind and Tibetan Buddhism, Gillian holds a degree in Psychology & Linguistics, is published in Human Communications, and received specialized training as a Miruspoint® Facilitator. Centre Space is her treasured vision for providing everyone the opportunity to *clear.connect.create!* Visit her at: yourcentrespace.com OR ignitepurepower.com. She also *really* loves running by her seaside home in Vancouver.

Gregg Taylor: Gregg's life-work is motivated by his personal mission statement: "To create spaces of grace for people's healing and growth." Having made his own journey to recovery from addiction and emotional turmoil, Gregg is known for being a stable and insightful "voice of reason," helping a growing sphere of people who are seeking reassurance, understanding, healing and freedom. With professional designations in Human Resources and Career Development, plus graduate studies in Counseling Psychology, Gregg is passionate about creating resources, programs and supports for people who desire personal healing and who long to be authentic. Gregg has been featured and quoted in local and national media, and recognized and awarded by his peers for his innovative practices and programs. For more, go to: greggtaylor.ca.

Gwenn Henkel is a Certified Medical and Master Hypnotherapist. As the result of an accident in 1995, Gwenn developed three debilitating, painful, chronic conditions. When drug therapies and physical therapy did not help, it was suggested she try hypnosis—and the rest is history! Through hypnosis, she discovered the way to control all of those conditions and renew her life again. Many doctors now refer their most challenging patients to her. Because of her compelling story, a full-page article was written about her in *Woman's World Magazine* in 2007, and she is now a regular contributing author for the *Californian Woman's World Magazine*. Her life purpose is to teach the World the power of the mind—including how hypnosis can help you to change your life!

Hilary Bowring is the owner at Divine Align, where she teaches meditation and offers energy healing and spiritual counseling. Her delight as a teacher is to help people establish a daily meditation practice so they can feel an inner state of calm no matter what life serves. This focus on meditation and the spiritual meaning of life came after her husband's sudden death. The impact of sudden death jolted her consciousness and brought her an understanding that life is about soul journeys for spiritual evolution. The transforming grace of meditation has moved her from deep grief to an uplifted state of mind. She loves to dance, chant and sing with others, always seeing the funnier side of life! For more about Hilary, go to: divinealign.com.

Jacob Nordby is a published author, speaker, conscious entrepreneur, and personal transformation mentor. He does personal coaching work with people who are moving through transitions in life. His other writings include a spiritual novel, *The Divine Arsonist: A Tale Of Awakening*, and as co-author in *Pearls of Wisdom: 30 Inspirational Ideas to Live Your Best Life Now* with Jack Canfield. He is currently writing *The Cosmic Compass: An Adventure of Inner Guidance*. Mr. Nordby is the founder and publisher of the popular e-magazine site, YourAwakenedSelf.com. His personal motto is: "The greatest gift you can offer the World is to awaken and walk in love." He has a great passion for helping others give birth to new purpose in life.

Janette Martin believes that each one of us is entitled to holistic wellness—and that we become what we believe about ourselves. She is a Registered Nurse, Cardiac Therapist, health and wellness coach/educator and personal care provider. She has a Bachelors degree in Biology with a minor in Theology, a Masters degree in Counselling Psychology and is currently a PhD candidate in Advanced Studies in Human Behaviour. Janette is the founder and lead consultant at Jemi Health & Wellness, which provides fitness training, disease management and health coaching/counseling to individuals and worksites. Her passion for people has led her to a heightened awareness of the importance of physical, mental and spiritual harmony resulting from healthy living. To learn more about the services offered by Jemi Health & Wellness go to: jemiwellness.com.

Janna Moll is the founder and president of Energy Medicine (EM) Specialists, a center of excellence offering treatment and advanced practice coursework—both here and internationally (EnergyMedicineSpecialists.com). She combines expertise in multiple energy disciplines (Healing Touch, Reiki, Polarity, Pranic Healing, EFT, Therapeutic Touch and Theta Healing, to name a few) with psychotherapy and coaching in her practice. Janna presents to national organizations on various topics related to energy healing and also trains medical intern students about its benefits. She has contributed advanced coursework for practitioners in the EM field (Hara Workshop, Advanced Chakra Workshop, EM in Surgery, etc.), and her specialty is making hard-to-understand topics easy. Janna is currently writing *Energy Medicine: the Big Picture*, a textbook for the practice of energy medicine.

Joe Rubino is the CEO and founder of the Center for Personal Reinvention and has been acknowledged as one of the World's foremost experts on the topic of elevating self-esteem. He is a life-changing personal development and success coach, with a focus on helping others restore self-esteem, achieve business success, maximize joy & fulfillment in life, and optimize productivity. He has written a number of best-selling books on these topics, including: *The Self-Esteem Book*, *The Success Code: Books I & II*, *The Magic Lantern*, *The Legend of the Light-Bearers*, *The Seven Blessings*, and *31 Ways to Champion Children to Develop High Self-Esteem*. To explore more about his life-changing work—championing people to restore their self-esteem—go to: CenterForPersonalReinvention.com OR theselfesteembook.com OR HighSelfEsteemKids.com.

Jonathan Yudis is an award winning independent filmmaker, certified Yogi Siromani, spiritual author, and family man. He was born and raised in Philadelphia. Jonathan graduated *summa cum laude* from New York University where he received his BFA in Film and Television. In 2009, Jonathan directed the award-winning media campaign for P:5Y—Peace In 5 Years, a global organization and collective dedicated to creating world peace by February 14th, 2014. Presently, he's promoting his new book and seminar, *The Divine Synthesis: Living Right Now*. In addition, he has two feature films: "*YOGANANDA*," based on the life of the great yogi Paramhansa Yogananda, and "*THE LOST YEARS*," based on the unknown life of Jesus Christ; both slated for production in 2012.

Kristen Moeller is a highly respected coach and speaker who holds a Masters degree in Counseling and has over 22 years in the field of personal development. Her best-selling book, *Waiting for Jack: Confession of a Self-Help Junkie – How to Stop Waiting and Start Living Your Life*, explores our pervasive human tendency to wait instead of living our dreams. As the creator of Author Your Brilliance™ mentoring programs and as the Executive Publisher for Imbue Press, Kristen found her home in the world of books. Her non-profit, the Chick-a-go Foundation, provides "pay-it-forward" scholarships for transformational educational training programs reaching people who otherwise cannot afford such opportunities. She resides in Colorado with her husband, two large dogs and an ornery cat.

L. Jon Porman is a Chiropractor of 17+ years with post-graduate training and certified as a Chiropractic Sports Physician. He has treated 600+ Professional and Olympic athletes from around the World and authored national articles on sports performance and injury rehabilitation. For more information, go to: SportsDocsAZ.com or call: 480-812-9000. He also has remarkable success with athletic performance, insomnia, anxiety, depression, ADD, ADHD and chronic pain utilizing Brain Wave Optimization™. He uses this new protocol not as a physician, but as an individual. For more information, go to: InfiniteBrainPotential.com. Dr. Porman also has a Motivational and Leadership company called Champion of Success, aimed at empowering individuals to reach their fullest potential. He speaks to athletes and companies inspiring them to achieve "Greatness." For more information, go to: ChampionOfSuccess.com.

Lee Johnson: Born in South Africa, graduating from Grosse Point High in Detroit, and now a Canadian living in Vancouver, Lee has an extremely colourful resume: high school teacher of English and Latin, psychotherapist, professional rock musician, and copywriter/creative director for many of the world's leading advertising agencies. His book: *How to Escape Your Comfort Zones*, displaced Nelson Mandela's *Long Walk to Freedom* at the top of best-seller lists for 8 weeks in South Africa. He co-wrote a musical "The Ancient Mariner" with Oliver Reed and Michael York as narrators, and a television series "Balltown" which teaches universal values to young children. Now a full time writer, Lee is working on a new book plus several innovative projects for television and film. His websites are: leejohnsonwriter.com OR lifebooklegacy.com.

Lionel Philippe is originally from France, but has retained his European flair since taking up residence in BC in 2000. He is deeply passionate about empowering people in both personal and corporate settings. In 2003, he was introduced to the Miruspoint® transformational work. One year later, he launched his own small business which specializes in stress management, coaching, professional and personal development. He takes great joy in helping his clients take responsibility for their own life experiences, equipping them with tools to take the necessary risks to achieve their heart's desires, to connect with and live from their deepest wisdom, and to rekindle their passion for life.

Lon and Sandy Golnick, co-founders of Relationship & Families By Design, are accomplished workshop leaders and coaches. They have successfully identified the source of breakdowns in relationships, and enable people to see it for themselves. They offer a new paradigm for relationships in which being related is completely natural. They also offer a model for relationships that is based on the design of games rather than a structure of survival. Together, Sandy and Lon have over 60 years of experience in training and developing people—both adults and young people—and they bring 48 years of marriage plus their experience of being parents of two and grandparents of six to their work with families. To learn more about the Golnick's, go to: familiesbydesign.com.

Lorri Dalton attended the University of Alberta in the Dental Hygiene program and spent 20 years in dental practice. After her third child was born, she began training seriously in track-and-field as a middle-distance runner. She competed in

University Masters' divisions as well as the World Masters' Games. She completed 2 levels in the NCCP coaching program in addition to the "RunJumpThrow Program," designed for school age children. Her interest for fitness and running led to a position as Assistant Coach with the Red Deer Titans city track team. Lorri continues to learn as a life-long goal and journey. Her passion today lies in supporting people through life transitions with emphasis in health, nutrition and fitness. Lorri resides in Sherwood Park, Alberta with her husband and 3 super-wonderful children.

Lynn Sumida is one of those lucky people who knew early in life that her calling was to work with people. She first obtained a Masters Degree in Social Work, then the real "tools of the trade"—Senior Faculty for the William Glasser Institute, training in the Satir Model of Family Therapy, and Trainer in Neuro-Linguistic Programming. Lynn is an outstanding teacher and facilitator, travelling globally to share her work. With experience in health, education and mental health, she opened a private practice in 1981, specializing in the treatment of trauma, abuse and ways to heal deep wounds. As President of Miruspoint Facilitators Inc™, Lynn has the opportunity to do all she loves—working with clients, training professionals, and creating a community which passionately champions the freedom of spirit.

Maureen Cubbon was born in Vancouver, BC, Canada. Finishing her education at Simon Fraser University and BCIT resulted in degrees in Criminology, Biochemistry and Forensics. Maureen currently resides in the Cayman Islands, which has been home for 11 years. There, she works on projects that help children discover the benefits of growing and preparing their own food, using the "garden-to-table" approach as a teaching tool. She proudly helped create and implement "Project Grow," a school garden initiative that schools in the Bahamas and the Cayman Islands have adopted. Maureen is also a passionate, self-trained chef, competing in the finale of the Amateur Chef Competition at the 2012 Food& Wine Cayman Cookout—cooking for the likes of Anthony Bourdain and Eric Ripert.

Marlyse Carroll is a meditation teacher, writer, speaker and artist of Swiss-French origin. She lives in Victoria, Australia. She is the co-founder of the Inner Peace Institute for Wellbeing, a non-sectarian educational organization specializing in personal transformation. Marlyse is also the author of the international best-seller *Am I Going Mad? The Unsettling Phenomena of Spiritual Evolution* (Inner Peace Publishing, 2007). Websites: amigoingmad.com.au OR innerpeace.com.au.

Michael Robins is a speaker and an author in the field of self-awareness and unlimited potential. He helps people experience their abundance and joy and offers an open community to support that potential, including two, weekly tele-conferences called *"The Abundance Empowerment Adventure"* and *"Tribe Victory."* He has created a process to experience self-realization called Supreme Purpose Activation (S.P.A.), which also assists in removing subconscious barriers to empower our lives. He is also the author of *Awakening: 13 Steps to Love, Freedom, and Power*, which illuminates the journey of self-realization, making it easier and more manageable by dividing it into specific, helpful steps. His passion is inspiring people to realize and share their magnificence, which helps both them and the world transform. His website is michaelrobins.me.

Molly McCord is a Consciousness Catalyst playing the roles of author, intuitive, astrologer, teacher and spiritual messenger. Her spiritual awakening began in 2001 when she was (unknowingly) learning about the power of personal consciousness through the Universal Spiritual Laws. Molly's consciousness-raising journey is captured in *My Life As A Trapeze Artist* where she shares the cosmic wisdom of launching, soaring, falling and beginning again—fearlessly and better than ever. She has a popular website, Conscious Cool Chic, and hosts a weekly blog talk radio show where she shares spiritual messages and astrological insights. Molly earned an M.A. in International Relations and Diplomacy as a formal avenue for studying and understanding Unity Consciousness from a global, historical perspective. To learn more, go to: mylifeasatrapezeartist.com OR consciouscoolchic.com.

Natalie Sisson is the adventurer behind *The Suitcase Entrepreneur,* a highly popular blog that shows you how to create a thriving online business you can run from anywhere. Natalie helps you create freedom in business and adventure in life, instead of being stuck in an office or working long hours for little in return. She uses online tools, social media and outsourcing to build the portable business and lifestyle you desire. She also offers a variety of digital products and programs, plus a wide variety of free resources to assist the "suitcase entrepreneur." Natalie is a contributor to *Forbes, Visa Business Network, Under30CEO* and many more major online publications. When she's not working on her business, she's travelling the World, living out of her suitcase and playing competitive Ultimate Frisbee.

Nina Talley-Kalokoh is a global citizen committed to expanding the depth of a peaceful humanity. Raised in the Shenandoah Valley of Virginia, USA, her travels throughout the United States, Central America, Europe and West Africa have infused her writing with vibrancy and authentic self-expression. Working in the field of leadership development, Nina engages with professionals around the world to provide customized training programs that enhance their management potential and highlight skills in emotional intelligence, appreciative inquiry and multi-cultural leadership. Yet it is as a life-long learner that she gains her deepest connections with others, whether it is in the capacity of facilitator, mother, volunteer, coach or musician. In the spirit of peace, possibilities are endless. Connect with Nina at: reimaginepeace.wordpress.com.

Ocean Bloom works internationally as a personal trainer, fitness instructor, choreographer, yoga instructor, actress, writer and speaker. After winning several World Championships in fitness competitions, Ocean had a feeling that there had to be a better way to integrate internal well-being with fitness. Ocean's desire to find the balance between physical fitness and nurturing the spirit inspired her to travel to Asia to study yoga, Ayruveda, martial arts, meditation and Thai Yoga Massage. Her interest is in transformational healing through an ancient form of therapeutic yoga massage and meditation. Ocean has appeared on numerous health and fitness magazine covers as a model and is a contributing author for *Status Fitness* and *Fresh* magazines. For more information, go to: oceanbloom.com.

Olaf Strassner is the Creative Director of OS Design, specializing in multi-disciplinary, communications design. As marketing changes through the growth of new communication channels, there is increasing demand for "multi-channel" creative experience. Over the last few years, Olaf's skills have evolved from classic advertising to brand identity, packaging and digital design. Coupled with his experience across a number of global brands, he is a highly flexible communications professional, fluent in a number of disciplines to meet the industry's highest standards. Olaf is a lead designer for strategic branding and complex visual identity systems; experienced in classic advertising, packaging, film making, motion design, music composing, web design and photography; a team leader and passionate hands-on designer. OlafStrassner.com

Petey Silveira has over 30 years of combined experience as a marriage and family therapist, author, radio show host, workshop leader and spiritual teacher. Trained in mental health counseling, past-life regression and hypnotherapy, Petey guides her clients to their "path of healing" and peace through the mind, body and soul connection. Petey is the author of *Musings To Help The Soul Remember*, a self-help journal comprised of 60 healing messages to create a profound shift in consciousness. As an expert member of the International Association for Regression Research and Therapies, Inc., Petey received her Master's degree in marriage and family therapy from the University of Virginia. She holds certification in NLP Hypnotherapy and has received extensive training in past-life regression from Dr. Brian Weiss. Visit newpathwaytohealing.com for more information.

Pilar Stella is a visionary author, speaker, conscious capitalist and peace activist. She has published two books: *Seeking Serenity* (seekingserenitybook.com), a kids' book about peace with ten Nobel Peace Laureates; and *BEing the Present* (beingthepresent.com), a book about living in the moment. Throughout her career, she has combined the best elements of capitalism with social good by leveraging resources and maximizing efficiencies across public, private and non-profit sectors to affect social, economic and environmental change. Her latest endeavor, OneGiving (onegiving.com), is a for-profit platform that standardizes giving to generate revenues, transparency, accountability and sustainability for corporations, celebrities, consumers and causes! When not working or writing, Pilar may be found surfing or leading Kundalini yoga and gong meditations in Santa Monica, CA. For more information about Pilar, go to: pilarstella.com.

Rita Soman is originally from India, currently living in Portland, Oregon with her husband. She has 25 years of experience as a Psychotherapist & Addictions Counselor. She has been incorporating PSYCH-K® in her practice for the past 7 years. She finds this process very effective and helpful in healing the root cause of one's problems related with physical, emotional and spiritual aspects of life. She feels very fulfilled watching her clients heal and succeed in just a few sessions. She credits Dr. Bruce Lipton and his book, *The Biology of Belief*, for connecting her to PSYCH-K®, and is thankful for his personal support, too. She works in person, by phone and Skype; she also teaches 2-day Basic PSYCH-K® workshops, nationally and internationally. She can be reached at ritasoman.com OR beliefmantra.com.

Russell Kennedy holds degrees in Neuroscience and Medicine. He is also an accomplished comedian and corporate speaker, with hundreds of appearances across North America. Dr. Kennedy uses his website as a portfolio of his work, highlighting his dedication to combining scientifically-proven Eastern practices with the latest in Western neuroscience. Using his trademark humour, Russ illustrates how our brains have been programmed by our environment to magnify our perception of stress and negative emotion, and shows how to use the brain's natural wiring to change how we perceive and, ultimately, think. In short, Russ will make you laugh and equip you with practical tools to help you SEE your stress rather than BE your stress. To learn more, go to: dr-russ.com.

Scott Simons defines himself as an "eco-preneur," meaning he puts people, purpose, and people before profit. In 2004, Scott and his mentor Steve Sims co-founded the Padua Center, an urban not-for-profit holistic health center. Padua's main activities include meditation, yoga, tai chi, and dialogue. Two years later, Scott co-created DESTA Black Youth Network, an outreach mission to young adults (18-25) in the black community. In 2006, he founded Organik Santé Corporative in response to the epidemic of stress in the workplace. Organik offers on-site services to businesses that make health and wellness accessible for their employees. Scott's mission is to inspire health in others, and he feels he's just getting started. To learn more, go to: beorganik.ca.

Sean Aiken is the creator of "The One Week Job Project": an inspiring journey across North America in which he worked 52 jobs in 52 weeks to find his passion. He trekked more than 55,000 miles and tried every job he could: bungee instructor, dairy farmer, advertising executive, baker, NHL mascot, stock trader, firefighter, and more. Sean's been featured in *The New York Times*, *Wall Street Journal*, *Time*, *Globe & Mail*, on CNN, "20/20," "The Rachael Ray Show," "Good Morning America," CBC, MTV, among other international media outlets. A book (*The One Week Job Project*) and a feature length documentary capture his amazing journey. Sean frequently speaks about his experience and is developing a program to empower others to discover their passion, too. Sean lives in Vancouver, BC.

Sophia Ducey is an ordained Minister, accomplished speaker, and teacher of the principles of various World traditions, leadership and cultural change. She has shared her gifts with organizations, churches and spiritual centers throughout the United States, Canada, Mexico, Russia and Ukraine. Sophia currently expresses her ardent commitment to individual and collective evolution of consciousness through workshops, keynotes, practice circles and spiritual services—incorporating Integral Life, Evolutionary Culture and Transparent Communication principles. She is passionate about celebrating the sacred through co-creating customized ceremonies, intertwining music with the reading and contemplation of sacred texts, and the practice of silent union with the Divine. Sophia loves to "play" with children to help them experience their own spiritual connection through meditation and prayer. Visit Sophia at: sophiaducey.com.

Stephanie Bennett Vogt, MA, is the author of *Your Spacious Self: Clear The Clutter and Discover Who You Are* and a contributing author in *Pearls of Wisdom* with Jack Canfield, et al. As New England's leading "space clearing" expert, she brings over thirty-five years of experience to SpaceClear, the teaching and consulting practice she founded in 1996—helping homes and their occupants come into balance. Stephanie teaches her inspirational clearing programs at centers worldwide, including Kripalu and the New England School of Feng Shui, plus shares her unique perspectives on simplifying, personal reinvention, and letting go as a course contributor at *DailyOM* and a columnist for the *Huffington Post*. Stephanie and her husband divide their time between Concord, Massachusetts and San Miguel de Allende, Mexico. For more, visit: spaceclear.com.

Stephen Thompson has been a teacher for over 30 years in the areas of Philosophy, Psychology, Sociology and plain, common-sense living. After a motorcycle accident in the early 1990's, it took 28 reconstructive surgeries and six years to fully heal. During his recovery process, Thompson was introduced to alternative healing modalities. His rapid recovery through such powerful mind-body techniques prompted several years of study with Psychological Kinesiology and intuitive training. His personal transformation led to the opening of The Personal Search and Growth Center in 1995. His success is founded on the principle that education without implementation is void. Therefore, he joins his authentic knowledge with practical tools for change that allow people to truly accept and apply the information they receive when learning with him.

Susan Phelan admires what is noble, truthful and beautiful in life. With her insightful and innovative approach, she offers individuals, groups and organizations a roadmap to reclaim their authenticity and strength. Her work focuses on personal and organizational transformation, healthy change and transition and spiritual coaching. Speaking from her heart with compassion, she guides people to reconnect with their vitality and passion to powerfully move forward in life. Susan is a Licensed Spiritual Practitioner (RScP), organization development consultant, workshop facilitator and coach. Also a certified Prime Potential© facilitator with Miruspoint®, she holds a Master's degree in organizational behavior with specialties in leadership and change management. She enjoys spending time with friends, appreciates nature, pursues spiritual interests and loves music of all kinds. Visit Susan's website: susanphelan.ca.

Ted Kuntz is a Psychotherapist in private practice in Vancouver, BC, and author of the best-selling book, *Peace Begins With Me*. The wisdom Ted shares doesn't come from his formal training; rather, it is the result of his journey as the father of a severely ill child. Ted's deeply personal story is an inspiration for all of us who want to reduce our pain and suffering and increase our peace and joy. Kuntz' passion is to create a peaceful world where we all belong. To learn more about Ted and his book, visit: peacebeginswithme.ca.

Vtec Janus is a motivational writer. His mission in life is to inspire people as he has been inspired—to know that joy and happiness are the essence of life. He is passionate to share his spiritual insights with the world. Vtec brings his unusual tale of a real-life miracle to life as the author of *When Reason Screams No and Intuition Screams Yes*, sharing his story of the wonder he discovered through a spiritual journey, perspective and insights to intuitive living. One of Vtec's life changing thoughts: "If you know how to forgive, life loses some of its terror." To learn more about Vtec and his calling, go to: janus.id.au.

Coming Soon!

From The Thought Publications, Inc.

The first volume of *The Thought That Changed My Life Forever* is just the beginning for us—and we hope for you, too!

We thrive in creating win-win-win-win scenarios. We created this book to give readers something that would inspire and provoke (a win); to give us the opportunity to make our creative dreams come true (another win); to shine a light on the brilliant work each of our contributors is doing in the World (win-check!); and finally, to do our part (collectively) to contribute to the awakening that is going on the planet right now (BIG win). In that spirit, we intend to fulfill on our promise and invite you to take the learning and inspiration you've received from these stories into your life to create your own new experiences. We know this takes focus, dedication and consistent effort. So, to help you with this, we've got some exciting "next steps" just for you.

First: We encourage you to share the book with a friend and to talk about it together. Help each other identify what you want most in your life—and remind each other often how to think about it to make it happen!

Second: We will be providing weekly tele-seminars for an entire year designed specifically to introduce each of our contributing authors to you and to give you a chance to learn more about the gifts they are offering to the World. Now you know why there are 52 of them! We will publish the schedule on our website (www. thethoughtpublications.com) so you can tune-in to listen for your favourites—perhaps one particular story sounded a lot like yours or maybe you'd like to ask for some professional guidance from the author directly. We want to give you access to those people who touched or awakened something in you. Join us!

Third: We'd like to meet you in person! We've created a very special event series called *"Food For Thought."* This is a showcase of special appearances, discussions, meditation and music with an opportunity to learn more, be further inspired, and to help support your local Food Bank (wherever the event takes place). These are planned for various locations as well as online via live-streaming webcasts. Find more details on our website.

Fourth: Connect with us! Our website will be an ongoing source of information, insights, and daily inspiration. Join our community and sign-up to receive special news updates and daily Tweeks (yes, Tweets that tweak your mind!). You can also learn more about what we're all up to around the globe and when you can expect...

Fifth: ...the next volume of *The Thought That Changed My Life Forever!* We are creating **The Thought Movement**—a series of books, events and initiatives that will touch you in unexpected and innovative ways! Whether it's more helpers and healers like we recruited this time OR moms, celebrities, artists or entrepreneurs, we know you'll love all we have planned for you. Stay tuned!

www.thethoughtpublications.com

All that we are is the result of what we have thought.
If a man speaks or acts with a pure thought,
happiness follows him, like a shadow that never leaves him.
— Buddha

CPSIA information can be obtained at www.ICGtesting.com
Printed in the USA
LVOW081426250113

317285LV00008B/966/P